Dish Do-Over

Dish Do-Over

JO LUSTED

SWAP IN GREEK YOGURT, BAKE YOUR BACON &
OTHER SECRETS TO DELICIOUS, GUILT-FREE COOKING

Photographs by Mike McColl

Collins

Published by Collins,
an imprint of HarperCollins Publishers Ltd

First edition

Those who might be at risk from the effects of salmonella poisoning
(the elderly, pregnant women, young children and those suffering from immune deficiency diseases)
should consult their doctor with any concerns
about eating raw eggs.

The recipes for Bacon Double-Cheeseburger Pizza, Butter Chicken, Chicken Fettuccine Alfredo,
Chicken Nuggets with Honey Mustard Sauce, Eggnog, Macaroni & Cheese, Mixed Berry Cheesecake,
Sausage Rolls, Shepherd's Pie, and Spinach & Artichoke Dip with Chili-Lime Baked Tortilla Chips were
featured on CBC's "Steven and Chris" and are reproduced with permission.

HarperCollins books may be purchased for educational, business
or sales promotional use through our Special Markets Department.

HarperCollins Publishers Ltd
2 Bloor Street East, 20th Floor
Toronto, Ontario, Canada
M4W 1A8

www.harpercollins.ca

Library and Archives Canada Cataloguing
Publication information is available upon request

ISBN 978-1-44342-312-0

Food styling by Mia Bachmaier

Printed and bound in Canada

DWF 9 8 7 6 5 4 3 2 1

To my mom and dad, Susan and Roland Lusted, and to my late grandparents, Chris and Mary Birch, and Charles and Dorothy Lusted

CONTENTS

Introduction

This book started as a dare from my foodie friends: Create a do-over version of not just any pizza but a bacon double-cheeseburger pizza. Two fast-food favourites together, one massive amount of fat, sodium and calories. But does it have to be? Do you have to give it up or give up the flavour? Not on my watch. Friends exclaim that my low-fat bacon double-cheeseburger pizza tastes like junk food but is better than the original!

My mother is a fantastic cook. She always made sure we had a home-cooked meal on the table. She made everything from scratch, including my favourite, macaroni and cheese. I didn't have Kraft Dinner till I was six. My grandmother and I always baked together, me standing on my little stool so I could reach the counter. And I remember watching, through the oven door, the cookies rise. We were a family of cooks that enjoyed good food.

So it wasn't too much of a surprise when I decided to go to chef school. Probably not a surprise either that you can gain weight when you're a chef: heavy cream, butter, pan-fried and breaded meats, fatty braised meats, butter sauces, decadent desserts, homemade bread and pastries, cheese, vegetables blanketed in butter and lots of refined starches like rice, pasta and white flour. After packing on the pounds and not feeling good, I knew it was time for a change. I started to look for healthier ways to eat my favourite foods. And like many people, I found I was eating a lot of "non-fat," "fat-free" or "low-calorie" food that was often heavily processed. I also got frustrated by so-called makeover recipes that used ingredients that weren't healthier, portion sizes that were reduced to hit a mythical calorie count or deceits like wrapping taco filling in lettuce and calling it a taco — or soggy oven "fries" that didn't taste at all like their deep-fried brethren.

I wanted to eat the classics — the favourites I grew up on — but without the fat, crazy sodium or calories, and without the garbage. I wanted real food that was still healthy and still tasted good. As it turned out, I wasn't alone. In 2012, "Dish Do-Over" launched on the television show *Steven and Chris*, and the response was overwhelming. Viewers told us their kids' favourites, their guilty pleasures and the restaurant favourites that they wanted to make healthier and at home. Requests poured in for chicken nuggets, macaroni and cheese, beef stroganoff, double chocolate cake, eggs Benedict, butter chicken, pad Thai, hamburgers and more.

Dish Do-Over features viewer favourites, plus many of my own family recipes reinvented. You won't find trickery here, just simple and smart swaps that anyone can do. As you'll see, the trick to making french fries in the oven is to soak the potatoes in hot water before baking them, to help draw out the starch. Dry them well and bake them at a high temperature, and they'll be crispy on the outside and fluffy on the inside.

The bacon double-cheeseburger pizza has more tricks, but they're fast and easy. Simply cooking the bacon in the oven instead of frying it saves fat and calories without cutting back on the amount of bacon on your pizza. Adding ground mushrooms to lean ground beef replaces the fat in full-fat ground beef (and no one notices the mushrooms, guaranteed). And the best thing of all? When you lose the fat, you actually are left with more flavour. Healthier food can taste better, and you can enjoy your favourites more often. You can transfer smart substitutions to other recipes: use the mushroom swap for anything with ground beef, such as lasagna, Bolognese sauce and tacos.

I believe that no one should ever feel guilty about eating and that you shouldn't have to make the choice between eating tasty food and enjoying good health. It also doesn't have to be difficult or intimidating to cook delicious food. Sacrificing flavour and your favourite foods is a surefire way to sabotage your mental state and healthy lifestyle goals — believe me, I've been there! Eating is just as much about the experience and the memory as it is about nutrition, perhaps more so. The key is balance. Being able to enjoy your favourite comfort foods prepared with wholesome ingredients is the perfect way to have your bacon double-cheeseburger pizza and eat it too.

Getting Started

I'm going to let you in on one of the biggest secrets of my professional cooking career: healthy cooking is most definitely, 100% assuredly, *not* complicated!

You don't have to be a trained chef to make lick-the-plate-clean dinners and delectable desserts, and you certainly don't need a nutrition degree to craft healthy, clean meals that nourish your body. It all comes down to ingredients and techniques, and once I help you get those down pat, you'll be fully equipped to start dishing out delicious, nutritious meals in a snap.

First things first: let's talk ingredients. The fresher your ingredients are, the better your food is going to look, smell and taste. And as a plus for all you busy cooks out there, the better your ingredients look, smell and taste, the less work you actually have to do in the kitchen. That's because food that's naturally fresh and full of nutrients is so delicious on its own, you hardly have to do anything to it to bring out the succulent flavour. The quality of your ingredients is particularly important when cooking healthy meals, since you're not masking the natural flavours with excess oil, salt or sugar. Even the saddest, driest little potato will undoubtedly taste incredible when deep-fried in fat and smothered in salt, but try turning that sorry spud into a clean, nutritious snack with a tablespoon of oil and pinch of salt and you'll get a different story. There's a reason that fresh summer corn on the cob needs only a few minutes in hot water to satisfy your taste buds — the sweet, creamy flavour is coming straight from nature, rather than from half a pound of butter and salt.

This brings me to my second rule for cooking delicious healthy meals: choose the right techniques. To let the natural flavour of your food shine, you need to know how to treat each ingredient in your kitchen. Don't worry: this is where I come in! In this chapter I show you the easiest, healthiest and simplest techniques for cooking the perfect hard-boiled egg and the best crispy bacon, among other things. I also give you recipes for the basics, such as homemade ketchup and whole-wheat pizza dough, to mention just two. And once you've got the basics covered, you'll be well on your way to transforming the calorie-heavy comfort foods you're used to reserving for special occasions into healthy flavourful meals you can enjoy every night of the week — think creamy pastas and pub-night classics!

Jo's Clean Staples

Don't let your old eating habits drag you down even before you get started. You need to rid your pantry and fridge of all the processed, refined stuff and replace it with natural foods with simple, uncomplicated ingredients. Here are a few of my clean staples:

• **Baby spinach and arugula (pre-washed).** With no washing or chopping required, they're always ready for slipping into eggs, pastas and soups.

• **Dried beans.** Dried beans are much cheaper and more nutritious than canned. Simply soak them overnight on the countertop (use 4 cups water for every cup of beans), then drain and simmer until tender.

• **Eggs.** Perfect for snacks and meals, eggs are full of protein, which helps keep you feeling full. I hard-boil enough to last me a week, so they're always on hand to make egg salad sandwiches (page 121) or simply to eat on their own with a dash of hot sauce.

• **Sea salt.** Ditch the table salt and embrace the power of the sea! Sea salt is minimally refined and retains most of its natural minerals. Kosher and Himalayan salts are also handy to have in the pantry, but sea salt is my go-to.

• **Spelt flour.** With its slightly sweet, nutty flavour, spelt flour is a tasty substitute for refined all-purpose flour. There are two types of spelt flour: white and whole-grain. Like white all-purpose wheat flour, white spelt flour has had the germ and bran removed. Still, both types of spelt flour are higher in protein than wheat flour, and whole-wheat spelt flour is higher in fibre and won't cause a significant spike in your blood sugars. Plus, spelt flour is lower in gluten, so suitable for those who have slight intolerances. Keep in mind, though, that it's not gluten-free, so not all people with gluten intolerances can tolerate it. Spelt flour is, however, more water soluble and more easily digested than wheat flour. Because it's more water soluble, less liquid is needed when baking with it and less kneading or mixing is required; overmixing can result in a crumbly texture.

• **Spices (fresh).** Go through your spices and discard any that aren't fragrant. Spices lose their potency after about 6 months, so you'll want to replace them with fresh for maximum flavour. Be sure to store them in a cool, dark place, as sunlight destroys the spices' natural oils.

• **Spice blends (salt-free).** These are great for one-step flavouring on a simple chicken breast or flank steak. Some blends to try are steak spice, chicken spice, Cajun and lemon-pepper.

• **Strong cheeses.** Varieties like low-fat aged cheddar, feta, pecorino and Parmesan pack more flavour into smaller amounts, so you can use less.

• **Tomato sauce (all-natural, jarred).** Read the label carefully and look for brands with short ingredient lists.

15 Must-Have Kitchen Tools

Healthy, delicious cooking starts with the right tools. Take a quick inventory of your kitchen to make sure you have everything you need to make cooking easy and fun. Here's what you should have on hand:

1. Good-quality knives. Your knife should glide through food with minimal resistance and, most importantly, it should feel comfortable in your hand. You'll need a bread knife, a paring knife and a chef's knife. Take your time when selecting the knives. Consider their size, weight and style, particularly that of the chef's knife, as this is the one you'll be using most often. A 6-inch blade is best suited to smaller hands, whereas larger hands benefit from an 8-inch blade. Go with what feels most comfortable — a good, well-suited knife should feel like an extension of your hand.

2. Non-stick pots and pans. You don't need a million pots and pans rattling around your kitchen! All you really need are four good pieces: a two-quart saucepan, a 6- to 8-quart stockpot or saucepan and a 6-inch and 12-inch skillet. When it comes to skillets, look for non-stick, as this keeps food from sticking, which lets you get away with using less oil in your cooking.

3. Rasp or Microplane. This is my all-time favourite kitchen tool. I use mine for grating everything from garlic, whole spices and lemon to cheese and dark chocolate. They're inexpensive and are guaranteed to save you time in the kitchen.

4. Lemon reamer. Lemon juice is full of flavour and can actually replace salt in many recipes, as the acidity enhances and balances the flavour of the other ingredients. To get the most juice from your lemons without taking an eye out, you need a lemon reamer. They're cheap, small and indispensable.

5. Salad spinner. Who wants a soggy salad? Not me, yet I'm always amazed at how few people actually own one of these. At about $20 a pop, these all-in-ones are the fastest way to wash and dry delicate greens and herbs. Plus, the basket doubles as a colander.

6. Tongs. These little guys will be your hands in the kitchen when dealing with hot food, so you want to stay away from the overly long varieties. The shorter the handle, the more control you have over the tongs. And don't bother with plastic models — stainless steel will last longer and stand up to heat.

7. Spatula. Look for one that is heatproof up to 450°F and that won't scratch non-stick surfaces. If you're a fish lover, consider getting a fish spatula too; these are extra-thin for slipping under delicate fillets.

8. Wooden spoon. There's something about stirring with a simple wooden spoon — it's classic, it's inexpensive and it will last far longer than plastic varieties.

9. Slotted spoon. Ideal for snatching veggies and short pasta from pots without taking the water with you.

10. Cutting board. Wooden and plastic boards are your best bet; avoid glass cutting boards, which are hard on your knives. Discard boards that are heavily scratched or indented, as harmful bacteria can harbour in the crooks and crannies. As an extra precaution, designate a separate board for meats to avoid contamination with raw vegetables.

11. Vegetable peeler. When you're cooking from scratch, a good peeler is a must. Look for sturdy models with a thin blade that will barely scrape the surface of your food, for minimal waste.

12. Whisk. Not just for baking, whisks are essential for whipping up homemade salad dressings and sauces.

13. Measuring cups and spoons. When you're new to cooking, precise measurement is key. To save on space, look for nesting models, and to prevent any melting mishaps, opt for heatproof.

14. Meat thermometer. This handy gadget instantly checks the internal temperature of foods, which is important for safely cooking large cuts of meat such as whole chickens and roast beef.

15. Parchment paper. I always keep a roll of parchment in my pantry for lining baking sheets — it prolongs their life and makes cleanup a breeze. Plus, it keeps food from sticking to the pans, which lets you get away with using less oil in your baking and roasting.

TOP TIME SAVERS

If you find you're spending a lot of time in the kitchen, you may want to consider investing in a few additional kitchen gadgets that will save time. Here are some of my favourites:

• *Food processor.* Available in a variety of sizes and at various price points, these powerhouses can knead dough, emulsify salad dressings, grate cheese and chop your veggies with the press of a button.

• *Immersion blender.* Skip the hassle of transferring soups and sauces to a blender and do the puréeing right in the pot with one of these hand-held mix masters.

• *Slow cooker.* Designed to cook food at a consistent temperature without supervision, slow cookers are a godsend for nine-to-fivers. Prep the ingredients the night before, throw them in the slow cooker in the morning and come home that evening to a perfectly cooked pot roast or stew.

• *Steamer basket.* Steam is hotter than water, so it cooks veggies more quickly, plus the vegetables' nutrients don't leach away into the cooking water, which happens when veggies are boiled.

Get to Know Your Ingredients

Most of the ingredients in this book can be found at your local grocery store. Here's a little bit more about some of them to explain why using them can help make your do-over recipes so tasty!

Avocado. This rich, buttery fruit is known for its smooth and creamy texture and mild nutty flavour. Common varieties are Hass, which have pebbled blackish skin, and Fuerte, which have smooth green skin. When ripe, the fruit yields slightly when gently squeezed. Avocados are an excellent source of healthy monounsaturated fats, which help lower your risk of heart disease by reducing levels of LDL (bad) cholesterol. Available year-round at supermarkets.

Bacon. This thinly sliced meat is cut from the pork belly and generally cured and brined in a mixture of salt, sugar and sodium nitrate for preservation and flavour. The healthiest option on the market is centre-cut bacon, as it tends to be less fatty. Fresh uncured varieties preserved naturally with celery salt are available. Find it in major supermarkets, delis and butcher shops.

Bitters. These are a family of highly concentrated liquors infused with natural herbs, barks, plants and roots. They are commonly added in small amounts to alcoholic beverages and cocktails for complexity of flavour, though they are also used as an herbal supplement to aid digestion. Available in major and specialty liquor stores, gourmet grocers and in the beverage section of most major supermarkets.

Buttermilk powder. Essentially dehydrated buttermilk, this pantry staple is a favourite among bakers for its convenience and cost-effectiveness, as it keeps for several months and can instantly be rehydrated to make the specific amount you need. Find it in the baking aisle of major supermarkets or bulk food stores.

Citric acid. This concentrated powder extracted from citrus fruits is used to add tartness to food and drinks, and is also commonly found in packaged foods as a preservative. Find it in bulk food or specialty baking stores.

Coconut water. This sweet water is found in the centres of young coconuts and has a slight nutty flavour. It is often used as a natural alternative to sports drinks because of its sodium and potassium content, as these electrolytes help prevent dehydration and restore nerve function after excessive sweating. Find it in the health and/or beverage section of major supermarkets or health food stores.

Cooking spray (olive oil). An essential pantry staple, olive oil cooking spray is perfect for misting pans for baking or skillets for sautéing, as it distributes an even coating of oil without adding too much fat. Find it in the oil section of major supermarkets, or purchase your own non-aerosol refillable mister in kitchen stores.

Dried shiitake mushrooms. Fresh shiitake mushrooms have a high water content and are prone to spoiling easily; dried shiitakes have all the flavour of fresh, and a far greater shelf life. Before using, reconstitute the dried form of this Asian mushroom in water until softened, and then remove the woody stems.

Dry-pressed cottage cheese. One of the best ingredients for cutting calories, dry-pressed cottage cheese, or dry curd cheese, is cottage cheese that has had no milk or cream added after the curds have formed. It's pressed dry, as the name suggests, and is a perfect substitute for ricotta cheese in recipes such as cannelloni and lasagna. It's also extremely low in fat and high in protein, but be sure to check the label: you're looking for one with less than 1% milk fat.

Dutch-process cocoa powder. This type of cocoa powder has been treated with an alkali to neutralize acid. It may be used in recipes that call for baking powder as the leavening agent; because of the cocoa's neutral acidity, baking soda doesn't react with it. Dutch-process cocoa powder has a reddish-brown colour and a milder flavour than regular cocoa powder, and it dissolves easily in liquid.

Fresh whole-wheat lasagna sheets. Fresh lasagna sheets are found in the refrigerated section of the grocery store, usually near the produce. They are great for layering or rolling in lasagna or cannelloni, and don't need to be parboiled before using. They can also be cut into ribbons, for a fettuccine-style pasta.

Honey (including raw honey). Honey is a wonderful alternative sweetener to refined white sugar. It is sweeter than sugar, so you can use less, and it naturally helps emulsify dressings, sauces and dips. It also provides moisture to baked goods. Most importantly, honey is more easily digested than white sugar. Liquid honey is best for cooking or baking, drizzling as a garnish or sweetening beverages. Whipped or creamed honey is best used as a spread. Not all honey is created equal. I prefer raw unpasteurized honey, which is available at local farmers' markets and health food stores. If you can't find unpasteurized honey locally, look for pure honey with no added sugars like corn syrup. Because honey gets its start as flower nectar, there are over 300 varieties, each unique in colour and flavour. Clover honey is the most common and is what most people think of in terms of colour and flavour. Don't worry if your honey crystallizes; it has not gone bad. Simply microwave for about 10 seconds, or warm in a pot of hot water for 30 seconds, and then stir. Honey does not need refrigeration, but it will absorb odours, so store in a cool, dark place away from highly scented food.

Low-fat aged cheddar cheese. This pungent variety of cheddar is a calorie-conscious cook's best option. The cheese is aged for anywhere from 9 months to 9 years to develop its sharp signature flavour, which lets you get away with using less without skimping on taste. Find it in the dairy section of major supermarkets or at specialty delis.

Molasses. A by-product of the sugar-making process, molasses is the thick, dark sugarcane syrup that sugar crystals are extracted from during the refining process. To fully extract the crystals from the juice, this liquid is boiled three times, each boiling process producing a different variety of molasses. With the first boiling comes light molasses, the sweetest and mildest variety. The second boiling produces dark molasses, a thicker, darker syrup that is less sweet and more robust in flavour. From the final boiling comes blackstrap molasses — at this processing point, most of the sugar has been extracted, so the result is a very thick, bitter syrup with very little sucrose and a high concentration of the sugarcane's nutrients, including iron, potassium, manganese and copper. Find molasses in the baking or syrup section of major supermarkets. If you can't find blackstrap molasses at your local grocery store, look for it in the health section or in specialty health food stores.

Organic icing sugar. Generally used for making icings, this sugar is made from organic evaporated cane juice that has been ground to a light, fine powder for easy blending. Most varieties include a small amount of cornstarch or tapioca starch to prevent the powder from caking. Find it in the organic or health section of major supermarkets or in the baking aisle of health food stores.

Organic sugar (organic evaporated cane juice). A healthier, unrefined version of granulated white sugar, this clean sweetener is made from the juice of organic sugar cane; once extracted, it is clarified and evaporated, then spun to remove most of the molasses content. Use as a 1:1 replacement for granulated white sugar. Find it in the organic or health section of major supermarkets or in the baking aisle of health food stores.

Panko bread crumbs. These Japanese-style bread crumbs are crispier, lighter and crunchier than traditional dried bread crumbs, partly because the crumb itself has a large surface area for absorbing liquids. Breading items with panko results in an airier crust and less absorbed oil. Look for whole-wheat and gluten-free varieties at specialty grocery and health food stores.

Passata. Common in Italian cooking, passata is a pure tomato purée that has been strained to remove seeds and skin. Unlike tomato sauce, passata contains no added ingredients and, unlike tomato paste, it has not been cooked to thicken. In supermarkets, passata is generally sold in tall glass containers alongside the tomato sauces, or in the Italian section of ethnic grocery stores. To make your own, simply whirl canned tomatoes in a blender or food processor and strain through a fine-mesh sieve.

Pure vanilla extract. This incredibly fragrant and flavourful alcohol-based liquid has been infused with crushed vanilla beans, then strained to produce a dark, clear extract. It is almost always used in baking to provide a warm, rich flavour. Find it in the baking aisle of supermarkets. Be wary of artificial vanilla extract; although it is half the price of the pure extract, this imitation flavouring contains no real vanilla and has a harsh, bitter flavour.

Rose water. Used in Asian and Middle Eastern cooking, this is the liquid remaining after distilling rose petals in water to make rose oil. It has a strong flavour that some find initially soapy, maybe because many North Americans associate rose with soaps and perfumes. Find it in the ethnic section of supermarkets, in health food stores and in Asian and Middle Eastern grocery stores.

Shirataki tofu noodles. These thin white noodles are made from a blend of konnyaku (a relative of the yam) starch and tofu. Generally purchased dry and rehydrated quickly, this low-carb pasta alternative absorbs the flavour of the soup or sauce it's added to and is popular in Asian cooking. Find it in the ethnic aisle of major supermarkets or in speciality Asian grocery stores.

Spelt flour. This ancient whole-grain flour is prized for its high nutritional content and nutty flavour. The grain is higher in protein than whole-wheat flour and more easily digestible, which allows its nutrients to be quickly absorbed by our bodies. In addition, it has a relatively low gluten content, so it may be tolerated by certain people with wheat intolerances. Find it in the health section of major supermarkets or in health food stores.

Sustainable seafood. Choosing the right seafood is as important to your cooking as selecting the freshest local vegetables. Sustainability is a major factor with seafood, and I encourage you to always select varieties that have been harvested in a way that is not harmful to the species and the environment. Health is another concern, so you should ensure that the seafood was harvested from a clean, unpolluted environment. Since sustainability is determined on a case-by-case basis depending on species and location of harvest, I recommend you check websites such as www.oceanwise.ca/seafood and www.seachoice.org to find which varieties are best, or find a trustworthy fishmonger that specializes in sustainability. Many grocery stores stock sustainable seafood; look for the symbols or labelling on packages and at the seafood counter.

Tequila. Sourced from the blue agave plant, this traditional Mexican liquor is produced by fermenting and distilling the plant's sap. Several varieties of tequila are available, but blanco is the one most commonly used in cooking, as it retains its peppery taste even when cooked. This distinctive flavour also makes it the best variety for mixing in drinks such as margaritas. For the best quality, look for brands made with 100% blue agave, which have no added sugar. Find it in stores selling liquor.

Vital wheat gluten. This powdered form of gluten is made by activating the gluten in flour, then isolating the gluten and dehydrating it into a powder. It is widely used to lend an extra fluffy texture to breads and doughs, particularly when the recipe calls for denser whole-wheat products. Find it in the health section of major supermarkets or in gourmet and health food stores.

Xanthan gum. This powdered thickener is used in gluten-free baking to replicate the rising and volumizing properties of gluten. Without gluten, baked goods tend to be dense and flat, but this natural corn-derived ingredient provides the structure needed to produce fluffy, aerated breads, muffins and cakes. Find it in the health section of major supermarkets or in the baking aisle of health food stores.

Jo's Kitchen Basics

My simple techniques for preparing key ingredients are essential for creating many of the reinvented family favourites in this book. Before you know it, you'll be baking your bacon and making perfect hard-boiled eggs every time.

Healthy and Delicious Bread Crumbs

Making bread crumbs is so simple, and it's one of the best things you can do to make your breaded, crusted or stuffed recipes taste that much better. All you need are 4 slices of slightly stale (but not rock hard) whole-wheat or whole-grain bread. Store-bought bread crumbs are awful bins of sawdust . . . Who wants to add that to their food?

For fresh bread crumbs, tear or cut bread into 1-inch chunks and pulse in food processor until coarse crumbs form.

For toasted dried bread crumbs, preheat oven to 350°F. Transfer fresh bread crumbs to a parchment-lined baking sheet and bake until golden, about 10 minutes. Toss with sea salt to taste, and mist with cooking spray, if desired. Cool and transfer to a resealable container.

Store fresh or dried bread crumbs in a resealable container in the freezer for up to 3 months.

Homemade Croutons

Making your own croutons reduces the calories and fat roughly by half. All you need are 4 slices of whole-grain bread (gluten-free, if desired), 2 tbsp of freshly grated Parmesan cheese, 1 tsp of Italian herb seasoning, and some sea salt and freshly ground black pepper.

Preheat oven to 350°F. Line a large baking sheet with parchment paper. Cut bread into 1-inch chunks, transfer to a bowl and mist with cooking spray, tossing and spraying again to coat evenly. Sprinkle with Parmesan and Italian herbs. Season with salt and pepper. Spread in a single layer on prepared baking sheet and bake, turning once, for about 10 minutes or until golden brown and crispy. Cool and store at room temperature in a resealable container. Croutons will keep for 1 week in your pantry or for up to 3 months in the freezer.

Toasted Panko Bread Crumbs

Toasting panko before breading is the secret to success in baking your formerly fried favourites like chicken nuggets and mozzarella sticks. It gives a nice golden colour and a crispier texture. You can use regular, whole-wheat or gluten-free panko bread crumbs — whichever you prefer.

Preheat oven to 350°F, and then line a large baking sheet with parchment paper. In a bowl, toss 2 1/2 cups of panko with 1 tsp of sea salt until combined. Transfer to prepared baking sheet and mist liberally with cooking spray. Mix and mist again to evenly coat crumbs. Bake for 5 to 8 minutes, until panko is medium golden brown. Cool, transfer to a resealable container and store in the fridge for up to 2 weeks or in the freezer for up to 3 months.

Toasted Nuts and Seeds

Nuts need only a light toasting to bring out their flavour. Preheat oven to 300°F. Arrange nuts in a single layer on a parchment-lined baking sheet and toast for 5 to 6 minutes, until light golden brown. Cool to room temperature. Store in a resealable container in the freezer for up to 3 months.

Perfect Hard-Boiled Eggs

What can be more important than knowing how to make a perfect hard-boiled egg? Follow my foolproof technique, and you'll get great results every time.

Place eggs in pot in a single layer; do not stack or they won't cook evenly. Cover eggs with cold water by at least 1 inch and bring water to a gentle boil over high heat. As soon as water begins to bubble, remove pot from heat, turn off burner, cover pot and rest for 8 minutes (10 minutes for extra-firm yolks). Rinse eggs under very cold running water or immerse in an ice bath for 10 minutes. If water in the ice bath warms, discard water and recover with more ice water.

Drain eggs and peel. To peel easily, crack fatter end of egg and peel under cold water (either in a bowl or running under the tap). Hard-boiled eggs in their shells will keep for up to 5 days in the fridge. Store in a container, and be sure to label the container with the date you boiled the eggs, to eliminate any guessing games.

Perfect Crispy Bacon

Repeat after me: "Bake your bacon!" Ladies and gentlemen, your oil-splattering bacon-frying days are over. Baking is the perfect — and the only — way to cook bacon. It drains all the fat, there's no splattering and you don't have to stand there and tend to it (while trying not to get grease spots on your favourite comfy sweatshirt).

Preheat oven to 350°F. Arrange bacon in a single layer on a baking rack set on a parchment-lined baking sheet. Bake for 20 to 25 minutes, until bacon is crispy, rotating sheet as needed so bacon cooks evenly. Pat off excess grease with paper towel. Discard fat.

Caramelized Onions

Sweet caramelized onions add a delicious burst of flavour, with virtually no fat — and making them is easy! Thinly slice 2 large Spanish onions. Heat a large non-stick skillet over medium-high heat; coat lightly with cooking spray. Add onions to pan. Cook, stirring frequently, for 1 to 2 minutes, until fragrant (pan will be very full, but don't worry, the onions will shrink as they cook). Reduce heat to medium-low and continue to cook, stirring occasionally, for about 60 minutes, until onions are very soft, sticky looking, and light caramel in colour. Remove from heat and allow to cool for 10 minutes at room temperature.

Essential Do-Over Recipes

Master these do-over recipes and you'll have a few simple swaps that you can rely on when creating your family's favourite meals.

Homemade Ketchup

MAKES ABOUT 1 1/3 CUPS (22 TBSP)
HANDS-ON TIME: 30 MINUTES
TOTAL TIME: 35 MINUTES

Let's face facts. Some things in life just taste better with ketchup: french fries, mac 'n' cheese, onion rings and a good grilled cheese sandwich. Most prepared ketchup has loads of sugar in it, thanks to high-fructose corn syrup, not the greatest thing to be pouring onto your food. Better-quality ketchups don't use these nasty sweeteners, but another option is to make your own. Although the calories are virtually identical, the do-over recipe is much healthier, with no corn syrup, refined white sugar or artificial sweeteners.

- 2 cups passata
- 1/3 cup honey
- 1/3 cup red wine vinegar
- 1/2 tsp onion powder
- 1/2 tsp sea salt, plus more to taste
- 1/4 tsp garlic powder
- 1/4 tsp ground allspice
- 1/4 tsp cayenne pepper

In a medium saucepan over medium heat, combine ingredients and bring to a simmer. Reduce heat to medium-low and cook, stirring occasionally, for 30 minutes or until reduced by half. Cool to room temperature and adjust seasoning to taste. Transfer to a resealable container and refrigerate. Ketchup will last for up to 2 months in the fridge.

Per Serving (1 tbsp)
Before: 20 calories, 10 g total fat
Dish Do-Over: 23 calories, 0 g total fat, 0 g saturated fat, 5.5 g carbohydrates, 0 g fibre, 5.4 g sugar, 0 g protein, 81 mg sodium, 0 mg cholesterol

Perfect Marinated Chicken Breasts

MAKES FOUR 4-OZ CHICKEN BREASTS
HANDS-ON TIME: 5 MINUTES
TOTAL TIME: 25 MINUTES

Having cooked and cooled chicken breasts on hand makes whipping up meals a breeze, but many marinades are loaded with oil. This simple all-purpose marinade adds lots of flavour without extra fat.

> 1 tbsp olive oil
> 3 tbsp fresh lemon juice
> 2 tsp Italian herb seasoning
> 2 garlic cloves, minced
> 1/4 tsp each sea salt and freshly ground black pepper
> 4 boneless, skinless chicken breasts (4 oz each)

In a resealable container or bag, combine oil, lemon juice, Italian herbs, garlic, salt and pepper. Add chicken, tossing to coat. Seal and refrigerate for up to 48 hours or freeze for up to 3 months.

To prepare from frozen, transfer to fridge and allow to defrost completely, about 48 hours.

Preheat oven to 400°F. Place chicken on a parchment-lined baking sheet and bake for 20 minutes or until cooked through.

Tip: Chicken breasts are often butterflied — sliced in half horizontally, with the two halves kept attached, thereby forming a butterfly (or heart) shape when laid flat — to make a pocket for stuffing the breast. Doing so also makes the breast thinner and uniform in thickness for fast, even cooking.

To butterfly, place boneless, skinless chicken breast on a cutting board, with one hand placed firmly on top. With a large knife held parallel to the board, cut through centre of chicken, leaving about 1 inch of flesh on the far edge so breast halves still hold together. Open up the breast like a book and stuff or season according to recipe.

Per Serving (one 4-oz breast)
Before: 327 calories, 16 g total fat
Dish Do-Over: 154 calories, 4.4 g total fat, 0.4 g saturated fat, 1.5 g carbohydrates, 0.25 g fibre, 0.2 g sugar, 25.9 g protein, 136 mg sodium, 67 mg cholesterol

Creamy Condensed Soup Substitute

MAKES ABOUT 2 1/2 CUPS CONDENSED SOUP
(THE EQUIVALENT OF 2 CANS)
HANDS-ON TIME: 15 MINUTES
TOTAL TIME: 30 MINUTES

Canned soup is a base for many classic recipes that our mothers and grandmothers made, some of which get the dish do-over treatment in this book. Although it's a convenient ingredient, canned soup contains

MSG and is loaded with sodium, sometimes 850 milligrams in just 1/2 cup! I use evaporated milk in this recipe because it's more stable and has less chance of splitting than regular low-fat milk. Whip up a batch of this soup on Sunday to make weekday meals a breeze.

1 tbsp grapeseed oil
1/2 cup minced onion
1 garlic clove, minced, or 1/4 tsp garlic powder
1/4 tsp sea salt
Flavour option of your choice (options follow)
1/4 cup whole-wheat or brown rice flour
1 cup low-sodium chicken stock
1 cup non-fat evaporated milk

Flavour Options
Celery: 1 cup minced celery
Chicken: 1 cup finely diced cooked chicken
Mushroom: 2 cups thinly sliced cremini mushrooms

In a saucepan, heat oil over medium heat. Add onion, garlic and salt and cook, stirring frequently, until onion is translucent. Stir in flavour option. If using mushrooms, cook for about 8 minutes until golden brown and softened.

Add flour and stir for 2 minutes, until golden brown. Stir in stock and milk. Bring to a gentle simmer, reduce heat to medium-low and simmer for 10 minutes, until thickened. Allow to cool before storing. Cover and refrigerate for up to 3 days.

Cream of Celery Soup
Per Serving (1/2 cup)
Before: 100 calories, 6 g total fat
Dish Do-Over: 106 calories, 3.1 g total fat, 0.4 g saturated fat, 14.5 g carbohydrates, 0.9 g fibre, 7.3 g sugar, 5.5 g protein, 276 mg sodium, 2 mg cholesterol

Cream of Chicken Soup
Per Serving (1/2 cup)
Before: 130 calories, 8 g total fat
Dish Do-Over: 156 calories, 5.1 g total fat, 0.9 g saturated fat, 13.6 g carbohydrates, 0.6 g fibre, 6.7 g sugar, 13.4 g protein, 258 mg sodium, 27 mg cholesterol

Cream of Mushroom Soup
Per Serving (1/2 cup)
Before: 120 calories, 9 g total fat
Dish Do-Over: 109 calories, 3.1 g total fat, 0.4 g saturated fat, 14.8 g carbohydrates, 1.2 g fibre, 7.2 g sugar, 6 g protein, 258 mg sodium, 2 mg cholesterol

Whole-Wheat Pizza Dough
MAKES TWO 1-LB DOUGH BALLS
HANDS-ON TIME: 30 MINUTES
TOTAL TIME: 2 HOURS

This might be the best pizza-dough-with-no-refined-white-flour that you've ever had. Its lovely airy texture is thanks to the secret ingredient, vital wheat gluten, which helps keep the dough soft and elastic. The reason most whole-wheat pizza dough recipes contain white flour or have a dense, cardboard-like texture is that the bran in whole-wheat flour cuts through the dough like little knives, flattening all that airiness and elasticity you worked so hard to create. This recipe makes 2 dough balls; freeze or refrigerate one for future use if you don't use them both at once.

1 tbsp honey
1 cup less 2 tbsp lukewarm water (105–110°F)
1 package (1/4 oz/7 g) regular active dry yeast (about 2 1/2 tsp)
2 1/2 cups whole-wheat flour
4 tsp vital wheat gluten
1 tsp sea salt
3 tbsp olive oil
2 tsp apple cider vinegar

In a large bowl, combine honey and 1/3 cup water. Sprinkle in yeast and allow to proof, undisturbed (do not stir or move the bowl), for 10 minutes or until foamy. (If yeast does not foam, it is dead and the dough will not rise. Discard and start again with fresh ingredients.)

While yeast is proofing, in another large bowl, whisk together 2 cups flour, wheat gluten and salt. Once yeast is foamy, add remaining water, 2 tbsp oil and vinegar to yeast mixture. Pour in flour mixture and gently fold in with a bowl scraper or spatula until just combined. (Mixture will form a very wet ball.) Coat the bottom of another large bowl with remaining oil (ensure bowl is large enough so that, when doubled in size, the dough will not reach the top). Transfer dough to bowl, rolling ball a bit to coat with oil. Cover bowl tightly with plastic wrap, set aside at room temperature and let dough rise for 1 hour. Dough will be very soft and sticky.

Lightly dust work surface with about 1/4 cup flour. Transfer dough to floured surface and roll lightly in flour. Gently knead dough for about 1 minute, dusting work surface with more flour as needed to prevent dough from sticking. Form dough into a ball and return to bowl. Cover bowl tightly with plastic wrap, set aside at room temperature and let dough rise for 30 minutes.

Transfer dough back to floured work surface and cut dough in half to form two balls. Dusting work surface with more flour as needed to prevent dough from sticking, lightly knead each ball for about 30 seconds. Reform into balls. Dough is now ready to be formed into a crust or saved for future use. To store, wrap each dough ball individually in plastic wrap. Dough can be kept refrigerated for 24 hours or frozen for up to 1 month.

To use from refrigerator: Remove dough from fridge and let warm at room temperature for about 10 minutes. Form a pizza crust.

To use from frozen: Thaw dough in fridge overnight. Remove dough from fridge and let warm at room temperature for about 10 minutes. Form a pizza crust.

Per Serving (1/8 dough ball)
Before: 183 calories, 5 g total fat
Dish Do-Over: 94 calories, 2.9 g total fat, 0.4 g saturated fat, 15 g carbohydrates, 2.4 g fibre, 1.2 g sugar, 3.2 g protein, 99 mg sodium, 0 mg cholesterol

Do-Over Whipped Cream
MAKES 2 CUPS
HANDS-ON TIME: 15 MINUTES
TOTAL TIME: 35 MINUTES

The purists out there will balk at this recipe, but here's my theory: whipped cream is a waste of calories and fat. There, I said it. Just half a cup of whipped cream tips the scales at 11 grams of fat and more than 100 calories. I'd rather have a few slices of bacon or a nice piece of dark chocolate instead, thank you very much. If you're craving a little fluffy stuff on top of your dish do-over dessert or milkshake, this simple recipe will do the trick with a fraction of the fat.

> 1 tsp unflavoured gelatin powder
> 1 cup skim milk
> 2 tbsp organic icing sugar
> 1 tsp pure vanilla extract

In a small bowl, combine gelatin with 2 tbsp milk and set aside for 5 minutes to soften.

Meanwhile, in a small saucepan, combine remaining milk, sugar and vanilla and bring to a simmer over medium heat. Remove from heat and add softened gelatin, stirring until gelatin is dissolved. Transfer mixture to a stand mixer or medium stainless-steel mixing bowl. Cover and refrigerate until mixture begins to thicken slightly, about 15 minutes.

Using whisk attachment or an electric whisk, beat on high speed for about 8 minutes, until thick and fluffy. Cover and refrigerate, or serve immediately. It will last for up to 24 hours refrigerated.

Note: Whipped cream must be stored in the fridge. It will deflate if left to stand at room temperature, though it can be re-whipped.

To re-whip: Divide whipped cream in half, whisk half of mixture until smooth and gently fold into remaining mixture. Serve immediately.

Per Serving (1/4 cup)
Before: 103.5 calories, 11 grams total fat
Dish Do-Over: 20 calories, 0 g total fat, 0 g saturated fat, 3.5 g carbohydrates, 0 g fibre, 3.5 g sugar, 1.3 g protein, 14 mg sodium, 1 mg cholesterol

Appetizers & Snacks

Buffalo Wings with Blue Cheese Dip

I grew up in the Niagara region, so frequent trips to Buffalo, New York, for its famous chicken wings and for bargain hunting was always something to look forward to on the weekends. The skin-to-meat ratio of a chicken wing makes it fatty enough on its own, but then we deep-fry them, toss them in hot sauce loaded with butter and dunk them in a blue cheese sauce that has as its base mayo and sour cream. For this do-over, I use skinless drumettes (the meaty upper part of a chicken wing) instead of full chicken wings, marinate them in a brine for extra juiciness and flavour, and lighten up both sauces. Even die-hard Buffalo wing purists would approve of these changes.

5 lb skinless chicken drumettes

BRINE
1/3 cup kosher or sea salt
1/4 cup honey
1/4 cup apple cider vinegar
1/8 tsp cayenne pepper
8 cups water

BLUE CHEESE DIP
1 cup non-fat plain Greek yogurt
1/2 cup crumbled blue cheese
1/4 cup thinly sliced green onions
2 tbsp skim milk or 1% buttermilk
1 small garlic clove, minced
Sea salt and freshly ground
    black pepper

BUFFALO WING SAUCE
1 cup cayenne pepper hot sauce
2 tbsp unsalted butter, softened
1 tbsp honey
1 tbsp apple cider vinegar
1/2 tsp cayenne pepper
1/4 tsp garlic powder
1/4 tsp each sea salt and freshly ground
    black pepper

SERVES 10
HANDS ON TIME: 30 MINUTES
TOTAL TIME: 1 HOUR, 15 MINUTES
+ 4 HOURS MARINATING TIME

Prepare brine: In a large resealable container, whisk salt, honey, vinegar and cayenne into water until dissolved. Add chicken, cover and refrigerate for at least 4 hours and up to 12 hours.

Meanwhile, prepare blue cheese dip: In a small bowl, combine yogurt, cheese, green onions, milk and garlic. Season with salt and pepper, cover and refrigerate.

Preheat oven to 425°F. Line a large baking sheet with parchment paper or foil and place a baking rack on top.

Drain wings, discarding brine. Arrange in a single layer on prepared baking sheet. Bake for 30 minutes. Remove from oven, turn wings over and continue to bake for another 20 minutes, until golden and crispy.

While wings are baking, prepare sauce: In a medium saucepan, whisk together hot sauce, butter, honey, vinegar, cayenne, garlic powder, salt and pepper. Warm over medium heat until barely simmering. Cover and set aside.

In a large bowl, toss chicken with sauce to coat. Serve with blue cheese dip and carrot and celery sticks.

PER SERVING
BEFORE: 411 CALORIES, 36 G TOTAL FAT
DISH DO-OVER: 256 CALORIES, 11.5 G TOTAL FAT
NUTRITIONAL INFORMATION: 4.7 G SATURATED FAT,
23 G CARBOHYDRATES, 0.1 G FIBRE, 4.8 G SUGAR,
31 G PROTEIN, 1604 MG SODIUM, 88 MG CHOLESTEROL

Spinach & Artichoke Dip

One of the most popular, and fattiest, appetizers . . . and always the hit of the party. By swapping in non-fat Greek yogurt and using low-fat versions of other creamy ingredients, I've created a version that will fool even the toughest critics. Serve with crudités and Chili-Lime Baked Tortilla Chips (recipe follows).

2 cups shredded low-fat mozzarella
    cheese
1/2 cup freshly grated Parmesan cheese
3/4 cup non-fat plain Greek yogurt
1/4 cup low-fat mayonnaise
3/4 cup low-fat cream cheese, softened
1 tsp dried oregano
Pinch cayenne pepper
Pinch freshly ground black pepper
1 cup (about 1/2 10-oz block) chopped
    frozen spinach, thawed, drained and
    squeezed dry
1 can (15 oz/398 mL) artichoke hearts,
    drained and coarsely chopped

SERVES 8
HANDS-ON TIME: 20 MINUTES
TOTAL TIME: 40 MINUTES

Reserve 1/3 cup mozzarella and 2 tbsp Parmesan. In a food processor, combine remaining mozzarella and Parmesan, yogurt, mayonnaise, cream cheese, oregano, cayenne and black pepper. Using a spatula, scrape cheese mixture into a large bowl. Stir in spinach and artichoke hearts.

Transfer dip to a shallow ovenproof baking dish, top with reserved cheeses, cover and refrigerate until needed. Will keep up to 3 days.

To serve, preheat oven to 400°F. Place dish on a baking sheet and heat in oven for 15 to 18 minutes, until hot and bubbling. Let rest at room temperature for 3 to 4 minutes before serving.

PER SERVING
BEFORE: 275 CALORIES, 21 G TOTAL FAT
DISH DO-OVER: 201 CALORIES, 12.9 G TOTAL FAT
*NUTRITIONAL INFORMATION: 6.9 G SATURATED FAT,
7.2 G CARBOHYDRATES, 1.6 G FIBRE, 1.5 G SUGAR,
15.3 G PROTEIN, 431 MG SODIUM, 38 MG CHOLESTEROL*

Chili-Lime Baked Tortilla Chips

Regular tortilla chips can add hundreds of calories to a dish that's already a caloric nightmare. The trick to crispy perfection with these chips is that, instead of oil, I mist them with flavourful lime-water.

2 tbsp fresh lime juice
1 tsp chili powder
1 tsp sea salt
20 6-inch corn tortillas

SERVES 8 (MAKES 160 CHIPS)
HANDS-ON TIME: 10 MINUTES
TOTAL TIME: 25 MINUTES

PER SERVING
BEFORE: 300 CALORIES, 16 G TOTAL
FAT/DISH DO-OVER: 227 CALORIES,
5 G TOTAL FAT
*NUTRITIONAL INFORMATION:
1.3 G SATURATED FAT, 35.5 G
CARBOHYDRATES, 2.6 G FIBRE,
0.1 G SUGAR, 7.6 G PROTEIN,
1.3 MG SODIUM, 0 MG CHOLESTEROL*

Pour lime juice into a small spray bottle and fill with 1/2 cup water; set aside. Combine chili powder and salt; set aside.

Set racks in top and bottom thirds of oven and preheat to 350°F. Line two large baking sheets with parchment paper.

Stack tortillas and cut into 8 wedges. Arrange in a single layer on prepared baking sheets. Mist with lime water. Dust with chili salt and bake for 15 minutes or until golden and crispy, switching and rotating baking sheets halfway through. (If chips are baking unevenly, remove individual chips as they are ready.)

Remove from oven and allow to cool completely. Store at room temperature in a sealed container for up to 1 week.

Fried Calamari with Yogurt Aioli & Tomato Sauce

Fried calamari is one of my favourite munchies, but like anything that takes a swim in hot oil, it's loaded with fat and calories. I've lightened things up by baking the calamari with a crunchy panko and corn-flour coating. Soaking the calamari in milk helps keep them tender.

1 lb calamari bodies, sliced into
　　1/4-inch-thick rings
2 1/2 cups 1% buttermilk or skim milk
3/4 cup whole-wheat or brown rice flour
1 cup non-fat plain Greek yogurt
1 garlic clove, minced
2 tbsp finely chopped fresh chives
2 tbsp Dijon mustard
2 tbsp fresh lemon juice
Freshly ground black pepper
3/4 cup egg whites (about 6 large)
1/4 tsp cayenne pepper
2 1/2 cups toasted panko bread crumbs
　　(page 17) (gluten-free, if desired)
1 1/2 cups corn flour
Sea salt
1 cup jarred all-natural tomato sauce

SERVES 8
HANDS-ON TIME: 35 MINUTES
TOTAL TIME: 50 MINUTES +
1 HOUR MARINATING TIME

Place calamari in medium bowl. Pour 2 cups buttermilk over top, ensuring rings are submerged. Cover and refrigerate for at least 1 hour and up to 8 hours.

For yogurt aioli, in a small bowl, whisk together yogurt, garlic, chives, Dijon and lemon juice. Season with salt and pepper, cover and refrigerate.

In a medium bowl, whisk together egg whites, remaining 1/2 cup buttermilk and cayenne. Place panko in a shallow dish and mix with corn flour.

Preheat oven to 400°F. Line a large baking sheet with parchment paper or foil and place a baking rack on top. Spray rack with cooking spray.

Drain calamari through a sieve and pat dry with paper towel. Working with a few rings at a time, coat calamari in rice flour by dredging on a plate or shaking in a resealable bag, then shaking off any excess. Dip into egg wash and then into panko mixture, pressing to coat each ring inside and out. Arrange in a single layer on baking rack. Repeat until all rings are coated. Lightly mist rings with cooking spray.

Bake in centre of oven for 6 minutes. Carefully flip each ring over, mist again with cooking spray and continue to bake for another 6 minutes or until crispy. Season with salt. Serve with yogurt aioli and tomato sauce for dipping.

PER SERVING
BEFORE: 207 CALORIES. 4.6 G TOTAL FAT
DISH DO-OVER: 329 CALORIES, 3.9 G TOTAL FAT
NUTRITIONAL INFORMATION: 0.6 G SATURATED FAT, 52.8 G CARBOHYDRATES, 3.2 G FIBRE, 21.6 G SUGAR, 19.8 G PROTEIN, 469 MG SODIUM, 31 MG CHOLESTEROL

Sausage Rolls

Betcha can't eat just one! I reached out to my Facebook friends and asked which holiday party food needed a do-over, and the clear winner was sausage rolls. I don't think I've been to a holiday party where a tray of these hasn't crossed my path. Phyllo and extra-lean turkey sausage instead of the traditional puff pastry and full-fat pork sausage transform these holiday favourites into a light and crispy treat.

1/4 cup rolled oats

2 cups quartered cremini mushrooms

1 chipotle pepper in adobo sauce, plus
    1 tsp sauce

2 garlic cloves, minced

1 tbsp chopped fresh rosemary

1/4 tsp each sea salt and freshly ground
    black pepper

4 extra-lean chicken or turkey sausages
    (1 lb total), casings removed

1 large egg

12 sheets phyllo pastry, thawed

3 tbsp Dijon mustard

1 tbsp sesame seeds

SERVES 20 (MAKES 80 PIECES)
HANDS-ON TIME: 40 MINUTES
TOTAL TIME: 1 HOUR + 1 HOUR
RESTING TIME

In a food processor, pulse oats to a fine powder. Add mushrooms, chipotle pepper, garlic, rosemary, salt and pepper. Pulse until mushrooms are coarsely ground. Add sausages and pulse to combine. Transfer mixture to a piping bag with a large round tip.

In a small bowl, whisk egg with 2 tbsp water.

Remove phyllo from wrapping and cover with a clean, damp kitchen towel. Lay 1 sheet on work surface, a short edge facing to you, and mist well with cooking spray. Add two more layers of phyllo, misting each layer with cooking spray. Cut phyllo in half lengthwise, to form 2 rectangles. Brush bottom lengthwise edge of a 3-sheet rectangle of phyllo with mustard. Squeeze about one-quarter of filling over top of Dijon. Brush top edge with egg wash. Starting at the bottom lengthwise edge, roll up phyllo around filling to form a 1-inch-wide tube, folding in ends and pinching to seal. Brush outside of roll with egg wash and sprinkle with sesame seeds. Repeat with remaining phyllo.

Transfer rolls to a baking sheet, cover loosely and refrigerate for 1 hour to allow filling to set.

Preheat oven to 425°F. Line a large baking sheet with parchment paper.

Using a very sharp knife, cut each roll into 10 pieces (each piece about 1 inch wide). Arrange on a prepared baking sheet and bake for about 20 minutes, until filling is cooked and pastry is golden brown and flaky.

PER SERVING
BEFORE: 240 CALORIES, 20 G TOTAL FAT
DISH DO-OVER: 100 CALORIES, 4 G TOTAL FAT
NUTRITIONAL INFORMATION: 0.8 G SATURATED FAT,
9.3 G CARBOHYDRATES, 0.7 G FIBRE, 0.3 G SUGAR,
6.2 G PROTEIN, 250 MG SODIUM, 26 MG CHOLESTEROL

Mini Corn Dogs with Grainy Mustard

This kids' favourite usually starts with a hot dog (loaded with fillers, fat and sodium) that is then battered and deep-fried. Some recipes suggest baking corn dogs, but regular batter won't stick well. The trick is to swap the batter for a fluffy dough and use all-natural cut turkey dogs.

24 4-inch wooden skewers, soaked in
    warm water for 3 minutes

1 cup skim milk
1 tsp honey
1 package (1/4 oz/7 g) regular active
    dry yeast (about 2 1/2 tsp)
2 tbsp olive oil, plus extra for coating
2 cups whole-wheat or spelt flour
1 cup fine yellow cornmeal, plus extra
    for dusting
4 tsp vital wheat gluten
1 tsp sea salt
1/4 tsp baking powder
1/2 tsp cayenne pepper
8 all-natural chicken or turkey dogs,
    cut into thirds, patted dry
    with paper towel
1/4 cup Dijon mustard
1/4 cup whole-grain mustard
1 large egg, beaten with 3 tbsp water
1/4 cup sesame seeds

MAKES 24 PIECES
HANDS-ON TIME: 55 MINUTES
TOTAL TIME: 1 HOUR, 10 MINUTES
+ 1 HOUR RISING TIME

PER SERVING
**BEFORE: 278 CALORIES, 17.2 G
TOTAL FAT / DISH DO-OVER: 133
CALORIES, 6.7 G TOTAL FAT**
*NUTRITIONAL INFORMATION:
1.8 G SATURATED FAT, 14 G CARBO-
HYDRATES, 2.1 G FIBRE, 0.9 G
SUGAR, 5.1 G PROTEIN, 281 MG
SODIUM, 16 MG CHOLESTEROL*

In a small saucepan over medium heat, warm milk until luke-warm, about 105°F. Transfer to a large bowl, stir in honey and sprinkle with yeast. Allow yeast to proof undisturbed (do not stir, or move the bowl) for 10 minutes or until foamy. (If yeast does not foam, it is dead, and the dough will not rise. Discard and start again with fresh ingredients.)

Once yeast is foamy, add oil, 1 1/2 cups flour, cornmeal, vital wheat gluten, salt, baking powder and cayenne. Blend mixture by scraping sides of bowl with a spatula, turning the bowl and folding ingredients into the centre until they form a ball of dough. Add more flour as needed if dough is sticky.

Turn dough out onto a floured work surface and begin to knead, dusting work surface with remaining flour as needed to prevent sticking. Knead for 5 minutes or until dough is smooth and elastic (it should spring back when poked with your finger). Place dough into a bowl lightly coated with oil and turn dough to coat completely. Cover bowl tightly with a clean, damp kitchen towel and let dough rise in a warm place for about 1 hour, until it is double in size.

While dough is resting, insert skewer into centre of each chicken dog piece, about halfway through. Cover and set aside.

In a small bowl, mix together Dijon and whole-grain mustard.

Preheat oven to 425°F. Line a large baking sheet with parchment paper and dust with about 2 tbsp cornmeal.

Once dough has risen, return dough to floured work surface and punch down to flatten slightly. Cut dough into 24 equal-sized pieces and cover with a clean, damp kitchen towel. Using a lightly floured rolling pin, roll 1 piece of dough until about 1 inch longer than the hot dog pieces and about 3 inches wide. Place 1 skewered hot dog in centre of dough. Roll up to enclose chicken dog completely, pinching dough to seal. Place on baking sheet, seam side down. Repeat with remaining dough and chicken dog pieces. Lightly brush each corn dog with egg wash and sprinkle with sesame seeds. Bake for 12 to 15 minutes, until very light golden brown and corn dogs are heated through. Serve with mustard mixture for dipping.

Ultimate Nachos

Nachos are happy food. Nachos mean party time. Nachos and beer are BFFs. However, one serving of nachos can pack more than your daily dose of sodium and fat, and over 900 calories, thanks to deep-fried tortillas, sour cream, guacamole, greasy beef and gobs of melted cheese. The good news is that you can have your beer and nachos too with these ultimate nachos. Combining the usual guacamole and sour cream into one sauce and swapping in Greek yogurt saves a boatload of calories, and beans add bulk and flavour to the meat. Every chip should be coated with toppings, so I must insist that you bake these in a single layer on a parchment-lined baking sheet.

1 lb extra-lean ground beef

1 medium yellow onion, diced

2 garlic cloves, minced

1 canned chipotle pepper in adobo sauce, minced, plus 1 tsp adobo sauce

1 tbsp chili powder

2 tsp ground cumin

1 cup canned black beans, drained and rinsed

1/3 cup low-sodium beef stock

Sea salt and freshly ground black pepper

1 package (7 oz/198 g) baked corn tortilla chips or 1 batch Chili-Lime Baked Tortilla Chips (page 31)

1 cup shredded low-fat aged cheddar cheese

1 cup shredded low-fat mozzarella cheese

4 medium plum tomatoes, seeded and diced

1/2 medium white onion, diced

1 fresh jalapeño or serrano chili pepper, finely diced (for less spice, remove seeds and ribs)

2/3 cup coarsely chopped fresh cilantro

6 tbsp fresh lime juice

2 ripe medium avocados, chopped

1 cup non-fat plain Greek yogurt

SERVES 8
HANDS-ON TIME: 40 MINUTES
TOTAL TIME: 40 MINUTES

Preheat oven to 400°F. Line a large baking sheet with parchment paper.

Heat a large non-stick skillet over medium-high heat; mist with cooking spray. Add beef to skillet and cook, breaking it up with a wooden spoon, for about 10 minutes, until lightly browned. Stir in yellow onion and garlic and cook, stirring frequently, for about 4 minutes, until onion is softened. Add chipotle and its sauce, chili powder and cumin and cook, stirring constantly, until fragrant, about 1 minute. Stir in beans and beef stock. Cook until beans are hot and liquid is absorbed. Remove from heat and season with salt and pepper.

Arrange chips in a single layer on prepared baking sheet. Top with half the cheese, then beef mixture, then remaining cheese. Bake for about 10 minutes, until cheese is melted and chips are light golden brown.

Meanwhile, prepare pico de gallo: In a medium bowl, mix together tomatoes, white onions, jalapeño, 1/3 cup cilantro and 2 tbsp lime juice. Season with salt and pepper.

In a food processor, pulse avocados, yogurt, remaining 1/3 cup cilantro and remaining 4 tbsp lime juice until combined but still a bit chunky. Alternatively, mash with a fork. Season with salt and pepper. Transfer to a bowl and cover; set aside.

Remove nachos from oven and top with pico de gallo. Serve with avocado purée on the side.

PER SERVING
BEFORE: 970 CALORIES, 63 G TOTAL FAT
DISH DO-OVER: 399 CALORIES, 16.4 G TOTAL FAT
NUTRITIONAL INFORMATION: 5.1 G SATURATED FAT, 37.4 G CARBOHYDRATES, 7.8 G FIBRE, 4.4 G SUGAR, 27.3 G PROTEIN, 517 MG SODIUM, 44 MG CHOLESTEROL

Layered Nacho Dip

Oh, nacho dip! One of my biggest party pitfalls: totally addictive and loaded with fat. My lightened-up version uses non-fat Greek yogurt, low-fat cheeses and a non-fried bean purée . . . *Olé!*

OLIVE SALSA

1/2 medium white onion, diced
1/2 red bell pepper, diced
1/2 green bell pepper, diced
1/3 cup jarred pickled jalapeño slices,
   drained and chopped
1 cup jarred sliced green pimento-
   stuffed olives, drained
1 cup jarred sliced black olives, drained
1/4 cup fresh lime juice

BLACK BEAN DIP

2 cans (19 oz/540 mL) black beans,
   drained and rinsed
1/2 cup coarsely chopped fresh cilantro
1/4 cup fresh lime juice
3 tbsp olive oil
3 tbsp water
1 tbsp ground cumin
2 tsp chili powder
1/2 tsp cayenne pepper or a few dashes
   hot sauce
Sea salt and freshly ground
   black pepper

GREEK YOGURT PURÉE

2 cups non-fat plain Greek yogurt
1 cup low-fat cream cheese, softened

AVOCADO PURÉE

2 ripe medium avocados, chopped
1 cup non-fat plain Greek yogurt
1/4 cup coarsely chopped fresh cilantro
3 tbsp fresh lime juice
Sea salt and freshly ground
   black pepper

NACHOS

4 cups shredded low-fat aged
   cheddar and mozzarella cheese
4 cups jarred all-natural salsa
8 cups baked tortilla chips

Prepare olive salsa: In a medium bowl, mix together onions, bell peppers, jalapeño, green and black olives and lime juice. Cover and set aside.

Prepare black bean dip: In a food processor, purée black beans, cilantro, lime juice, oil, water, cumin, chili powder and cayenne until smooth, adding more water 1 tbsp at a time if needed. Season with salt and pepper, transfer to a bowl and cover.

Prepare Greek yogurt purée: Clean food processor, then add yogurt and cream cheese and purée until smooth. Transfer to a bowl and cover.

Prepare avocado purée: In food processor, pulse avocados, yogurt, cilantro and lime juice and until combined but still a bit chunky. Season with salt and pepper, transfer to a bowl and cover.

To build dip, reserve 1/2 cup each shredded cheese mixture and olive salsa. Spread half of yogurt purée into bottom of a large glass bowl or a 9- × 13-inch baking dish and smooth with a spatula. Using a slotted spoon to drain any liquid, top with half of olive salsa. Dollop half of jarred salsa on top of olives, then sprinkle with half of shredded cheeses. Dollop half of avocado purée on top, smoothing with a spatula into a thin layer. Top with half of black bean dip, smoothing with spatula. Repeat layers using remaining dip and purées. Top with reserved shredded cheese and olive salsa. Serve immediately with chips on the side, or cover and refrigerate for up to 4 hours.

SERVES 16
HANDS-ON TIME: 45 MINUTES
TOTAL TIME: 45 MINUTES

PER SERVING
BEFORE: 490 CALORIES, 36 G TOTAL FAT
DISH DO-OVER: 333 CALORIES, 15.2 G TOTAL FAT,
NUTRITIONAL INFORMATION: 5.1 G SATURATED FAT,
32.8 G CARBOHYDRATES, 8.1 G FIBRE, 4.9 G SUGAR,
19.3 G PROTEIN, 1128 MG SODIUM, 22 MG CHOLESTEROL

Three-Cheese Garlic Bread

When I was a kid, I often got up before my parents and made toast with melted cheese for myself for breakfast, a practice frowned upon by my mom. To this day, bread and any sort of cheese are my stranded-on-a-desert-island foods, but enjoyed in moderation, cheesy garlic bread is an irresistible possibility. Garlic bread is usually drenched in butter, the soft bread soaking it in like a sponge. Here, I use a whole-grain baguette and make a cheese spread with non-fat Greek yogurt and low-fat cheeses, to slather on the bread.

1 whole-wheat or gluten-free baguette
3 tbsp unsalted butter
4 garlic cloves, minced
2 green onions, minced
3/4 cup shredded low-fat aged
    cheddar cheese
3/4 cup shredded low-fat mozzarella
    cheese
1/3 cup non-fat plain Greek yogurt
1/4 cup freshly grated Parmesan cheese
1/2 tsp Italian herb seasoning
1/4 tsp cayenne pepper
Sea salt and freshly ground
    black pepper

SERVES 8
HANDS-ON TIME: 20 MINUTES
TOTAL TIME: 35 MINUTES

Preheat oven to 400°F. Line a large baking sheet with parchment paper.

Slice baguette in half crosswise and then in half lengthwise.

In a small saucepan or non-stick skillet, melt butter over medium heat. Add garlic and cook, stirring constantly, until fragrant, about 2 minutes. Transfer to a large bowl and allow to cool to room temperature. Stir in green onions, cheddar, mozzarella, yogurt, Parmesan, Italian herbs and cayenne. Season with salt and pepper.

Spread mixture evenly over cut sides of bread and place on prepared baking sheet. Bake for 12 to 15 minutes, until cheese is golden brown and bubbling and edges of bread are golden brown.

PER SERVING
BEFORE: 402 CALORIES, 22 G TOTAL FAT
DISH DO-OVER: 207 CALORIES, 8.8 G TOTAL FAT
NUTRITIONAL INFORMATION: 5.1 G SATURATED FAT,
22.7 G CARBOHYDRATES, 2.6 G FIBRE, 0.6 G SUGAR,
11 G PROTEIN, 386 MG SODIUM, 23 MG CHOLESTEROL

Baked Potato Skins

Potato skins are one of the most fat-laden options on the menu. Even I was shocked that one serving of potato skins can have 62 grams of fat. Naturally, something had to be done! I started with baking instead of deep-frying the potatoes, filled them with veggies and brought in our pal non-fat Greek yogurt to really slash the fat. I didn't mess with the bacon too much, but feel free to omit it, to make these vegetarian. You can use sweet potatoes or fluffy russet potatoes for this recipe. My first choice is sweet potatoes, as they have more flavour and are loaded with nutrients.

8 small sweet or russet potatoes, scrubbed
1/2 red bell pepper, diced
1/2 medium red onion, diced
1 cup frozen corn kernels, thawed and drained
1 tbsp fresh lime juice
Sea salt and freshly ground black pepper
1/2 tsp cumin
1/2 tsp smoked paprika
1 cup shredded low-fat aged cheddar cheese
1 cup non-fat plain Greek yogurt
4 slices Perfect Crispy Bacon (page 17) (use low-sodium, and all-natural, nitrate-free if possible), crumbled
3 green onions, thinly sliced

MAKES 16 PIECES
HANDS-ON TIME: 40 MINUTES
TOTAL TIME: 1 HOUR, 25 MINUTES

Preheat oven to 425°F. Line a large baking sheet with parchment paper or foil.

Pierce potatoes several times with a fork and arrange on prepared baking sheet. Bake for about 1 hour, until flesh is tender when pierced with a knife. Set aside to cool completely.

Meanwhile, in a large bowl, mix bell pepper, onion and corn with lime juice. Season with salt and pepper.

Cut baked potatoes in half lengthwise and, using a spoon, scoop out flesh, leaving a 1/4-inch-thick shell. Save flesh for another use (try my Perfect Mashed Potatoes, page 85, or Loaded Baked Potato Soup, page 99). Return potatoes, cut side up, to baking sheet and mist with cooking spray. Sprinkle with cumin and paprika. Season with salt and pepper. Bake in oven for about 10 minutes, until crispy.

Remove from oven and divide corn mixture between skins. Top with cheddar. Bake for another 8 minutes or until filling is hot and cheese is melted and bubbling. Remove from oven and dollop each skin with 2 tbsp yogurt. Sprinkle with bacon bits and green onion.

PER SERVING
BEFORE: 769 CALORIES, 62 G TOTAL FAT
DISH DO-OVER: 125 CALORIES, 1.3 G TOTAL FAT
NUTRITIONAL INFORMATION: 0.5 G SATURATED FAT, 23 G CARBOHYDRATES, 3.4 G FIBRE, 8.9 G SUGAR, 6.3 G PROTEIN, 115 MG SODIUM, 4 MG CHOLESTEROL

Sweet & Sour Meatballs

Versions of this party favourite have been passed around for decades. It's the perfect potluck dish, except for some offending ingredients: frozen meatballs, grape jelly and ketchup, which are full of fat, refined sugar and sodium. Bring this retro crowd-pleaser to any potluck party and everyone will be asking for the recipe.

MEATBALLS

1 large egg
2 garlic cloves, minced
1/2 medium yellow onion, grated
1/4 cup fresh whole-wheat
   bread crumbs
2 tbsp Dijon mustard
1 tbsp Italian herb seasoning
1/2 tsp each sea salt and freshly
   ground black pepper
1 lb extra-lean ground beef
1 lb lean ground pork

SAUCE

1 tbsp olive oil
1/2 medium yellow onion, finely
   chopped
1 garlic clove, minced
1/4 cup tomato paste
1/4 cup apple cider vinegar
1 cup passata
1/2 cup honey
1/2 cup sugar-free all-natural cherry or
   black currant preserves
Sea salt and freshly ground
   black pepper

SERVES 10 (MAKES 40 PIECES)
HANDS-ON TIME: 25 MINUTES
TOTAL TIME: 1 HOUR

Preheat oven to 425°F. Line a large baking sheet with parchment paper.

Prepare meatballs: In a large bowl, whisk egg until frothy. Stir in garlic, onion, bread crumbs, Dijon, Italian herbs, salt and pepper. Add beef and pork and mix by hand to combine.

Roll mixture into 2-tbsp balls. Transfer to prepared baking sheet and mist all over with cooking spray. Bake until browned on top, about 15 minutes. Remove from oven; drain and discard pan juices.

Reduce oven temperature to 350°F.

While meatballs are baking, prepare sauce: In a medium saucepan, heat oil over medium heat. Add onion and garlic and sauté, stirring frequently, until softened. Stir in tomato paste and cook, stirring constantly, for about 4 minutes, until colour changes to a deep red. Deglaze pan with vinegar, stirring and scraping up any brown bits from bottom of pan with a wooden spoon. Stir in passata, honey and jam. Increase heat to high and bring mixture to a boil. Reduce heat to medium-low and simmer for 5 minutes, until thickened.

Transfer meatballs to a baking dish and pour sauce over top, stirring to coat. Bake for 20 minutes, stirring once. Serve with small skewers.

PER SERVING
BEFORE: 477 CALORIES, 15 G TOTAL FAT
DISH DO-OVER: 100 CALORIES, 4 G TOTAL FAT
*NUTRITIONAL INFORMATION: 0.8 G SATURATED FAT,
9.3 G CARBOHYDRATES, 0.7 G FIBRE, 0.3 G SUGAR,
6.2 G PROTEIN, 250 MG SODIUM, 26 MG CHOLESTEROL*

Falafel with Tahini Yogurt Sauce

Falafels are full of lots of naturally healthy good stuff. Then they go for an oil bath. But good news: you can achieve the same crispiness as deep-frying without all the extra fat.

FALAFEL

1 can (15 oz/398 mL) chickpeas, drained and rinsed
1/2 medium white onion, chopped (about 3/4 cup)
3 garlic cloves, minced
3 tbsp chopped fresh flat-leaf parsley
3 tbsp chopped fresh cilantro
3 tbsp whole-wheat panko bread crumbs
1 tbsp fresh lemon juice
1 tbsp olive oil
1 1/2 tsp ground cumin
1 tsp ground coriander
1 tsp baking powder
1 tsp sea salt
1/8 tsp cayenne pepper

TAHINI YOGURT SAUCE

1 cup non-fat plain Greek yogurt
1/4 cup tahini paste
2 tbsp fresh lemon juice
1/2 tsp ground cumin
Sea salt and freshly ground black pepper

SERVES 6 (MAKES ABOUT 18 BALLS + 1 1/4 CUPS SAUCE)
HANDS-ON TIME: 25 MINUTES
TOTAL TIME: 55 MINUTES

Preheat oven to 425°F.

Spread chickpeas in a single layer on a paper towel–lined baking sheet and pat dry with paper towel.

In a food processor, pulse chickpeas, onion, garlic, parsley and cilantro until chickpeas are coarsely chopped. Scrape mixture into a bowl. Stir in panko, lemon juice, oil, cumin, coriander, baking powder, salt and cayenne.

Form mixture into 2-tbsp balls, flatten slightly and place on a parchment-lined baking sheet. Mist falafels with cooking spray and bake for 20 minutes. Remove from oven, flip over and mist again with cooking spray. Bake for another 15 minutes or until golden brown and crispy.

Meanwhile, prepare sauce: In a medium bowl, whisk together yogurt, tahini, lemon juice, cumin, salt and pepper until smooth.

Serve baked falafel with sauce on the side for dipping.

Serving Suggestion: Serve 3 falafels in half a 4- or 6-inch whole-wheat pita with diced Roma tomatoes, diced English cucumber, thinly sliced radishes, chopped romaine lettuce and crumbled low-fat feta cheese.

PER SERVING (INCLUDING 3 TBSP YOGURT TAHINI SAUCE)
BEFORE: 560 CALORIES, 62 G TOTAL FAT
DISH DO-OVER: 221 CALORIES, 9.6 G TOTAL FAT
NUTRITIONAL INFORMATION: 1.3 G SATURATED FAT, 25.8 G CARBOHYDRATES, 4.9 G FIBRE, 5.6 G SUGAR, 10 G PROTEIN, 527 MG SODIUM, 2 MG CHOLESTEROL

Jalapeño Poppers

Usually stuffed with cheese and deep-fried, these pub favourites have been lightened up with white beans and cheese for that same creamy taste, and I use panko bread crumbs for that crispy deep-fried flavour. The secret to getting the golden deep-fried look is to mist the panko with cooking spray and toss with salt before baking. Remember to always wear gloves when handling hot peppers.

2 cups toasted whole-wheat panko bread crumbs (page 17) (gluten-free, if desired)

1/2 cup egg whites (about 4 large)

1/4 cup 1% buttermilk

1/2 cup whole-wheat or brown rice flour

10 medium jalapeño peppers

1 cup shredded low-fat aged cheddar cheese

1/2 cup canned white beans, drained and rinsed

1/4 cup low-fat cream cheese, softened

2 green onions, thinly sliced

2 tbsp chopped fresh cilantro

1/2 tsp ground cumin

Sea salt and freshly ground black pepper

1/3 cup non-fat plain Greek yogurt

1/3 cup jarred all-natural salsa

SERVES 10 (MAKES 20 POPPERS)
HANDS-ON TIME: 35 MINUTES
TOTAL TIME: 1 HOUR

Preheat oven to 400°F. Line a large baking sheet with parchment paper.

Prepare breading station: Place panko in a shallow dish. In a medium bowl, whisk together egg whites and buttermilk. Spread flour on a small plate.

Wearing gloves, cut each jalapeño in half. Scrape out and discard seeds and membrane. Place peppers cut side up on a prepared baking sheet.

In a food processor, pulse cheddar, beans, cream cheese, green onions, cilantro and cumin until mixture is almost smooth. Season with salt and pepper.

Wearing gloves, spoon about 2 tsp mixture into the centre of each jalapeño half. Smooth tops of mixture and return jalapeños to baking sheet, filling side up.

Carefully dredge jalapeños in flour to coat completely, gently shaking off excess flour. Dip into egg wash and then into panko, pressing gently to adhere.

Place poppers cut side up on baking sheet and bake for about 20 minutes, until cheese is melted and poppers are golden brown and crispy. Cool at room temperature for 5 minutes before serving. Arrange on a platter and serve immediately with yogurt and salsa for dipping.

PER SERVING
BEFORE: 420 CALORIES, 30 G TOTAL FAT
DISH DO-OVER: 141 CALORIES, 2.5 G TOTAL FAT
NUTRITIONAL INFORMATION: 1.2 G SATURATED FAT, 19.8 G CARBOHYDRATES, 3.3 G FIBRE, 2.3 G SUGAR, 9 G PROTEIN, 376 MG SODIUM, 6 MG CHOLESTEROL

Mozzarella Sticks

Cheese strings are the secret to this dish do-over for kids. Regular low-fat mozzarella will work but won't have the same melty stretchability that cheese strings have. Plus, cheese strings are the perfect size for this recipe.

3/4 cup egg whites (about 6 large)

3/4 cup 1% buttermilk

1/4 tsp cayenne pepper

2 1/2 cups toasted whole-wheat panko bread crumbs (page 17) (gluten-free, if desired)

3/4 cup whole-wheat or brown rice flour

1/2 tsp garlic powder

1/2 tsp dried Italian herb seasoning

1/2 tsp sea salt

8 oz low-fat mozzarella cheese strings, cut into 16 pieces and frozen

1 cup jarred all-natural tomato sauce

SERVES 8 (MAKES 16 STICKS)
HANDS-ON TIME: 30 MINUTES
TOTAL TIME: 35 MINUTES

Tip: Prepare ahead and freeze in a single layer on a baking sheet. Cook from frozen as directed, adding 3 minutes to total cooking time.

Preheat oven to 400°F. Line a large baking sheet with foil or parchment paper and place a baking rack on top. Spray rack with cooking spray.

In a medium bowl, whisk together egg whites, buttermilk and cayenne. Place panko in a shallow dish.

In another medium bowl, whisk together flour, garlic powder, Italian herb seasoning and salt. Transfer to a resealable bag or container, add cheese, seal and shake to evenly coat strings.

Working with 2 or 3 cheese strings at a time, shake off excess flour and dip in egg wash, gently turning to coat completely. Dip in panko, turning to coat completely and gently pressing panko onto cheese. Repeat egg wash and panko steps to double-coat cheese with breading. Place breaded cheese on baking rack. Repeat with remaining cheese strings. Lightly mist with cooking spray.

Bake in centre of oven for 5 minutes. Remove from oven, carefully flip each cheese stick and mist again with cooking spray. Return to oven and bake for another 5 minutes or until crispy on all sides.

In a small saucepan over medium heat, heat sauce, stirring often, until hot and bubbling. Alternatively, warm sauce in a microwave-safe container, covered, for about 1 minute, until hot and bubbling. Serve cheese sticks with tomato sauce on the side for dipping.

PER SERVING
BEFORE: 302 CALORIES, 14 G TOTAL FAT
DISH DO-OVER: 235 CALORIES, 6.7 G TOTAL FAT
NUTRITIONAL INFORMATION: 1.8 G SATURATED FAT, 27.8 G CARBOHYDRATES, 4.6 G FIBRE, 4 G SUGAR, 14.3 G PROTEIN, 520 MG SODIUM, 18 MG CHOLESTEROL

Vegetable Samosas

Samosa dough usually has a lot of fat, since it uses ghee or vegetable oil. Using buttermilk instead reduces the fat, and whole-wheat pastry flour adds fibre and keeps the dough light and flaky. To save time, you could use phyllo or spring roll wrappers.

DOUGH

2 cups whole-wheat pastry flour
1 tsp cumin seeds
1 tsp sea salt
1/4 cup cold unsalted butter, cubed
3/4 cup 1% buttermilk

FILLING

1 cup peeled and diced Yukon Gold
  potatoes
1 cup peeled and diced sweet potato
1 tbsp coconut or grapeseed oil
1 tsp fennel seeds
1 tsp cumin seeds
1 tsp coriander seeds
1 tsp turmeric
1 medium yellow onion, diced
2 garlic cloves, minced
2 medium green chili peppers,
  seeded and minced
1 tbsp grated fresh ginger
1 package (10 oz/300 g) frozen
  chopped spinach, thawed and
  squeezed of excess water
1/2 cup frozen peas, thawed and
  drained
2 tbsp fresh lemon juice
3 tbsp chopped fresh cilantro
Sea salt and freshly ground
  black pepper
1 large egg, beaten with 1 tbsp water

CILANTRO MINT CHUTNEY

1 1/2 cups gently packed mint leaves
1 1/2 cups gently packed cilantro leaves
1/4 cup fresh lime juice
1 tbsp grated fresh ginger
Sea salt and freshly ground
  black pepper

Prepare dough: In a food processor or in a medium bowl and using a pastry blender, combine flour, cumin seeds and salt. Pulse or cut in butter to fine crumbs. Pulse or stir in buttermilk until a ball begins to form. Press dough into a disc; wrap in plastic wrap and refrigerate for 1 hour. [*Make-ahead:* Refrigerate for up to 24 hours.]

Meanwhile, prepare filling: In a medium saucepan, cover potatoes and sweet potatoes with salted water, bring to a boil and cook until tender when pierced with a knife, about 10 minutes. Drain well.

In a large non-stick skillet, heat oil over medium-high heat. Add fennel seeds, cumin seeds, coriander seeds and turmeric and cook, stirring constantly, until fragrant and seeds begin to pop, about 1 minute. Add onion, garlic, chilies and ginger and sauté for 2 to 3 minutes, stirring, until onion is translucent. Transfer to a large bowl. Stir in boiled potatoes, spinach, peas, lemon juice and cilantro. Season with salt and pepper; set aside to cool.

Preheat oven to 400°F. Line a large baking sheet with parchment paper.

Roll dough into a short cylinder shape. Cut dough into 4 pieces, then each into 3 pieces, to get 12 pieces in total; form each piece into a flat round. On a floured work surface, roll out each piece to a 6-inch circle; cut in half. Working with 1 piece at a time, moisten half of the cut edge with water. Form a cone shape by overlapping cut edges by 1/4 inch.

Hold cone in your hand and fill with rounded 1 tbsp potato mixture. Moisten top inside edges of pastry; press to seal. Trim jagged edges and crimp with fork to seal. Transfer samosa to prepared baking sheet and brush with egg wash. Repeat with remaining dough pieces.

Bake samosas for about 25 minutes, until golden brown and heated through.

SERVES 12 (MAKES 24 PIECES)
HANDS-ON TIME: 1 HOUR
TOTAL TIME: 1 HOUR, 15 MINUTES
+ 1 HOUR CHILLING TIME

Meanwhile, prepare chutney: In a food processor, pulse mint, cilantro, lime juice, ginger and 1/4 cup water until almost smooth, adding 1 tbsp water at a time up to 1/3 cup until mixture is the consistency of a thin sauce. Season with salt and pepper and transfer to a bowl.

Serve baked samosas with chutney on the side.

PER SERVING
BEFORE: 372 CALORIES, 19.2 G TOTAL FAT
DISH DO-OVER: 200 CALORIES, 6.3 G TOTAL FAT
*NUTRITIONAL INFORMATION: 3.7 G SATURATED FAT,
31.8 G CARBOHYDRATES, 5.8 G FIBRE, 6.3 G SUGAR,
6.3 G PROTEIN, 239 MG SODIUM, 26 MG CHOLESTEROL*

Baba Ganoush

Another sneaky saboteur! Most packaged baba ganoush contains mayonnaise to help give it its creamy texture — and a whopping 20 grams of fat per 1/4-cup serving. My do-over cuts the mayo and oil for a much fresher and figure-friendly version, with beautiful pomegranate seeds as a finishing touch and bright pop of flavour. While it's not traditional, if you'd like the dip a little creamier, add the yogurt.

1 large eggplant (about 1 lb)
1/4 cup non-fat plain Greek yogurt
    (optional)
3 tbsp tahini
3 tbsp fresh lemon juice
1 garlic clove, minced
1/2 tsp ground cumin
1/2 tsp smoked paprika
Sea salt and freshly ground black
    pepper
1/4 cup chopped fresh flat-leaf parsley
1/3 cup fresh pomegranate seeds
    (optional)

SERVES 5 (MAKES 1 1/3 CUPS)
HANDS-ON TIME: 20 MINUTES
TOTAL TIME: 50 MINUTES

Preheat oven to 450°F or outdoor grill to medium-high heat.

To roast, pierce eggplant several times with a fork and place on a parchment-lined baking sheet. Roast in oven, turning once, until skin is charred and eggplant is tender throughout when pierced with a knife, about 20 minutes.

To grill, place on grill and cook, turning frequently, for about 12 minutes, until skin is charred and eggplant is soft. Cool at room temperature for 10 minutes.

Cut eggplant in half, scoop out flesh with a spoon and drain in a colander, lightly pressing flesh down with the spoon to remove excess water. Transfer eggplant to a food processor and add yogurt (if using), tahini, lemon juice, garlic, cumin and paprika; purée until smooth. Season with salt and pepper.

Add 3 tbsp parsley, pulsing to combine. Transfer to a bowl and top with remaining parsley and pomegranate seeds (if using).

Serve with fresh veggies or pita for dipping.

PER SERVING
BEFORE: 80 CALORIES, 20 G TOTAL FAT
DISH DO-OVER: 83 CALORIES, 5 G TOTAL FAT
*NUTRITIONAL INFORMATION: 0.7 G SATURATED FAT,
9.3 G CARBOHYDRATES, 2.8 G FIBRE, 2.5 G SUGAR,
2.3 G PROTEIN, 13 MG SODIUM, 0 MG CHOLESTEROL*

Chipotle Red Pepper-Topped Hummus

Every gal's favourite snack . . . am I right, ladies? While the fat and calories come from healthy sources, this is one of those foods that can sabotage your efforts to maintain a healthy weight, one scoop at a time. I love that packaged hummus lists the nutritional info as a 2-tbsp serving — when was the last time you ate only two tablespoons of hummus? Their 4.5 grams of fat and 70 calories may seem innocent enough, but they translate to 18.7 grams of fat and 291 calories in a more realistic 1/2-cup serving size.

I adore the topped hummus served in Middle Eastern restaurants and now available in grocery stores. My do-over for this protein-packed dip trades the olive oil and some of the tahini for non-fat Greek yogurt to keep it creamy and a spicy topping to kick things up a bit. For classic hummus, simply eliminate the topping.

HUMMUS

1 can (15 oz/398 mL) chickpeas,
   drained and rinsed
1 garlic clove, minced
1/4 cup fresh lemon juice
1/4 cup non-fat plain Greek yogurt
3 tbsp tahini
1 tsp ground cumin
Sea salt and freshly ground
   black pepper

CHIPOTLE RED PEPPER TOPPING

1/3 cup diced jarred roasted red pepper
1 green onion, thinly sliced
1 tbsp olive oil
1 tsp minced chipotle pepper in
   adobo sauce
Sea salt and freshly ground
   black pepper

SERVES 4
HANDS-ON TIME: 15 MINUTES
TOTAL TIME: 15 MINUTES

Prepare hummus: In a food processor, purée chickpeas, garlic, lemon juice, yogurt, tahini and cumin until smooth, adding water 1 tbsp at a time up to 1/4 cup until hummus is the consistency of a smooth paste. Season with salt and pepper, then transfer to a bowl.

Prepare topping: In a small bowl, mix together bell pepper, green onion, oil and chipotle pepper. Season with salt and pepper. Scoop topping onto hummus, piling it in the centre. Serve with fresh vegetables for dipping.

PER SERVING (1/2 CUP)
BEFORE: 291 CALORIES / 18.7 G TOTAL FAT
DISH DO-OVER: 246 CALORIES, 10.8 G TOTAL FAT
*NUTRITIONAL INFORMATION: 4.7 G SATURATED FAT,
35.5 G CARBOHYDRATES, 2.6 G FIBRE, 0.1 G SUGAR,
7.6 G PROTEIN, 369 MG SODIUM, 0 MG CHOLESTEROL*

Tip: For grab-n-go servings, portion hummus and topping into small Mason jars in 1/2-cup servings. Will keep for 3 days, refrigerated.

Popcorn

Popcorn can be a healthy, delicious and filling snack if you avoid the packaged variety, including microwave popcorn, which is loaded with fat and salt. And besides, it's so easy and fast to make your own.

1/2 cup popcorn kernels
Olive oil cooking spray or 1 tsp olive oil
2 flat-bottom paper lunch bags

TOPPINGS:

PIZZA

1/4 cup freshly grated Parmesan cheese
2 tsp Italian herb seasoning
1/2 tsp sea salt
1/2 tsp garlic powder
1/2 tsp smoked paprika
1/4 tsp cayenne pepper

DILL PICKLE

2 tsp dried dill
1/2 tsp sea salt
1/2 tsp garlic powder
1/2 tsp onion powder
1/2 tsp citric acid

RANCH

2 tbsp buttermilk powder
1/2 tsp onion powder
1/2 tsp sea salt
1/2 tsp garlic powder
1/4 tsp dried dill
1/4 tsp dry mustard

SERVES 4 (MAKES 10 CUPS)
HANDS-ON TIME: 5 MINUTES
TOTAL TIME: 10 MINUTES

In a small bowl, combine ingredients for the topping of your choice.

In another small bowl, mist popcorn kernels with cooking spray. Toss with seasoning mix. Divide popcorn between the two bags and fold the top of each bag over twice to close. Place one bag in the microwave and cook on high for 2 to 3 minutes or until about 5 seconds elapse between pops. Carefully remove bag, shake well and open carefully. Repeat with the second bag.

Note: The popped corn will emit very hot steam when the bag is opened. Do not allow children to open the bag, and do not place your face directly over the bag when opening.

Alternative: If using an air popper, place topping in a large bowl. Mist popcorn with cooking spray as it pops into the bowl, and mix well with the topping after all the popcorn has popped.

PIZZA
PER SERVING (ABOUT 2 1/2 CUPS)
BEFORE: 295 CALORIES, 25 G TOTAL FAT
DISH DO-OVER: 129 CALORIES, 3.6 G TOTAL FAT
NUTRITIONAL INFORMATION: 1.1 G SATURATED FAT, 20.3 G CARBOHYDRATES, 4 G FIBRE, 0.4 G SUGAR, 5.2 G PROTEIN, 276 MG SODIUM, 3 MG CHOLESTEROL

DILL PICKLE
PER SERVING (ABOUT 2 1/2 CUPS)
BEFORE: 133 CALORIES, 7.2 G TOTAL FAT;
DISH DO-OVER: 110 CALORIES, 2.3 G TOTAL FAT
NUTRITIONAL INFORMATION: 0.3 G SATURATED FAT, 20.5 G CARBOHYDRATES, 3.7 G FIBRE, 0.4 G SUGAR, 3.4 G PROTEIN, 0.3 MG SODIUM, 0 MG CHOLESTEROL

RANCH
PER SERVING (ABOUT 2 1/2 CUPS)
BEFORE: 150 CALORIES, 10 G TOTAL FAT
DISH DO-OVER: 122 CALORIES, 2.3 G TOTAL FAT
NUTRITIONAL INFORMATION: 0.4 G SATURATED FAT, 21.6 G CARBOHYDRATES, 3.7 G FIBRE, 0.4 G SUGAR, 4.5 G PROTEIN, 214 MG SODIUM, 3 MG CHOLESTEROL

Salads & Sides

Caesar Salad

I have always loved creamy Caesar salad. When I was growing up, my parents and I would go out for dinner on Friday nights to a local family-run restaurant, and I would order the Caesar salad every time — it was a little bit of an obsession. Caesar salad dressing is essentially emulsified eggs and oil, the same as mayonnaise, and pretty much all fat: just 3 tablespoons of full-fat Caesar dressing contain around 30 grams of fat and 270 calories. I've made a just as creamy version with a fraction of the fat using non-fat Greek yogurt.

There are lots of crunchy crouton alternatives, like toasted nuts or roasted chickpeas, but one of my favourite parts of the salad is a classic garlicky bread crouton, so we're using my lightened-up whole-grain version of those too.

DRESSING

1/2 cup non-fat plain Greek yogurt
1/2 cup freshly grated Parmesan cheese
2 anchovy fillets, minced
1 garlic clove, minced
1 tbsp fresh lemon juice
1 tbsp apple cider vinegar
1 tsp Dijon mustard
1 tsp Worcestershire sauce
1/4 tsp each sea salt and freshly ground
    black pepper
2 or 3 dashes hot sauce

SALAD

12 cups chopped romaine lettuce
1 cup Homemade Croutons (page 15)
4 slices all-natural pork or turkey
    bacon, cooked until crispy
    (page 17) and coarsely chopped

SERVES 4
HANDS-ON TIME: 30 MINUTES
TOTAL TIME: 60 MINUTES

Prepare dressing: Whisk together yogurt, 1/4 cup Parmesan, anchovies, garlic, lemon juice, vinegar, Dijon, Worcestershire sauce, salt, pepper and hot sauce until smooth. [*Make-ahead:* Dressing can be prepared up to 3 days in advance, covered and refrigerated.]

Prepare salad: In a large bowl, combine lettuce, croutons and bacon. Toss with prepared dressing. Sprinkle with remaining 1/4 cup Parmesan.

PER SERVING
BEFORE: 490 CALORIES, 26 G TOTAL FAT
DISH DO-OVER: 284 CALORIES, 10.2 G TOTAL FAT
NUTRITIONAL INFORMATION: 4.8 G SATURATED FAT, 32.5 G CARBOHYDRATES, 4.6 G FIBRE, 19.3 G SUGAR, 18.2 G PROTEIN, 590 MG SODIUM, 24 MG CHOLESTEROL

Cobb Salad

This is a salad that almost doesn't require a recipe. However, due to the mind-blowing 65 grams of fat that most classic versions contain, I decided it was warranted. I've swapped bacon for smoky ham, used egg whites — throwing in just one yolk — cut down on the avocado and lightened up the dressing. All of this while bumping up the amount of vegetables keeps the good parts of this salad without the high-fat price tag.

DRESSING

3 tbsp red or white wine vinegar
1 tbsp fresh lemon juice
1 tbsp Dijon mustard
2 tsp honey
1 tsp Worcestershire sauce
1 garlic clove, minced
3 tbsp olive oil
Sea salt and freshly ground
   black pepper

SALAD

4 Perfect Hard-Boiled Eggs (page 17)
1/2 head iceberg lettuce, cored and
   coarsely shredded by hand
1/2 head romaine lettuce, coarsely
   chopped
1/2 bunch watercress, thick stems
   discarded
1 cup diced smoked cooked ham
   (about 6 oz)
1/2 ripe large avocado, diced and tossed
   with 1 tbsp fresh lemon juice
4 oz Perfect Marinated Chicken Breasts
   (page 21), cooled and diced
1 1/2 cups diced cucumber
1 1/2 cups halved grape tomatoes
1/2 cup crumbled blue cheese
   (about 2 oz)
3 tbsp chopped fresh chives

SERVES 4
HANDS-ON TIME: 1 HOUR,
10 MINUTES
TOTAL TIME: 1 HOUR,
10 MINUTES

Prepare dressing: In a small bowl, whisk together vinegar, lemon juice, Dijon, honey, Worcestershire sauce and garlic. Whisk in oil until combined. Season with salt and pepper.

Prepare salad: Peel eggs and cut in half lengthwise. Remove 3 yolks and reserve for another use. Dice remaining yolk and whites; set aside.

Combine lettuces and watercress in a large bowl and gently toss with three-quarters of dressing to coat completely. Transfer to a large platter. Arrange ham, eggs, avocado, chicken breast, cucumber, tomatoes and cheese in straight rows on top of greens. Drizzle with remaining dressing and sprinkle with chives.

PER SERVING
BEFORE: 880 CALORIES, 65 G TOTAL FAT
DISH DO-OVER: 431 CALORIES, 25.4 G TOTAL FAT
NUTRITIONAL INFORMATION: 7 G SATURATED FAT, 17.2 G CARBOHYDRATES, 5.8 G FIBRE, 9.1 G SUGAR, 35.2 G PROTEIN, 1010 MG SODIUM, 123 MG CHOLESTEROL

Tip: Don't throw out leftover cooked egg yolks! I save them to add to salads for good extra fat and protein. They will last for 2 days in the fridge, but if you're over-loaded with yolks, just pop them into a resealable bag or container and freeze.

Greek Salad

You've heard it before: salads are the secret saboteurs of weight management. Greek salad looks so innocent — loads of veggies with a little vinaigrette and feta cheese — but did you know that just 1 cup can contain as much as 42 grams of fat? Here, I've simply lightened up the vinaigrette, added chicken for protein and swapped in low-fat feta.

3 tbsp olive oil

3 tbsp fresh lemon juice

2 tbsp red wine vinegar

2 tsp dried oregano

2 garlic cloves, minced

Sea salt and freshly ground
    black pepper

2 boneless, skinless chicken breasts
    (4 oz each), butterflied

2 medium vine-ripened tomatoes,
    coarsely diced

1 medium English cucumber, coarsely
    diced

1 red, orange or yellow bell pepper,
    coarsely diced

1/2 red onion, coarsely diced

1/2 cup pitted Kalamata or brine-cured
    black olives

1/4 cup chopped fresh flat-leaf parsley

1 cup crumbled low-fat feta cheese
    (about 4 oz)

SERVES 4
HANDS-ON TIME: 35 MINUTES
TOTAL TIME: 35 MINUTES + 1 HOUR
MARINATING TIME

In a small bowl, whisk together oil, lemon juice, vinegar, oregano and garlic. Season with salt and pepper. Place chicken in a resealable bag or container. Add one-quarter of dressing, turning chicken to coat. Seal and refrigerate for at least 1 hour and up to 24 hours.

Meanwhile, in a large bowl, mix together tomatoes, cucumber, bell pepper, onion, olives and parsley. Add remaining dressing and gently toss to coat. Cover and refrigerate. [*Make-ahead:* Salad can be prepared up to 24 hours in advance.]

Heat a greased grill or non-stick grill pan to medium-high. Discard marinade and grill chicken turning once, for about 8 minutes, until cooked through. Allow to cool to room temperature, then dice.

To serve, toss chicken with salad and top with crumbled feta

PER SERVING
BEFORE: 658 CALORIES, 42 G TOTAL FAT
DISH DO-OVER: 303 CALORIES, 18.2 G TOTAL FAT
NUTRITIONAL INFORMATION: 6.1 G SATURATED FAT, 13.3 G CARBOHYDRATES, 2.6 G FIBRE, 6.6 G SUGAR, 23.9 G PROTEIN, 771 MG SODIUM, 52 MG CHOLESTEROL

Tip: To make this vegetarian, substitute 1 cup drained and rinsed canned chickpeas for the chicken. Toss dressing and chickpeas together with vegetables.

Pasta Salad

No one will miss the mayo in this deli classic. Brown rice pasta also lightens things up and is easier to digest than white pasta.

1 1/2 cups brown rice pasta
1 cup diced celery
1 cup diced red bell pepper
1/3 cup finely diced dill pickle
1/3 cup grated peeled carrot
1/4 cup finely diced red onion, soaked in cold water for 5 minutes, then drained
1/3 cup non-fat plain Greek yogurt
3 tbsp chopped fresh flat-leaf parsley
2 tbsp apple cider vinegar
2 tbsp Dijon mustard
2 tbsp honey
Sea salt and freshly ground black pepper

SERVES 6
HANDS-ON TIME: 20 MINUTES
TOTAL TIME: 20 MINUTES + 1 HOUR CHILLING TIME

Bring a large pot of salted water to a boil and cook pasta according to package instructions. Drain, rinse under cold water and place in a large bowl. Add celery, bell pepper, dill pickle, carrot, onion, yogurt, parsley, vinegar, mustard and honey to pasta and stir well. Season with salt and pepper. Cover and refrigerate for at least 1 hour before serving to allow flavours to blend. Will last for 2 days in the fridge.

PER SERVING
BEFORE: 470 CALORIES, 33 G TOTAL FAT
DISH DO-OVER: 263 CALORIES, 2.1 G TOTAL FAT
NUTRITIONAL INFORMATION: 0.5 G SATURATED FAT, 57.1 G CARBOHYDRATES, 2.2 G FIBRE, 8.3 G SUGAR, 6.5 G PROTEIN, 221 MG SODIUM, 1 MG CHOLESTEROL

Potato Salad

Potato salad is a quintessential summer favourite, but not so fabulous on the old waistline. Mayo is pretty much the biggest offender here, and more is needed if using really starchy potatoes. Greek yogurt is the obvious swap. Also, I use Yukon Gold potatoes, which are a perfect all-purpose spud because they are the ideal combo of a creamy and a waxy potato. Their smooth texture and buttery flavour allow you to use less dressing, and their ability to hold their shape after cooking makes them beautiful for potato salad.

2 lb Yukon Gold potatoes
  (about 6 potatoes), each cut
  into 8 pieces
3 tbsp apple cider vinegar
1/2 tsp sea salt, plus more to taste
1 cup non-fat plain Greek yogurt
4 Perfect Hard-Boiled Eggs (page 17),
  peeled and chopped
2 celery ribs, finely diced
2 medium dill pickles, finely diced
  (about 1/3 cup)
3 green onions, thinly sliced
2 tbsp yellow mustard
Freshly ground black pepper
1 tsp smoked paprika

SERVES 8
HANDS-ON TIME: 30 MINUTES
TOTAL TIME: 30 MINUTES + 1 HOUR
CHILLING TIME

Place potatoes in a medium saucepan and cover with salted water by 1 inch. Bring to a boil over high heat, reduce heat to medium and simmer uncovered until potatoes are tender when pierced with a knife, about 15 minutes. Drain well in a colander, then place in a large bowl. Add vinegar and 1/2 tsp salt to hot potatoes and mix well. Set aside to cool to room temperature.

Meanwhile, in a medium bowl, combine yogurt, egg, celery, pickle, green onions and mustard. When potatoes are cool, gently stir yogurt mixture into potatoes and season with salt and pepper. Cover and refrigerate for at least 1 hour and ideally overnight, as this salad is even better the next day. Sprinkle with paprika just before serving.

PER SERVING
BEFORE: 420 CALORIES, 32 G TOTAL FAT
DISH DO-OVER: 146 CALORIES, 3 G TOTAL FAT
NUTRITIONAL INFORMATION: 0.9 G SATURATED FAT,
22 G CARBOHYDRATES, 2.1 G FIBRE, 2.3 G SUGAR,
8.4 G PROTEIN, 271 MG SODIUM, 110 MG CHOLESTEROL

Broccoli, Cheddar & Ham Salad

My sister makes this delicious salad for many family get-togethers. I try to convince myself that because it's mostly broccoli, it's not so bad for me — oh, the little white lies we tell ourselves. I've swapped mayo for Greek yogurt, switched to low-fat cheese and reduced the amount, and traded bacon for ham.

1 large head broccoli, cut into small
   florets (about 6 cups)
3/4 cup non-fat plain Greek yogurt
2 tbsp honey or organic sugar
1 tbsp apple cider vinegar
1/2 tsp garlic powder
1 cup diced smoked cooked ham
   (about 6 oz)
1 cup shredded low-fat aged cheddar
   cheese
1/3 cup dried cranberries
3 green onions, thinly sliced
Sea salt and freshly ground
   black pepper
1/4 cup toasted sunflower seeds or
   slivered almonds (page 17)

SERVES 8
HANDS-ON TIME: 20 MINUTES
TOTAL TIME: 20 MINUTES + 1 HOUR
CHILLING TIME

Bring a large pot of salted water to a boil. Add broccoli florets and cook for about 90 seconds, until bright green and tender-crisp. Drain and rinse under cold water or in an ice bath. Arrange in a single layer on a kitchen towel–lined baking sheet, gently patting dry with another kitchen towel to remove excess moisture.

In a large bowl, combine yogurt, honey, vinegar and garlic powder. Add ham, cheese, cranberries, green onions and drained broccoli and gently mix until broccoli is coated with dressing. Season with salt and pepper. Cover and refrigerate for at least 1 hour before serving.

To serve, gently stir in sunflower seeds.

PER SERVING
BEFORE: 340 CALORIES, 21 G TOTAL FAT
DISH DO-OVER: 146 CALORIES, 4.7 G TOTAL FAT
NUTRITIONAL INFORMATION: 1.3 G SATURATED FAT,
14.3 G CARBOHYDRATES, 2.3 G FIBRE, 9.2 G SUGAR,
13.8 G PROTEIN, 518 MG SODIUM, 16 MG CHOLESTEROL

Blue Cheese Wedge Salad

Crisp iceberg lettuce is a must for this beautiful, simple salad. I've lightened up the dressing with Greek yogurt and buttermilk, and by making homemade croutons and baking the bacon, drastically and easily reduced the calories and fat. I use the stinkiest blue cheese I can find for this salad, as it's one of the star ingredients. Ask your cheesemonger for a little chunk of something pungent and crumbly.

1 cup non-fat plain Greek yogurt

1/3 cup 1% buttermilk

1/2 cup crumbled blue cheese

1/4 cup finely chopped fresh chives

1 tbsp fresh lemon juice

1 tbsp honey

1 garlic clove, minced, or 1/4 tsp garlic powder

Dash hot sauce

Sea salt and freshly ground black pepper

1 medium head iceberg lettuce

1 batch Homemade Croutons (page 15)

1 cup grape tomatoes, halved lengthwise

1/2 medium Vidalia or sweet onion, thinly sliced

2 slices Perfect Crispy Bacon (page 17), crumbled

SERVES 4
HANDS-ON TIME: 30 MINUTES
TOTAL TIME: 35 MINUTES

For the dressing, in a medium bowl, whisk together yogurt, buttermilk, 1/4 cup cheese, chives, lemon juice, honey, garlic and hot sauce. Season with salt and pepper. [*Make-ahead:* Dressing can be prepared up to 48 hours in advance, covered and refrigerated.]

Remove any wilted outer leaves from lettuce. To loosen core, strike entire head of lettuce, core side down, on a flat surface. Pull core out and discard. Cut lettuce into 4 wedges and arrange cut side up on serving dishes.

Drizzle dressing over each wedge. Top with remaining 1/4 cup cheese, croutons, tomatoes, onion and bacon.

PER SERVING
BEFORE: 419 CALORIES, 37 G TOTAL FAT
DISH DO-OVER: 284 CALORIES, 10.2 G TOTAL FAT
NUTRITIONAL INFORMATION: 4.8 G SATURATED FAT, 32.5 G CARBOHYDRATES, 4.6 G FIBRE, 19.3 G SUGAR, 18.2 G PROTEIN, 590 MG SODIUM, 24 MG CHOLESTEROL

Spinach Salad with Bacon Dressing

You will not find raspberry dressing, candied nuts or goat cheese in this recipe. This is a classic salad with a warm dressing made from . . . bacon fat! I know you'll think I'm nuts, but hear me out: We're using way less bacon fat than the original version, loading up on the spinach and removing most of the egg yolks to help keep the calories in check. If you're really freaked out about eating bacon fat, replace it with olive or coconut oil; I won't be offended.

4 slices Perfect Crispy Bacon (page 17),
   1 tbsp fat reserved

1/3 cup red wine vinegar

1 tbsp honey

1 tbsp Dijon mustard

1 small garlic clove, minced

Sea salt and freshly ground
   black pepper

10 cups lightly packed, fresh baby
   spinach (11-oz/310-g package)

8 medium white mushrooms,
   thinly sliced

1/2 medium Vidalia or sweet onion,
   thinly sliced

4 Perfect Hard-Boiled Eggs
   (page 17), peeled and quartered

SERVES 4
HANDS-ON TIME: 15 MINUTES
TOTAL TIME: 25 MINUTES

Crumble or chop bacon into small pieces.

In a small saucepan, heat bacon fat over medium-low heat. Stir in vinegar, honey, Dijon and garlic. Season with salt and pepper. Remove from heat and cover to keep warm.

In a large bowl, gently toss spinach, mushrooms and onion with dressing to coat. Divide salad among serving bowls and top with bacon and eggs.

PER SERVING
BEFORE: 460 CALORIES, 35 G TOTAL FAT
DISH DO-OVER: 202 CALORIES, 11.6 G TOTAL FAT
NUTRITIONAL INFORMATION: 3.8 G SATURATED FAT,
12.5 G CARBOHYDRATES, 2.6 G FIBRE, 7.9 G SUGAR,
12.5 G PROTEIN, 329 MG SODIUM, 225 MG CHOLESTEROL

Latkes

Any recipe that involves frying potatoes is going to be trouble. For my version, I use a fraction of the oil, thanks to the help of a non-stick pan, and I choose yogurt and unsweetened applesauce for the toppings. Be sure to remove any dark brown bits from the bottom of the pan after each batch is cooked so they don't burn.

1 1/2 lb russet potatoes, peeled
    (about 3 1/2 cups grated)
3/4 lb parsnips, peeled
1 small yellow onion, minced
1 large egg white
1 large egg
3 tbsp fresh whole-wheat bread crumbs
1 tsp baking powder
1/2 tsp sea salt
1/4 tsp freshly ground black pepper
1 cup unsweetened applesauce
1/2 cup non-fat plain Greek yogurt

SERVES 8
HANDS-ON TIME: 35 MINUTES
TOTAL TIME: 40 MINUTES

Preheat oven to 350°F. Line a large baking sheet with parchment paper.

Grate potato and parsnips into a large bowl of cold water. Allow to soak for 2 minutes after all are grated. Drain well in a colander. Transfer to a large, clean kitchen towel. Working over the sink, gather ends of the towel; twist and squeeze very hard to wring out as much liquid as possible. Open towel on work surface; use your fingers to gently loosen vegetables. Wring out once more.

In a large bowl, whisk together onion, egg white, egg, bread crumbs, baking powder, salt and pepper. Add vegetables and mix well.

Heat a large non-stick skillet over medium-high heat; mist with cooking spray. Working in batches, drop 2-tbsp dollops of latke mixture into pan, gently flattening with a spatula. Cook for about 2 minutes per side, until golden brown, misting tops of latkes with cooking spray before flipping. Transfer to prepared baking sheet.

Once all latkes are cooked, transfer baking sheet to oven and bake for about 5 minutes, until latkes are heated through. Serve with applesauce and yogurt on the side.

PER SERVING
BEFORE: 283 CALORIES, 8 G TOTAL FAT
DISH DO-OVER: 144 CALORIES, 2.7 G TOTAL FAT
NUTRITIONAL INFORMATION: 0.4 G SATURATED FAT,
25.9 G CARBOHYDRATES, 3.1 G FIBRE, 6 G SUGAR,
5.1 G PROTEIN, 181 MG SODIUM, 24 MG CHOLESTEROL

Scalloped Potatoes

One of my mom's signature dishes is her fabulous scalloped potatoes. Everyone fights for the bubbly layer of cheese on top! I've swapped in brown rice flour to thicken, and used skim milk. Yukon Gold potatoes are my go-to. The key to perfect scalloped potatoes is slicing the potatoes very thin; a mandolin is your best friend here.

2 tbsp unsalted butter

1 medium onion, finely diced

3 garlic cloves, minced

3 tbsp whole-wheat or brown rice flour

1 tsp coarsely chopped fresh thyme
    (or 1/2 tsp dried)

2 cups skim milk

1 tsp sea salt

1/2 tsp freshly ground black pepper

1/4 tsp freshly grated nutmeg

2 lb Yukon Gold potatoes

1 cup shredded low-fat aged
    cheddar cheese

1/4 cup grated Parmesan cheese

SERVES 6 TO 8
HANDS-ON TIME: 25 MINUTES
TOTAL TIME: 1 HOUR, 45 MINUTES
+ 5 MINUTES RESTING TIME

Preheat oven to 350°F.

In a medium saucepan, melt butter over medium heat. Add onion and garlic and cook, stirring, for about 2 minutes, until onion is softened. Add flour and thyme and cook, stirring, for about 1 minute, until flour is golden brown. Slowly whisk in milk and cook, whisking constantly, until simmering and thickened, about 6 minutes. Remove from heat and season with salt, pepper and nutmeg.

Mist a 9- × 13-inch baking dish with cooking spray. Using a mandolin, very sharp knife or food processor fitted with an 1/8-inch slicing blade, slice potatoes and layer in baking dish, overlapping slices slightly. Pour sauce over potatoes, gently lifting potatoes with the back of a knife or thin spatula to ease sauce in between layers.

Cover with foil and bake for 50 to 60 minutes. Uncover, sprinkle with both cheeses and return to oven, uncovered. Bake for 30 minutes or until potatoes are tender when centre of casserole is pierced with a knife and cheese is golden brown. Let rest at room temperature for 5 minutes before serving.

PER SERVING
BEFORE: 288 CALORIES, 10.4 G TOTAL FAT
DISH DO-OVER: 186 CALORIES, 5.1 G TOTAL FAT
*NUTRITIONAL INFORMATION: 3.1 G SATURATED FAT,
26.8 G CARBOHYDRATES, 2 G FIBRE, 4.7 G SUGAR,
9.1 G PROTEIN, 359 MG SODIUM, 15 MG CHOLESTEROL*

Creamed Spinach

This steakhouse classic is the perfect example of turning a beautiful, fresh, healthy vegetable into something full of fat by adding a few offending ingredients: cream or whole milk, butter and all-purpose flour. I've swapped these saboteurs for tangy low-fat cream cheese and increased the amount of spinach. I prefer regular spinach over baby spinach in this recipe, simply because baby spinach is delicate and has a tendency to get mushy quickly. If you love the convenience of prepackaged baby spinach, just reduce the initial wilting time to 30 seconds.

3 packages (10 oz/284 g each) fresh
    spinach, stems trimmed
Sea salt and freshly ground
    black pepper
1/2 medium yellow onion, finely diced
2 garlic cloves, minced
1/4 tsp dried thyme, oregano or
    Italian herb blend
1/2 cup low-fat cream cheese, cubed
    and softened
3 tbsp skim or 1% milk
Pinch freshly grated nutmeg

SERVES 4
HANDS-ON TIME: 25 MINUTES
TOTAL TIME: 25 MINUTES

Wash spinach well and drain, but do not pat dry or spin in a salad spinner. Heat a large saucepan over high heat; add spinach and a pinch of salt. Cook, stirring frequently, for 1 minute or until spinach is just wilted. Transfer to a sieve, drain well and let stand until cool enough to handle.

Remove excess liquid from spinach by squeezing small handfuls at a time in your hands, by gently wringing in a clean kitchen towel or cheesecloth, or by pressing against the sieve using a wooden spoon or spatula, discarding excess liquid. Coarsely chop drained spinach.

Wipe empty saucepan clean with a clean kitchen towel and set over medium heat; mist with cooking spray. Add onion, garlic and thyme and cook, stirring frequently, until onion is softened and translucent, about 3 minutes. Reduce heat to medium-low and add cream cheese, milk and nutmeg. Cook, stirring frequently, until cream cheese is well combined with milk, about 1 minute. Stir in spinach and season with salt and pepper. Cook until just heated through, about 1 minute.

Note: Creamed spinach can be prepared in advance, covered and refrigerated, then warmed over medium heat until heated through, but it's best enjoyed immediately.

PER SERVING
BEFORE: 295 CALORIES, 21 G TOTAL FAT
DISH DO-OVER: 128 CALORIES, 6.2 G TOTAL FAT
NUTRITIONAL INFORMATION: 3.4 G SATURATED FAT,
11.5 G CARBOHYDRATES, 4.8 G FIBRE, 2 G SUGAR,
9.4 G PROTEIN, 225 MG SODIUM, 17 MG CHOLESTEROL

Creamy Coleslaw

I once catered for a wedding where the bride and groom just could not agree on creamy or vinegar coleslaw. This debate also happened on a regular basis in my house when I was growing up, so my mom acquiesced and made both to keep the peace. Cool, refreshing coleslaw is an essential salad for summer BBQs in my books, but even just 1/2 cup can add 16 grams of fat to your plate. I've cut the full-fat mayo and opted for a lighter, buttermilk-based dressing with all the tang and flavour of the original. Salting the cabbage ahead of time is the key to leaching a lot of water out of the leaves so the dressing isn't runny.

1 medium green cabbage, thinly sliced
   (about 8 cups lightly packed)
2 medium carrots, peeled and grated
1 small red onion, thinly sliced
1 tsp sea salt, plus more to taste
1/4 cup 1% buttermilk
1/4 cup non-fat plain Greek yogurt
3 tbsp chopped fresh flat-leaf parsley
2 tbsp apple cider vinegar
2 tbsp Dijon mustard
2 tbsp honey
Freshly ground black pepper

SERVES 8
HANDS-ON TIME: 20 MINUTES
TOTAL TIME: 20 MINUTES +
90 MINUTES DRAINING TIME

In a large bowl, toss cabbage, carrot and onion with 1 tsp salt. Transfer to a large colander set over a bowl and allow to drain for 90 minutes. Rinse well under cold water and place in a thin layer on a kitchen towel–lined baking sheet, gently patting with another kitchen towel to dry completely.

While the cabbage mixture is draining, in a large bowl, whisk together buttermilk, yogurt, parsley, vinegar, Dijon and honey. Add cabbage mixture, tossing to coat well. Season with salt and pepper.

PER SERVING
BEFORE: 300 CALORIES, 14 G TOTAL FAT
DISH DO-OVER: 69 CALORIES, 0.5 G TOTAL FAT
NUTRITIONAL INFORMATION: 0.1 G SATURATED FAT, 15.1 G CARBOHYDRATES, 2.8 G FIBRE, 10.8 G SUGAR, 3.2 G PROTEIN, 145 MG SODIUM, 1 MG CHOLESTEROL

Tortilla Chip–Crusted Onion Rings

Isn't it wonderful how you can turn a humble workhorse ingredient, like onions or potatoes, into something spectacular? Rather than a panko crust, I opted for baked tortilla chips, which make a beautiful, crispy coating. You could also have some fun and swap baked potato chips in place of the tortillas.

5 cups baked tortilla chips
   (about 7-oz/200-g package)
1 cup cornmeal
1 tsp garlic powder
1/4 tsp cayenne pepper
1 cup corn or brown rice flour
1 cup 1% buttermilk
1 tsp sea salt, plus more to taste
2 large Spanish onions

SERVES 4
HANDS-ON TIME: 25 MINUTES
TOTAL TIME: 40 MINUTES

Position racks in top and bottom thirds of oven and preheat oven to 450°F. Line two large baking sheets with parchment paper.

In a food processor, pulse tortilla chips, cornmeal, garlic powder and cayenne until tortilla chips are fine crumbs. Divide between two shallow bowls; set one bowl aside. (Dividing the mixture in half helps keep the breading dry; use one bowl until coating becomes too wet to stick to onions, then switch.)

Whisk together 1/4 cup flour, buttermilk and 1 tsp salt. Transfer to a shallow bowl. Transfer remaining 3/4 cup flour to a separate shallow bowl.

Slice onions into 1/2-inch-thick rings, separate each ring and reserve small inner rings (about 1/4 onion) for another use.

Dip an onion ring into flour, shaking off excess. Using a fork, transfer to buttermilk mixture, turning to coat completely, then drop into tortilla mixture. Using your hands, turn onion to coat, gently pressing tortilla coating onto ring to adhere. Place on prepared baking sheet. Repeat with remaining rings, arranging in a single layer on the baking sheets.

Mist onion rings with cooking spray and bake in preheated oven for about 16 minutes, switching and rotating baking sheets halfway through cooking time, until golden brown and crispy. Season with salt. Serve with Homemade Ketchup (page 19) or your favourite dip.

PER SERVING
BEFORE: 276 CALORIES, 16 G TOTAL FAT
DISH DO-OVER: 435 CALORIES, 4.2 G TOTAL FAT
NUTRITIONAL INFORMATION: 0.7 G SATURATED FAT, 89.5 G CARBOHYDRATES, 6.8 G FIBRE, 9.6 G SUGAR, 9.6 G PROTEIN, 627 MG SODIUM, 2 MG CHOLESTEROL

Sweet Potato Fries with Garlic Yogurt Aioli

The problem with most sweet potato fry recipes is that the fries are soggy, even the deep-fried ones! Egg whites and cornmeal are the trick to crispy, oven-baked sweet potato fries.

SWEET POTATO FRIES

3 medium sweet potatoes
1/4 cup egg whites (about 2 large)
1/2 tsp sea salt
1/2 tsp ground cumin
1/4 tsp cayenne pepper
1 tbsp finely ground cornmeal

GARLIC YOGURT AIOLI

3/4 cup non-fat plain Greek yogurt
1/4 cup low-fat olive oil mayonnaise
1 garlic clove, minced
1 tbsp Dijon mustard
1 tbsp fresh lemon juice
Sea salt and freshly ground
    black pepper

SERVES 4
HANDS-ON TIME: 20 MINUTES
TOTAL TIME: 45 MINUTES

Position racks in top and bottom thirds of oven and preheat oven to 450°F. Line two large baking sheets with parchment paper.

Peel and slice sweet potato into 1/2-inch-thick wedges.

In a large bowl, whisk together egg whites, salt, cumin and cayenne until foamy. Add potato wedges and toss to coat. Sprinkle with cornmeal and gently toss to coat.

Mist prepared baking sheets with cooking spray. Arrange sweet potatoes in a single layer on baking sheets. Bake for about 30 minutes, flipping potatoes over and switching and rotating baking sheets halfway through cooking time, until golden brown and crispy.

Meanwhile, prepare aioli: Whisk together yogurt, mayonnaise, garlic, Dijon and lemon juice. Season with salt and pepper, cover and refrigerate until needed.

Serve fries with aioli on the side for dipping.

PER SERVING
BEFORE: 472 CALORIES, 36 G TOTAL FAT
DISH DO-OVER: 219 CALORIES, 6.4 G TOTAL FAT
NUTRITIONAL INFORMATION: 0.6 G SATURATED FAT,
32.4 G CARBOHYDRATES, 4.1 G FIBRE, 9.9 G SUGAR,
8.7 G PROTEIN, 438 MG SODIUM, 8 MG CHOLESTEROL

Poutine

Poutine snobs may balk at my do-over of their beloved late-night snack, but we all know that this delicious Quebec favourite is an artery-clogging hot mess. I'm using baked french fries, vegetarian gravy and (gasp!) low-fat cheese instead of the traditional full-fat curds.

FRENCH FRIES

3 medium russet potatoes
1/2 tsp sea salt

GRAVY

3 tbsp unsalted butter
1 medium yellow onion, diced
2 garlic cloves, smashed
1 cup thinly sliced cremini mushrooms
1 small carrot, peeled and diced
1 celery rib, diced
3 sprigs fresh thyme
2 tbsp tomato paste
3 tbsp whole-wheat or brown rice flour
1 cup dry red wine
2 bay leaves
4 cups low-sodium vegetable stock
1 tbsp fresh lemon juice
Sea salt and freshly ground
    black pepper
8 oz low-fat medium white cheddar
    cheese

SERVES 4
(MAKES ABOUT 2 1/2 CUPS GRAVY)
HANDS-ON TIME: 50 MINUTES
TOTAL TIME: 1 HOUR, 10 MINUTES
+ 30 MINUTES SOAKING TIME

PER SERVING
BEFORE: 710 CALORIES,
38 G TOTAL FAT
DISH DO-OVER: 400 CALORIES,
14.5 G TOTAL FAT
NUTRITIONAL INFORMATION:
8.1 G SATURATED FAT,
45.4 G CARBOHYDRATES,
2.9 G FIBRE, 6.8 G SUGAR,
19.9 G PROTEIN, 718 MG SODIUM,
35 MG CHOLESTEROL

Slice potatoes into 1/4-inch-thick fries and place in a large bowl. Cover fries with hot tap water by 1 inch and let soak for at least 30 minutes.

For gravy: Meanwhile, in a large, high-sided non-stick skillet, melt butter over medium-high heat. Add onion, garlic and mushrooms and cook, stirring frequently, for about 3 minutes, until onion is translucent and mushrooms are softened. Add carrot, celery and thyme and cook, stirring constantly, until fragrant, about 1 minute. Add tomato paste and cook, stirring frequently, until dark and richly caramelized, about 15 minutes.

Add flour to pan and cook, stirring constantly, until brown and fragrant, about 3 minutes. Deglaze pan with red wine, stirring and scraping up any brown bits from bottom of pan with a wooden spoon. Add bay leaves and stir in stock. Bring to a boil, reduce heat to medium-low and simmer uncovered for about 20 minutes, until reduced and thickened. (You may wish to start making the fries while the gravy reduces.) Strain through a fine-mesh sieve, pushing out all liquid with the bottom of a ladle. Stir in lemon juice and season with salt and pepper. Set aside; reheat before serving, if needed.

For french fries: Position rack in bottom third of oven and preheat oven to 475°F. Line a large baking sheet with parchment paper. Drain fries well in a colander and spread out in a single layer on clean, dry kitchen towels. Pat dry with more kitchen towels. Return fries to clean and dried bowl. Mist fries with cooking spray, tossing and spraying again to coat well. Toss with salt to season.

Arrange fries in a single layer on prepared baking sheet and bake for 12 minutes. Remove from oven and, using a spatula, flip fries over. Bake for another 10 minutes, until golden brown and crispy. Season with salt.

Break cheese into irregular-shaped 1/4-inch to 1/2-inch pieces. Place hot fries in a large bowl and top with half the cheese, all the gravy, then remaining cheese. Serve immediately.

Perfect Mashed Potatoes

You don't need piles of butter and 35% cream to make fluffy, creamy mashed potatoes. A few simple techniques and swaps will do the trick. Steaming reduces the amount of water absorbed by the potatoes, and Yukon Gold have a naturally creamy texture. Adding the butter before the milk coats the starch in a thin layer of fat, keeping the water in the milk from soaking into the potatoes. Invest in a ricer or food mill, and you'll never go back to mashing again.

6 medium Yukon Gold potatoes
   (about 2 lb), peeled, cut into 1-inch
   chunks, rinsed and drained
3 tbsp unsalted butter
Sea salt and freshly ground
   black pepper
1/2 cup 1% buttermilk, warmed

SERVES 8
HANDS-ON TIME: 20 MINUTES
TOTAL TIME: 40 MINUTES

Tip: Serve with vegetarian gravy (page 83) for a lightened-up classic side dish, perfect for holiday dinners.

In a steamer insert over a pot of boiling water, cover and steam potatoes for 20 to 25 minutes. Drain off water; remove pot from heat.

For the fluffiest potatoes, use a ricer or food mill to process potatoes into a pot (work in batches if necessary). Alternatively, mash with a potato masher until just smooth. With a spatula, gently stir in butter with a pinch of salt. Add warm buttermilk. Season with pepper and additional salt.

PER SERVING
BEFORE: 237 CALORIES, 9 G TOTAL FAT
DISH DO-OVER: 122 CALORIES, 4.5 G TOTAL FAT
*NUTRITIONAL INFORMATION: 2.8 G SATURATED FAT,
18.9 G CARBOHYDRATES, 1.3 G FIBRE, 1.5 G SUGAR,
2.1 G PROTEIN, 21 MG SODIUM, 12 MG CHOLESTEROL*

Green Bean Casserole

I think everyone's mom or grandma made this dish at least once! Using canned condensed soup, frozen green beans and canned fried onions, the original recipe is a quick and easy family favourite, though high in fat and sodium thanks to those canned convenience items. I've swapped in crispy baked shallots for the canned onions, used my creamy condensed soup substitute and opted for fresh green beans for a more vibrant, crunchy dish. Prep the onions and soup substitute ahead of time and you can throw this dish together in just about the same amount of time as the original.

1 cup thinly sliced shallots
1 cup 1% buttermilk
1/4 tsp cayenne pepper
1 cup corn flour
1/2 cup cornmeal
1/4 tsp sea salt, plus more to taste
Freshly ground black pepper
5 cups roughly chopped haricots verts
   or green beans
1 1/3 cups mushroom Creamy
   Condensed Soup Substitute (page 21)
1 tsp low-sodium soy sauce or tamari
1/4 tsp freshly grated nutmeg

SERVES 6
HANDS-ON TIME: 45 MINUTES
TOTAL TIME: 1 HOUR

Tip: For a broccoli casserole, substitute 4 cups broccoli florets for the beans.

Tip: Add protein with 1/2 cup black beans or chickpeas, or 8 oz cooked and sliced boneless, skinless chicken breast, lean beef or salmon.

Preheat oven to 400°F.

In a bowl, mix together shallots, buttermilk and cayenne, ensuring shallots are coated with buttermilk. In a separate bowl, combine corn flour, cornmeal and 1/4 tsp salt. Drain shallots in a sieve, reserving buttermilk. Transfer shallots to corn-flour mixture, tossing to coat well. Using a dry sieve, gently shake excess flour from shallots and arrange in a single layer on prepared baking sheet. Bake for 12 to 15 minutes, until golden brown and crispy. Season with salt and pepper.

While shallots are cooking, blanch beans in a pot of salted boiling water for 2 minutes. Refresh in ice water, drain and transfer to a 9- x 9-inch baking dish.

In a bowl, combine mushroom soup, reserved buttermilk, soy sauce, pepper and nutmeg. Season with salt and pour over beans. Sprinkle beans with crispy shallots. Cover and bake for about 12 minutes, until hot and bubbling, then uncover and bake for another 5 minutes until lightly golden.

PER SERVING
BEFORE: 251 CALORIES, 17 G TOTAL FAT
DISH DO-OVER: 194 CALORIES, 2.4 G TOTAL FAT
NUTRITIONAL INFORMATION: 0.5 G SATURATED FAT, 36.9 G CARBOHYDRATES, 3.6 G FIBRE, 7.4 G SUGAR, 7.6 G PROTEIN, 430 MG SODIUM, 2 MG CHOLESTEROL

Soups, Stews & Chilies

Creamy Mushroom Soup

One of the easiest ways to make soup taste luxurious is by adding cream. It should come as no surprise that this technique packs loads of fat into each humble bowl. In this soup, I've removed the cream, butter and white flour yet achieved the same richness and texture with a few fat-saving tricks. I use lots of mushrooms, roasting them first to develop the flavour, and add zucchini, which melts right in to help thicken the broth. Then I top each bowl with a dollop of non-fat Greek yogurt to complement the woodsy mushrooms with its bright tangy flavour.

2 cups quartered medium cremini

2 cups quartered white mushrooms

2 cups shiitake mushrooms, stems removed

2 large Portobello mushrooms, stems removed, caps sliced 1 inch thick

2 tsp chopped fresh thyme (or 1 tsp dried)

Sea salt and freshly ground black pepper

1 tbsp olive oil

1 medium onion, diced

3 garlic cloves, minced

2 medium zucchini, ends trimmed, diced (about 1 cup)

1/3 cup dry red wine

4 cups low-sodium chicken or vegetable stock

2 tbsp fresh lemon juice

1/3 cup non-fat plain Greek yogurt

2 tbsp finely chopped fresh chives

SERVES 4
HANDS-ON TIME: 25 MINUTES
TOTAL TIME: 45 MINUTES

Preheat oven to 400°F. Line a large baking sheet with parchment paper.

Arrange mushrooms on prepared baking sheet and mist with cooking spray. Sprinkle with half of thyme and season with salt and pepper. Roast, stirring occasionally, for 20 minutes, until tender and golden.

In a large saucepan, heat oil over medium-high heat. Add onion, garlic, zucchini and remaining thyme and sauté until vegetables are soft, about 5 minutes. Stir in roasted mushrooms. Stir in wine and simmer until evaporated, about 1 minute. Add stock and bring to a boil. Reduce heat to medium-low and simmer uncovered for 20 minutes.

Purée soup with an immersion blender. Season with lemon juice, salt and pepper. Ladle soup into serving bowls and top each with yogurt and chives.

PER SERVING
BEFORE: 337 CALORIES, 24 G TOTAL FAT
DISH DO-OVER: 136 CALORIES, 4.4 G TOTAL FAT
NUTRITIONAL INFORMATION: 0.5 G SATURATED FAT, 16.6 G CARBOHYDRATES, 4.5 G FIBRE, 7.4 G SUGAR, 10.3 G PROTEIN, 615 MG SODIUM, 1 MG CHOLESTEROL

New England Clam Chowder

One of my favourite things to order at any oyster bar worth its salt is a steaming cup of creamy clam chowder. Traditionally made with salt pork or bacon, cream and flour, this dish can be transformed into a beautifully svelte version of its former self by using smoked ham, 1% milk and brown rice flour.

2 cans (10 oz/283 g each) baby clams
1 tbsp olive oil
2 oz smoked ham, finely diced
    (about 1/3 cup)
1 large yellow onion, diced
4 celery ribs, diced
3 garlic cloves, minced
1/4 cup brown rice flour
2 medium Yukon Gold potatoes,
    diced (about 2 cups)
2 sprigs fresh thyme
1 bay leaf
1 1/2 cups low-sodium chicken or
    vegetable stock
2 cups 1% milk
2 tbsp chopped fresh flat-leaf parsley
    or chives
Sea salt and freshly ground
    black pepper

SERVES 4
HANDS-ON TIME: 30 MINUTES
TOTAL TIME: 45 MINUTES

Drain clams, reserving juice. Set clams and juice aside.

In a large saucepan, heat oil over medium heat. Add ham and cook for about 2 minutes, until lightly browned. Add onion, celery and garlic and cook for about 5 minutes, until translucent and softened. Add flour and cook, stirring, for about 1 minute, until lightly browned. Add potatoes, thyme, bay leaf, reserved clam juice and stock. Bring to a simmer, reduce heat to low and cook, uncovered and stirring occasionally, until potatoes are tender when pierced with a knife, about 15 minutes. [*Make-ahead:* Prepare to this point up to 24 hours in advance, cover and refrigerate. Bring to a simmer before proceeding with recipe.]

Stir in milk and bring to a gentle simmer over medium heat; do not boil. Reduce heat to medium-low and cook, stirring occasionally, for about 5 minutes, until thickened slightly. Add reserved clams and cook until clams are just heated through, about 2 minutes. Season with parsley, salt and pepper.

Serve with hot sauce and crunchy brown rice crackers.

PER SERVING
BEFORE: 730 CALORIES, 36 G TOTAL FAT
DISH DO-OVER: 340 CALORIES, 7.1 G TOTAL FAT
*NUTRITIONAL INFORMATION: 1.7 G SATURATED FAT,
40.3 G CARBOHYDRATES, 3 G FIBRE, 10 G SUGAR,
28.5 G PROTEIN, 744 MG SODIUM, 59 MG CHOLESTEROL*

Beef & Bean Chili

There is much debate over whether beans belong in chili. I say, bring on the beans! They add fibre and nutrients, cut down on the fat and are much less expensive than meat. In short, beans rock. I use kidney and pinto beans here, but feel free to use black beans or whatever variety you have in your pantry. To cut down on the fat, I replace regular ground beef with extra-lean ground beef or sirloin. When choosing sirloin, be sure to look for extra-lean or lean, or check the nutritional content; otherwise, it could be just as calorie-dense as regular ground beef. A great chili is all about the layering of flavour, so I've added tons of aromatic spices and a bit of cocoa powder for a rich undertone. Top it all off with non-fat Greek yogurt instead of full-fat sour cream, and with low-fat cheddar instead of full-fat, and you've got a hearty bowl of chili that won't tip the scales.

1 tbsp olive oil

1 medium onion, diced

3 garlic cloves, minced

1 1/2 lb extra-lean ground beef or sirloin

3 tbsp tomato paste

2 tbsp chili powder

2 tbsp cocoa powder

1 tbsp ground cumin

2 tsp dried oregano

1 chipotle pepper in adobo sauce, minced, plus 1 tsp adobo sauce

1/4 tsp each sea salt and freshly ground black pepper, plus more to taste

1 can (28 oz/796 mL) unsalted diced tomatoes

2 cups passata

1 1/2 cups low-sodium beef stock

1 can (15 oz/398 mL) kidney beans, drained and rinsed

1 can (15 oz/398 mL) pinto beans, drained and rinsed

1 cup non-fat plain Greek yogurt

1 cup shredded low-fat aged cheddar cheese

3 green onions, thinly sliced

1/4 cup chopped fresh cilantro

SERVES 8
HANDS-ON TIME: 25 MINUTES
TOTAL TIME: 55 MINUTES

In a large saucepan, heat oil over medium-high heat. Add onion and garlic and cook, stirring frequently, until softened, about 5 minutes. Add beef and cook, breaking up with a wooden spoon and stirring frequently, until browned and no liquid remains in pan, about 5 minutes.

Add tomato paste, chili powder, cocoa powder, cumin, oregano, chipotle pepper and adobo sauce, and 1/4 tsp each salt and pepper and cook, stirring constantly, until fragrant, about 1 minute. Stir in diced tomatoes, passata and stock and bring to a boil. Reduce heat to medium-low and simmer, uncovered and stirring occasionally, for about 20 minutes, until thickened. Stir in kidney and pinto beans and simmer for another 10 minutes until heated through. Season with salt and pepper.

Spoon chili into bowls and garnish with yogurt, cheese, green onions and cilantro. Serve with hot sauce and Chili-Lime Baked Tortilla Chips (page 31) or your favourite packaged baked tortilla chips for dipping.

Note: Chili is even better the next day, after the flavours have had time to blend. This chili tastes best prepared at least a day — and up to 3 days — in advance. Cover and refrigerate; reheat over low heat when ready to serve.

PER SERVING
BEFORE: 628 CALORIES, 24 G TOTAL FAT
DISH DO-OVER: 333 CALORIES, 10.8 G TOTAL FAT
NUTRITIONAL INFORMATION: 3.9 G SATURATED FAT, 28 G CARBOHYDRATES, 7.4 G FIBRE, 8.1 G SUGAR, 31.7 G PROTEIN, 778 MG SODIUM, 52 MG CHOLESTEROL

Vietnamese Beef Pho

A giant bowl of aromatic pho could possibly be one of the most perfect soups on the planet. At first glance, it seems a very innocent soup, but the broth contains an absurd amount of white rice noodles, and some versions include fatty beef brisket or beef balls. Don't fret, the cleverly disguised offending ingredients are easily replaced. I've used lean beef, along with low-sodium and low-fat beef stock, and opted for brown rice or low-carb shirataki noodles instead of the refined white rice variety.

1 tsp grapeseed oil

1 medium onion, halved

1 4-inch-piece ginger, quartered

3 garlic cloves, smashed

2 star anise

1 3-inch cinnamon stick

1 tsp fennel seeds

4 whole cloves

6 cups low-sodium beef stock

2 cups water

1 lb shirataki or brown rice vermicelli noodles

8 oz lean beef flank steak, eye of round or sirloin (raw), chilled in freezer for 20 minutes

8 sprigs fresh cilantro

8 sprigs fresh basil

8 sprigs fresh mint

4 cups bean sprouts

2 limes, cut into wedges

2 to 3 red chili peppers, thinly sliced (optional)

Sriracha sauce

Low-sodium tamari or soy sauce

SERVES 4
HANDS-ON TIME: 30 MINUTES
TOTAL TIME: 40 MINUTES

In a large saucepan, heat oil over medium heat. Add onion, ginger and garlic and cook, stirring frequently, until garlic is golden. Stir in star anise, cinnamon stick, fennel seeds and cloves. Add stock and water, increase heat to high and bring to a boil. Reduce heat to medium-low and simmer for 8 minutes, to allow flavours to blend. Strain broth through a fine-mesh sieve, discarding solids; return broth to pot and bring to a boil. [*Make-ahead:* Broth can be prepared up to 48 hours in advance, covered and refrigerated. Bring to a boil before proceeding with recipe.]

Add noodles to broth and cook according to package instructions. Scoop noodles from broth using a fine-mesh sieve and divide among serving bowls. Remove beef from freezer and thinly slice across the grain into pieces about 1/8 inch thick. Place beef on noodles (the broth will cook it). Arrange herbs, bean sprouts, lime wedges and chilies (if using) on a large platter to serve alongside soup, with Sriracha and tamari, for guests to garnish their bowls. Pour broth into bowls and serve immediately.

PER SERVING
BEFORE: 700 CALORIES, 15 G TOTAL FAT
DISH DO-OVER: 574 CALORIES, 9 G TOTAL FAT
NUTRITIONAL INFORMATION: 2.9 G SATURATED FAT, 100 G CARBOHYDRATES, 4.5 G FIBRE, 5.8 G SUGAR, 28.6 G PROTEIN, 1011 MG SODIUM, 27 MG CHOLESTEROL

French Onion Soup

If there was ever a dish with a rags-to-riches story, this is it. French onion soup was once considered peasant food, as onions were cheap and plentiful. The secret to a robust onion soup is slow cooking the onions over low heat, which magically brings out their natural sugars, making them soft, sweet and intensely flavourful. I've used a fraction of the oil in place of the copious amount of butter normally used to caramelize the onions, and replaced the white-flour crostini and thick blanket of cheese on the top of the bowl with whole-grain crostini covered in low-fat Swiss cheese and pungent Parmesan.

SOUP

1 tbsp olive oil
4 cups thinly sliced leeks, white
   and light green parts only
   (about 3 large leeks), rinsed
   well and drained
2 large Spanish onions, thinly sliced
2 large Vidalia or sweet onions,
   thinly sliced
1/4 cup dry red wine
8 cups low-sodium beef or chicken
   stock
3 sprigs fresh thyme
2 bay leaves

CROSTINI

4 slices whole-grain baguette,
   each about 4 inches long and
   1/4 inch thick
1 garlic clove
1/2 cup shredded low-fat Swiss cheese
2 tbsp shredded Parmesan cheese
Sea salt and freshly ground
   black pepper
1/4 cup thinly sliced fresh chives

SERVES 4
HANDS-ON TIME: 25 MINUTES
TOTAL TIME: 1 HOUR, 45 MINUTES

For soup: In a large saucepan, heat oil over medium-high heat. Add leeks and Spanish and Vidalia onions. Cook, stirring frequently, for 2 to 3 minutes, until onions are softened slightly. Reduce heat to medium, cover saucepan with tight-fitting lid and allow onions to sweat (release water) for 15 to 20 minutes, stirring twice. Remove lid and cook for another 10 minutes. Reduce heat to medium-low and continue to cook for 20 minutes, stirring and scraping bottom of pan with a wooden spoon every 10 minutes, until onions caramelize and turn rich golden brown.

Increase heat to high, pour in wine and stir until liquid is evaporated. Add stock, thyme and bay leaves and bring to a boil. Reduce heat to medium and simmer uncovered for 30 minutes.

For crostini: Position rack in top third of oven and preheat broiler to high. Line a large baking sheet with parchment paper or foil.

Place baguette slices on prepared baking sheet and toast in oven for about 30 seconds to 1 minute per side, until very golden brown. Cut garlic clove in half and rub cut side onto both sides of each piece of baguette. Sprinkle with cheeses and broil for about 1 minute, until cheese is melted and light golden brown.

Remove bay leaves and thyme from soup. Season with salt and pepper. Ladle soup into bowls, float 1 crostini on top of each bowl and garnish with chives. Serve immediately.

PER SERVING
BEFORE: 580 CALORIES, 20 G TOTAL FAT
DISH DO-OVER: 307 CALORIES, 6 G TOTAL FAT
*NUTRITIONAL INFORMATION: 1.6 G SATURATED FAT,
50.5 G CARBOHYDRATES, 7.5 G FIBRE, 21.9 G SUGAR,
16.8 G PROTEIN, 1384 MG SODIUM, 7 MG CHOLESTEROL*

Loaded Baked Potato Soup

Whenever "Loaded Baked Potato" appears on a menu, it usually means loaded with salted butter, full-fat sour cream, full-fat cheese and greasy bacon. Delicious? You bet! But not exactly on the healthy side of things. I've lightened things up by using non-fat Greek yogurt and low-fat aged cheddar, and cooked the bacon super crispy by draining off all the excess fat. For an even lighter meal, enjoy this potato leek soup without the toppings.

1 tbsp olive oil

4 cups sliced leeks, white and light green parts only (about 3 large leeks), rinsed well and drained

2 tsp chopped fresh thyme (or 1/2 tsp dried)

1 tsp sea salt, plus more to taste

1 1/4 lb Yukon Gold potatoes, peeled and diced

6 cups low-sodium chicken or vegetable stock

2 bay leaves

1 cup 1% milk

Freshly ground black pepper

2 tbsp fresh lemon juice

3/4 cup non-fat plain Greek yogurt

1 cup shredded low-fat aged cheddar cheese

3 slices Perfect Crispy Bacon (page 17), crumbled

3 green onions, thinly sliced

SERVES 6
HANDS-ON TIME: 35 MINUTES
TOTAL TIME: 55 MINUTES
(BACON NOT INCLUDED)

In a large saucepan, heat oil over medium heat. Add leeks, thyme and 1 tsp salt and cook, stirring frequently, until softened, 5 to 7 minutes. Add potatoes, stock and bay leaves. Increase heat to high and bring to a boil. Reduce heat to medium-low and simmer uncovered until potatoes are tender when pierced with a knife, about 15 minutes. Remove from heat and allow to cool for 5 minutes. Discard bay leaves.

Using an immersion blender or working in batches using a blender (do not use a food processor or soup will become gluey), purée soup until smooth. [*Make-ahead:* Prepare soup to this point up to 48 hours in advance, cover and refrigerate.] Return soup to medium heat, stir in milk and cook for 2 to 3 minutes, until heated through. Season with salt, pepper and lemon juice.

Ladle soup into bowls and top with yogurt, cheese, bacon and green onions.

PER SERVING
BEFORE: 500 CALORIES, 40 G TOTAL FAT
DISH DO-OVER: 212 CALORIES, 5.5 G TOTAL FAT
NUTRITIONAL INFORMATION: 1.9 G SATURATED FAT, 26.8 G CARBOHYDRATES, 2.1 G FIBRE, 5.6 G SUGAR, 15.4 G PROTEIN, 1079 MG SODIUM, 11 MG CHOLESTEROL

Cream of Asparagus Soup

This was my all-time favourite soup as a child. This healthier version is still at the top of my list, and the short roster of ingredients makes it a simple make-ahead meal. I've swapped the cream for non-fat evaporated milk to keep the velvety texture, used plenty of fresh asparagus and added a hint of lemon juice to boost the flavour.

6 cups low-sodium chicken or
　　vegetable stock
2 lb fresh asparagus
1 tbsp olive oil
1 cup sliced leek, white and light green
　　parts only, rinsed well and drained
3 medium shallots, thinly sliced
1/3 cup non-fat evaporated milk
1 tbsp fresh lemon juice
Sea salt and freshly ground
　　black pepper

SERVES 6
HANDS-ON TIME: 30 MINUTES
TOTAL TIME: 1 HOUR

In a large saucepan over high heat, bring stock to a boil. Reduce heat to a simmer.

While stock is coming to a boil, snap woody ends from asparagus and add to stock. Trim tips from asparagus about 1 1/2 inches long and set aside. Cut remaining asparagus into 1 1/2–inch pieces and set aside. Simmer stock uncovered for 25 minutes, then remove asparagus ends with a fine-mesh sieve or slotted spoon and discard. Add reserved asparagus tips to stock and blanch for 30 seconds. Remove stock from heat and, using a fine-mesh sieve or slotted spoon, transfer tips to an ice bath. Once chilled, place tips on a clean kitchen towel to drain.

In a large saucepan, heat oil over medium heat. Add leeks and shallots and cook, stirring frequently, until softened, about 10 minutes. Stir in reserved asparagus pieces. Add stock and bring to a boil. Reduce heat to medium-low and simmer uncovered for 5 to 8 minutes or until asparagus is very tender. Remove from heat and, using an immersion blender or working in batches using a blender or food processor, purée soup until smooth. Pass through a fine-mesh sieve to remove any fibrous bits.

Return soup to saucepan over medium heat. Stir in evaporated milk and heat, stirring occasionally, until just simmering, about 3 minutes. Season with lemon juice, salt and pepper. [*Make-ahead:* Soup can be prepared to this point up to 48 hours in advance, covered and refrigerated. To serve, bring to a simmer over medium heat.]

Stir in reserved asparagus tips and heat for 1 minute before serving.

PER SERVING
BEFORE: 299 CALORIES, 21.9 G TOTAL FAT
DISH DO-OVER: 88 CALORIES, 2.6 G TOTAL FAT
NUTRITIONAL INFORMATION: 0.4 G SATURATED FAT, 10.5 G CARBOHYDRATES, 2.6 G FIBRE, 5.2 G SUGAR, 7.9 G PROTEIN, 631 MG SODIUM, 1 MG CHOLESTEROL

Italian Wedding Soup

Contrary to what the name might lead you to believe, this soup is not traditionally served at Italian weddings. It is called wedding soup because it's the marriage of ingredients that makes it so delicious. Extra-lean turkey or chicken instead of beef and pork lightens up the meatballs, and whole-wheat bread crumbs instead of white help bind the mixture together. Instead of using several whole eggs, I gently stir a mixture of whole egg and egg whites into the finished broth, for beautiful ribbons of egg with less fat.

MEATBALLS

1 large egg
1 small yellow onion, grated
1 cup fresh whole-wheat bread crumbs
1 garlic clove, minced
1/4 cup chopped fresh flat-leaf parsley
1/4 cup freshly grated Parmesan cheese
1/4 tsp each sea salt and freshly
   ground black pepper
1 lb extra-lean ground turkey or
   chicken

BROTH

1 tbsp olive oil
1 medium yellow onion, diced
2 medium carrots, peeled and diced
2 garlic cloves, minced
8 cups low-sodium chicken stock
1 lb escarole or curly endive, coarsely
   chopped
1 large egg
1/2 cup egg whites (about 4 large)
2 tbsp freshly grated Parmesan cheese,
   plus more for serving (optional)
Sea salt and freshly ground black
   pepper
Chili flakes (optional)

SERVES 4
HANDS-ON TIME: 30 MINUTES
TOTAL TIME: 45 MINUTES

Prepare meatballs: In a large bowl, whisk egg, then stir in onion, bread crumbs, garlic, parsley, Parmesan, salt and pepper. Add ground turkey and mix by hand to combine. Scoop into 1 1/2–tbsp balls and transfer to a parchment-lined baking sheet. Cover and refrigerate.

Prepare broth: In a large saucepan, heat oil over medium-high heat. Add onion, carrots and garlic and cook, stirring frequently, until softened, about 3 minutes. Add stock and bring to a boil. Stir in escarole and meatballs and simmer until escarole is wilted and meatballs are cooked through, about 8 minutes.

While meatballs are simmering, in a small bowl, whisk together egg, egg whites and Parmesan. When meatballs are cooked, remove soup from heat. Gently stir soup in a circular motion and add egg mixture in a thin stream, continuing to stir until eggs form long strands; do not overstir. Season with salt and pepper. Divide among serving bowls and garnish with Parmesan and chili flakes (if using).

PER SERVING
BEFORE: 340 CALORIES, 22 G TOTAL FAT
DISH DO-OVER: 405 CALORIES, 18.8 G TOTAL FAT
NUTRITIONAL INFORMATION: 5.6 G SATURATED FAT,
19.3 G CARBOHYDRATES, 6.3 G FIBRE, 6.7 G SUGAR,
40 G PROTEIN, 1711 MG SODIUM, 189 MG CHOLESTEROL

Beef Stew

Have you ever made stew and put the leftovers in the fridge overnight, only to find a layer of fat coating the top the next day? Most of that is fat coming out from a cut of stewing beef with a lot of marbling. A lean cut of beef like chuck shoulder or eye of round doesn't contain that fat and is perfect for stewing because it becomes fork-tender. Prepare this stew ahead of time, portion and freeze or refrigerate for quick and easy comfort food any day of the week.

2 lb chuck shoulder or eye of round beef, trimmed of all visible fat, cut into 1-inch chunks

3 tbsp whole-wheat or gluten-free all-purpose flour

1/4 tsp each sea salt and freshly ground black pepper, plus more to taste

2 tbsp grapeseed oil

3 tbsp tomato paste

1 large yellow onion, chopped

2 medium carrots, peeled and cut into 1/2-inch pieces

2 celery ribs, cut into 1/2-inch pieces

3 garlic cloves, minced

1 tsp smoked paprika

Pinch cayenne pepper

3 tbsp balsamic vinegar

4 cups low-sodium beef stock

2 bay leaves

2 medium Yukon Gold potatoes or 1 large peeled sweet potato, cut into 1-inch pieces

3/4 cup frozen green peas, thawed and drained

SERVES 8
HANDS-ON TIME: 30 MINUTES
TOTAL TIME: 2 HOURS, 30 MINUTES

Pat beef dry with paper towel. In a resealable bag, combine beef with flour, salt and pepper and toss to coat well. Heat half the oil in a large Dutch oven or heavy-bottomed saucepan over medium-high heat. Add half of prepared beef and cook, turning occasionally, until brown on all sides. Using tongs or a slotted spoon, transfer beef to a bowl or baking sheet. Repeat with remaining oil and beef.

Add tomato paste to pan and cook, stirring constantly, until dark red-brown. Add half each of onion, carrots and celery and cook for about 3 minutes, stirring frequently and scraping up brown bits from bottom of pan, until onion is softened. Add garlic, paprika and cayenne and cook, stirring constantly, until fragrant, about 1 minute.

Return browned beef and any drippings to pan. Stir in vinegar, stock and bay leaves. Bring to a gentle simmer, reduce heat to medium-low, cover and simmer for about 1 1/2 hours, stirring occasionally, until beef is almost tender.

Stir in reserved vegetables and potatoes, cover and simmer for another 30 minutes, until potatoes and carrots are tender when pierced with a knife. Add peas and simmer uncovered for 5 minutes until cooked through. Remove bay leaves. Season with salt and pepper.

PER SERVING
BEFORE: 628 CALORIES, 24 G TOTAL FAT
DISH DO-OVER: 289 CALORIES, 11.3 G TOTAL FAT
NUTRITIONAL INFORMATION: 3.4 G SATURATED FAT, 19.3 G CARBOHYDRATES, 3 G FIBRE, 4.6 G SUGAR, 27.5 G PROTEIN, 471 MG SODIUM, 65 MG CHOLESTEROL

Broccoli Cheddar Soup

It's easy to eat your greens when they're combined with cheese! This heartwarming soup forgoes the usual heavy cream or whole milk, full-fat cheese and white flour in favour of low-fat milk, low-fat cheese and gluten-free rice flour, leaving your belly happy and free of excess calories.

1 tbsp olive oil

2 medium yellow onions, coarsely chopped

2 celery ribs, chopped

3 garlic cloves, smashed

1/4 cup brown rice flour

4 cups low-sodium chicken stock

1 head broccoli, stems and florets chopped

2 cups 1% milk or unsweetened plain almond milk

1 cup shredded low-fat aged cheddar cheese

1/4 cup freshly grated Parmesan cheese

1/4 tsp freshly grated nutmeg

Sea salt and freshly ground black pepper

SERVES 6
HANDS-ON TIME: 30 MINUTES
TOTAL TIME: 50 MINUTES

In a large saucepan, heat oil over medium heat. Add onions, celery and garlic and cook, stirring frequently, until onions are tender and translucent, about 5 minutes. Stir in flour and cook, stirring constantly, until lightly browned. Whisk in half of stock, until smooth. Add broccoli and remaining stock. Increase heat to medium-high and bring to a boil. Reduce heat to medium-low and simmer for 10 minutes or until broccoli is tender. Allow to cool slightly, about 10 minutes.

Using an immersion blender, or working in batches using a blender or food processor, purée soup until almost smooth. [*Make-ahead:* Soup can be prepared to this point up to 48 hours in advance, covered and refrigerated.]

Return pan to stove and warm over medium heat. Whisk in milk and cook, stirring frequently, until steaming and just barely bubbling, about 10 minutes. Stir in cheeses and season with nutmeg, salt and pepper.

PER SERVING
BEFORE: 403 CALORIES, 29 G TOTAL FAT
DISH DO-OVER: 212 CALORIES, 6.6 G TOTAL FAT
NUTRITIONAL INFORMATION: 2.7 G SATURATED FAT, 17.7 G CARBOHYDRATES, 0.9 G FIBRE, 8.8 G SUGAR, 17.8 G PROTEIN, 569 MG SODIUM, 14 MG CHOLESTEROL

Beer Cheddar Soup

Yes, you are reading this correctly! Typically made with crisp, fresh lager, piles of aged cheddar cheese and whole milk or cream, the regular version of this creamy favourite tips the scales at a whopping 48 grams of fat per serving. Still using regular beer, I've swapped the cream for non-fat evaporated milk to keep the silky texture and used low-fat in place of full-fat cheese. I've also increased the spices to round out the flavour and added a dash of smoked paprika instead of frying up bacon to add to the soup.

1 tbsp grapeseed oil

1 medium yellow onion, finely diced

2 garlic cloves, minced

1 tbsp chopped fresh thyme
(or 1 tsp dried)

1 tsp smoked paprika

1 tsp dry mustard

1/4 tsp cayenne pepper

1/4 cup brown rice flour

1 12-oz bottle lager

2 cups low-sodium chicken stock

1 1/2 cups non-fat evaporated milk

2 cups shredded low-fat aged cheddar
cheese

1/4 cup freshly grated Parmesan cheese

1/4 tsp freshly grated nutmeg

Sea salt and freshly ground
black pepper

4 tsp finely sliced fresh chives

SERVES 6
HANDS-ON TIME: 25 MINUTES
TOTAL TIME: 25 MINUTES

In a large saucepan, heat oil over medium heat. Add onion and garlic and cook, stirring frequently, until softened, about 4 minutes. Add thyme, paprika, mustard and cayenne and cook, stirring constantly, until fragrant, about 1 minute. Stir in flour and cook, stirring constantly, until lightly browned, about 2 minutes.

Whisk in half of beer until smooth, then simmer uncovered until thickened slightly, about 3 minutes. Whisk in remaining beer, stock and evaporated milk. Bring to a simmer and cook, stirring frequently, until thickened, about 5 minutes. Whisk in cheeses and season with nutmeg, salt and pepper. Garnish with chives.

PER SERVING
BEFORE: 587 CALORIES, 48 G TOTAL FAT
DISH DO-OVER: 212 CALORIES, 6.6 G TOTAL FAT
NUTRITIONAL INFORMATION: 2.7 G SATURATED FAT,
17.7 G CARBOHYDRATES, 0.9 G FIBRE, 8.8 G SUGAR,
17.8 G PROTEIN, 569 MG SODIUM, 14 MG CHOLESTEROL

Corn Chowder

I absolutely love slightly sweet, smoky corn chowder, especially on a cold, rainy day. In this recipe, I replace the usual excessive amount of butter, bacon and cream with a respectable amount of olive oil, 1% milk and smoked paprika for smoky flavour without any calories. I also load this soup with veggies, making this a nutrient-dense version of the classic.

3 cups fresh corn kernels (or frozen, thawed and drained)

4 cups low-sodium chicken stock

1 cup 1% milk or unsweetened plain almond milk

1 tbsp olive oil

1 medium yellow onion, diced

1 small carrot, peeled and diced

1 celery rib, diced

2 garlic cloves

2 tsp chopped fresh thyme (or 1/2 tsp dried)

1 tsp smoked paprika

1/4 cup brown rice flour

1 medium Yukon Gold potato, diced

1 bay leaf

1 medium red bell pepper, diced

1 tbsp fresh lemon juice

Hot sauce

Sea salt and freshly ground black pepper

2 tbsp chopped fresh flat-leaf parsley or chives

SERVES 6
HANDS-ON TIME: 25 MINUTES
TOTAL TIME: 40 MINUTES

In a blender, purée 1 cup corn kernels and 1 cup each stock and milk until smooth. Set aside.

In a medium saucepan, heat oil over medium heat. Add onion, carrot, celery, garlic and thyme and cook, stirring frequently, until softened, about 6 minutes. Add paprika and flour and cook, stirring constantly, until fragrant, about 1 minute. Add potato, bay leaf and remaining 3 cups stock, increase heat to high and bring to a boil. Reduce heat to medium and simmer for 10 minutes or until potatoes are tender when pierced with a knife. [*Make-ahead:* Soup can be prepared to this point up to 48 hours in advance, covered and refrigerated. Warm soup over medium heat before proceeding with recipe.]

Stir in prepared corn purée, remaining 2 cups corn kernels and bell pepper and bring to a gentle simmer, about 5 minutes. Remove from heat, discard bay leaf and season with lemon juice, hot sauce, salt and pepper. Ladle into serving bowls and sprinkle with chives.

PER SERVING
BEFORE: 533 CALORIES, 42 G TOTAL FAT
DISH DO-OVER: 187 CALORIES, 3.8 G TOTAL FAT
NUTRITIONAL INFORMATION: 0.8 G SATURATED FAT, 34.7 G CARBOHYDRATES, 3.8 G FIBRE, 7.3 G SUGAR, 7.4 G PROTEIN, 437 MG SODIUM, 2 MG CHOLESTEROL

Sandwiches

Philly Cheesesteaks

A classic sandwich that's been popular for over 70 years, the Philly Cheesesteak normally has really fatty beef topped with cheese sauce and fried onions, and is dripping with grease. Top sirloin steak gives you lots of flavour without a lot of fat. Be sure, though, to slice the beef super thin and against the grain, to get the flavour without having to use a fatty cut of meat.

1 lb flank, top round or top sirloin steak, trimmed of all visible fat
1 tbsp olive oil
2 tbsp whole-wheat or brown rice flour
1/2 tsp dry mustard
1 1/2 cups skim or 1% milk
2 cups shredded low-fat mozzarella cheese
1/4 cup freshly grated Parmesan cheese
Pinch freshly grated nutmeg
Sea salt and freshly ground black pepper
4 gluten-free or whole-wheat hoagie-style rolls
3 cups thinly sliced cremini mushrooms
1 large white onion, thinly sliced
2 garlic cloves, minced
1 green bell pepper, thinly sliced

SERVES 4
HANDS-ON TIME: 45 MINUTES
TOTAL TIME: 1 HOUR

Wrap steak tightly in plastic wrap and freeze for 30 to 45 minutes. This will make it easier to slice thinly.

For cheese sauce, in a medium saucepan, heat oil over medium heat. Add flour and mustard and cook, stirring constantly for 1 minute. Slowly whisk in milk and cook, stirring frequently, until milk is just barely simmering (small bubbles will form at edge of pan) and is thickened enough to coat the back of a spoon. Remove from heat and whisk in cheeses. Season with nutmeg, salt and pepper. Cover to keep warm.

Cut rolls in half lengthwise, leaving one side attached. Hollow out buns, leaving a 1-inch crust. Reserve torn bread to make fresh bread crumbs (see page 15).

Remove steak from freezer, unwrap and thinly slice against the grain. Season with salt and pepper.

Heat a large non-stick skillet over medium-high heat; mist with cooking spray. Add mushrooms to pan and cook, stirring frequently, until golden brown, about 6 minutes. Transfer to a large bowl and cover to keep warm. Add onion, garlic and bell pepper to pan and cook, stirring frequently, until vegetables are softened, about 8 minutes. Add to mushrooms and season with salt and pepper. Cover to keep warm.

Return pan to heat and mist with cooking spray. Add beef and cook, stirring frequently, until browned and no pink remains, 1 to 2 minutes. Mix meat with vegetables and scoop into buns. Top with cheese sauce.

PER SERVING
BEFORE: 965 CALORIES, 39.5 G TOTAL FAT
DISH DO-OVER: 603 CALORIES, 25.7 G TOTAL FAT
NUTRITIONAL INFORMATION: 11.6 G SATURATED FAT, 47.3 G CARBOHYDRATES, 6.5 G FIBRE, 13.8 G SUGAR, 48 G PROTEIN, 867 MG SODIUM, 90 MG CHOLESTEROL

Slow Cooker Pulled Pork Sandwiches

Perhaps the ultimate set-it and forget-it meal. It takes only minutes to make this slow cooker favourite that you can serve with a tangy coleslaw. Many people use a fatty pork shoulder for pulled pork, but you don't need to. Searing the meat first gives it a ton of flavour, so don't skip this step.

PULLED PORK

2 lb boneless centre-cut pork loin, trimmed of visible fat

Sea salt and freshly ground black pepper

1 medium yellow onion, diced

6 garlic cloves, minced

2 tbsp chili powder

1 tbsp smoked paprika

2 tsp ground cumin

1/2 tsp cayenne pepper

1 cup low-sodium chicken stock

1 1/2 cups jarred all-natural tomato sauce

1/3 cup apple cider vinegar

1/4 cup honey

TANGY COLESLAW

1/2 medium head green cabbage, cored and shredded (about 6 cups)

1/2 medium red onion, very thinly sliced

2 medium carrots, peeled and grated

1 tsp sea salt, plus more to taste

1/4 cup apple cider vinegar

2 tbsp grapeseed or vegetable oil

1 tbsp yellow mustard

1 tbsp honey

Freshly ground black pepper

8 whole-grain kaiser rolls, halved

SERVES 8
HANDS-ON TIME: 40 MINUTES
TOTAL TIME: 4 TO 8 HOURS
(DEPENDING ON SLOW COOKER)

Liberally season pork on all sides with salt and pepper, rubbing seasoning into meat. Heat a large non-stick skillet over medium-high heat; mist with cooking spray. Sear pork on all sides until browned, about 3 minutes per side.

Transfer pork to slow cooker and return pan to heat. Add onion and garlic and cook, stirring frequently, until softened, 2 to 3 minutes. Add chili powder, paprika, cumin and cayenne and cook, stirring constantly, until fragrant, about 1 minute. Deglaze pan with stock, scraping any brown bits from bottom of pan with a wooden spoon. Remove from heat and stir in tomato sauce, vinegar and honey. Pour mixture over pork. Cover with lid and cook until pork is tender and can be pulled apart easily with a fork, 4 to 6 hours on high heat, 6 to 8 hours on low heat. (*Note:* slow cookers vary, so adjust time accordingly.)

Transfer pork to a cutting board, cover loosely with foil and let rest for 10 minutes. Turn slow cooker to high heat and allow sauce to simmer uncovered while pork is resting, skimming off and discarding any visible fat. Using tongs or two forks, shred pork and return to slow cooker, mixing until pork is coated with sauce. Heat pork for 5 minutes; season with salt and pepper.

While pork is cooking, prepare coleslaw: In a large bowl, toss cabbage, onion and carrots with 1/2 tsp salt. Let stand for 1 hour. Drain vegetables in a colander, gently pressing to extract excess water. Add vinegar, oil, mustard and honey to cabbage mixture, mixing well. Season with salt and pepper, then cover and refrigerate.

To serve, top buns with pork and coleslaw.

PER SERVING
BEFORE: 937 CALORIES, 63 G TOTAL FAT
DISH DO-OVER: 454 CALORIES, 10.8 G TOTAL FAT
NUTRITIONAL INFORMATION: 2.1 G SATURATED FAT, 57.6 G CARBOHYDRATES, 9.6 G FIBRE, 22.6 G SUGAR, 35.6 G PROTEIN, 604 MG SODIUM, 60 MG CHOLESTEROL

Monte Cristo Sandwiches

The Americanized version of the French croque monsieur sandwich, the Monte Cristo sandwich is typically dipped in batter and fried in a lot of oil. Swapping the batter for crushed brown rice crisp cereal still gives you the crispiness and deep-fried flavour.

1 large egg

1/2 cup egg whites (about 4 large)

3 tbsp skim milk

Pinch freshly grated nutmeg

Pinch sea salt

2 cups coarsely crushed brown rice crisp cereal

4 tsp non-fat plain Greek yogurt

4 tsp Dijon mustard

8 slices whole-grain bread

4 oz all-natural smoked turkey breast, thinly sliced

4 oz all-natural Black Forest ham, thinly sliced

4 oz shredded low-fat Swiss cheese (or 4 1-oz slices)

1/4 cup organic icing sugar

1/2 cup all-natural no-sugar-added raspberry or black currant jam

SERVES 4
HANDS-ON TIME: 25 MINUTES
TOTAL TIME: 25 MINUTES

Tip: To crush cereal, pulse in a food processor until cereal resembles a coarse flour. Alternatively, place in a resealable bag, squeezing out all the air before sealing. Lay the bag on a work surface and crush by rolling over it with a rolling pin, can or jar. To prevent the bag from breaking, I like to drape a clean kitchen towel over it before rolling.

Preheat oven to 250°F. Line a large baking sheet with parchment paper.

In a shallow dish, whisk together egg, egg whites and milk. Season with nutmeg and salt. In a separate shallow dish, place crushed cereal.

In a small bowl, mix together yogurt and Dijon. Spread about 1 tsp of the mixture on one side of each bread slice; place, yogurt spread side up, on work surface. Layer turkey, ham and cheese on 4 bread slices. Top each with remaining 4 bread slices, yogurt spread side down, pressing gently.

Heat a large non-stick skillet or griddle over medium heat; mist with cooking spray.

Using a spatula, carefully dip one side of a sandwich into egg mixture (egg mixture should go about halfway up the bottom slice of bread when immersed). With your hand on the top of the sandwich and spatula underneath, carefully flip to immerse the other side in egg, then gently transfer to crushed cereal, turning once to coat. Transfer to a small plate or baking sheet. Repeat with second sandwich. Mist both sandwiches with cooking spray on both sides and transfer to hot pan. Sear sandwiches, turning once, until golden brown and crispy, about 4 minutes per side. Transfer to prepared baking sheet and place in oven to keep warm. Repeat with remaining sandwiches.

To serve, dust with icing sugar and serve with a dollop of jam for dipping.

PER SERVING
BEFORE: 508 CALORIES, 15 G TOTAL FAT
DISH DO-OVER: 577 CALORIES, 10.1 G TOTAL FAT
NUTRITIONAL INFORMATION: 2.7 G SATURATED FAT, 82.3 G CARBOHYDRATES, 8.1 G FIBRE, 38.3 G SUGAR, 38.7 G PROTEIN, 1128 MG SODIUM, 79 MG CHOLESTEROL

Reuben Sandwiches

How can you go wrong with a fried sandwich piled with fatty corned beef, cheese and Russian mayo dressing? Perhaps it's not surprising that a classic Reuben has 967 calories and 70 grams of fat — it's almost like eating *two* fast food double-stacked burgers. With a few simple swaps and a much lighter dressing that uses Greek yogurt, you can't miss with this Reuben.

RUSSIAN DRESSING

1/2 cup non-fat plain Greek yogurt

1/4 cup Homemade Ketchup (page 19) or organic ketchup

2 tbsp minced dill pickle

4 tsp minced green onion (about 1 green onion)

1 tsp prepared horseradish

1/4 tsp Worcestershire sauce

Sea salt and freshly ground black pepper

SANDWICHES

8 slices dark rye bread

2 tbsp unsalted butter, softened

8 oz lean corned beef, thinly sliced

8 oz Montreal smoked turkey breast, thinly sliced

1 1/3 cups sauerkraut, drained

4 slices low-fat Swiss or Jarlsberg cheese (4 oz)

SERVES 4
HANDS-ON TIME: 20 MINUTES
TOTAL TIME: 20 MINUTES
(KETCHUP NOT INCLUDED)

Prepare dressing: In a bowl, stir together yogurt, ketchup, pickle, green onion, horseradish and Worcestershire sauce. Season with salt and pepper.

Prepare sandwich: Butter bread slices on one side and arrange, butter side down, on a cutting board. Spread dressing over top bread slices. Top 4 slices with corned beef, turkey, sauerkraut and cheese. Top each with remaining 4 bread slices, dressing side down.

Heat a large non-stick skillet or griddle over medium heat; mist with cooking spray. Cook sandwiches for 5 to 7 minutes per side, flipping once with a spatula, until bread is crispy and filling is heated through.

Note: If working in batches, preheat oven to 350°F. After searing each sandwich, place on a parchment-lined baking sheet and warm in oven for about 5 minutes, until heated through.

PER SERVING
BEFORE: 967 CALORIES, 70 G TOTAL FAT
DISH DO-OVER: 385 CALORIES, 12.8 G TOTAL FAT
NUTRITIONAL INFORMATION: 6 G SATURATED FAT, 41.6 G CARBOHYDRATES, 5.6 G FIBRE, 10.7 G SUGAR, 25.5 G PROTEIN, 1624 MG SODIUM, 51 MG CHOLESTEROL

Cubano-Style Sandwiches

The Cubano is the Cuban version of a ham and cheese sandwich. It's especially popular in Florida — I first had one in South Beach. Authentic Cuban rolls are hard to find (and some may even say it's not a Cubano without them); look for rolls with a crispy crust and soft, airy centre. I've stayed true to the double-pork filling, and used lean pork loin to cut some of the fat.

6 garlic cloves, minced

1/2 small yellow onion, grated

1/3 cup fresh orange juice

3 tbsp fresh lime juice

2 tsp ground cumin

1 tsp dried oregano

1/2 tsp each sea salt and freshly
   ground black pepper

1 lb boneless centre-cut pork loin,
   trimmed of visible fat

4 whole-wheat hoagie rolls

4 tbsp yellow mustard

8 oz Black Forest ham, thinly sliced
   (about 8 slices)

2 medium dill pickles, thinly sliced

4 oz low-fat Swiss cheese

SERVES 4
HANDS-ON TIME: 45 MINUTES
TOTAL TIME: 1 HOUR, 15 MINUTES
+ 1 HOUR MARINATING TIME

In a resealable bag or container, combine garlic, onion, orange juice, lime juice, cumin, oregano, salt and pepper. Add pork loin to marinade, turning to coat completely. Seal and refrigerate, turning occasionally to marinate evenly, for at least 1 hour and up to 6 hours.

Preheat oven to 350°F. Line a 9- x 9-inch baking pan with parchment paper.

Heat a large non-stick skillet over medium-high; mist with cooking spray. Remove pork from marinade, discarding marinade. Sear pork for about 2 minutes per side, until golden brown. Transfer to prepared baking pan and roast for 18 to 20 minutes or until cooked through. Let rest at room temperature for 10 minutes, then thinly slice. [*Make-ahead:* Pork can be roasted up to 48 hours in advance, covered and refrigerated until ready to slice and use.]

To assemble sandwiches, slice each roll in half lengthwise, leaving one side intact. Lightly spread with mustard, then stuff with ham, pork, pickles and cheese.

Heat a large non-stick skillet or griddle over medium heat; mist with cooking spray. Place sandwiches in skillet and press down with a heavy weight to press flat, like a panini. Cook, turning once, for about 8 minutes, until golden brown and crispy and cheese is melted. Slice each sandwich in half diagonally.

Note: You can use a heavy cast-iron pan to press down the sandwiches. If you don't have a cast-iron pan, use a small baking sheet weighted with a few cans of beans on top. Or you can use a brick wrapped in several layers of foil.

PER SERVING
BEFORE: 692 CALORIES, 29.5 G TOTAL FAT
DISH DO-OVER: 484 CALORIES, 11.4 G TOTAL FAT
*NUTRITIONAL INFORMATION: 3.4 G SATURATED FAT,
43.1 G CARBOHYDRATES, 6.6 G FIBRE, 8.5 G SUGAR,
54.1 G PROTEIN, 1687 MG SODIUM, 93 MG CHOLESTEROL*

Egg Salad Sandwiches

As a child I professed to hate hard-boiled eggs, so my mom called egg salad "Dinosaur Dip" — and I loved it. For this sandwich, I swap full-fat mayonnaise for non-fat Greek yogurt and use mostly egg whites to cut down on the total fat.

12 Perfect Hard-Boiled Eggs
(page 17)
2 celery ribs, finely diced
2 tbsp coarsely chopped fresh dill
(optional)
2 green onions, thinly sliced
2 tsp dry mustard
3 tbsp non-fat plain Greek yogurt
Pinch cayenne pepper or a few dashes
hot sauce
Sea salt and freshly ground
black pepper
8 slices whole-grain bread
1 1/3 cups thinly sliced iceberg lettuce

SERVES 4
HANDS-ON TIME: 20 MINUTES
TOTAL TIME: 40 MINUTES

Peel eggs, reserving 8 yolks for another use. Place egg whites and remaining 4 yolks in a food processor. Add celery, dill (if using) and green onions and pulse until finely chopped. Transfer to a large bowl and add mustard, yogurt, cayenne, salt and pepper, stirring with a spatula to combine.

Top 4 bread slices with egg salad and lettuce. Sandwich with remaining bread slices.

PER SERVING
BEFORE: 485 CALORIES, 34 G TOTAL FAT
DISH DO-OVER: 366 CALORIES, 9.5 G TOTAL FAT
NUTRITIONAL INFORMATION: 2.4 G SATURATED FAT,
42.3 G CARBOHYDRATES, 7.3 G FIBRE, 8 G SUGAR,
26.9 G PROTEIN, 567 MG SODIUM, 216 MG CHOLESTEROL

Crispy Fish Sandwiches

Fish is naturally low in fat until you deep-fry it, smother it with mayonnaise and top it with cheese. You can make this fast-food favourite at home with all of the flavour and without giving up the health benefits of eating fish.

1/3 cup non-fat plain Greek yogurt
2 tbsp minced dill pickle
1 tbsp chopped capers
2 tsp fresh lemon juice
4 tsp Dijon mustard
Dash hot sauce
1/2 tsp sea salt, plus more to taste
1/4 tsp freshly ground black pepper,
    plus more to taste
1/2 cup egg whites (about 4 large)
1 1/4 cups fresh whole-wheat or regular
    panko bread crumbs (gluten-free,
    if desired)
1/3 cup whole-wheat flour
1 1/2 lb Pacific cod, halibut or
    Mediterranean sea bass fillets,
    cut into 3-oz pieces
4 whole-grain hamburger or thin
    sandwich buns, toasted
4 large leaves leaf lettuce
4 slices or 1 cup shredded low-fat aged
    cheddar cheese (about 4 oz)

SERVES 4
HANDS-ON TIME: 30 MINUTES
TOTAL TIME: 35 MINUTES

Preheat oven to 400°F. Line a large baking sheet with parchment paper.

For tartar sauce, in a small bowl, whisk together yogurt, pickle, capers, lemon juice, 2 tsp Dijon and hot sauce. Season with salt and pepper to taste.

Prepare breading station: In a separate bowl, whisk together egg whites and remaining 2 tsp Dijon. On a shallow plate, combine panko, 1/2 tsp salt and 1/4 tsp pepper. Place flour in a second shallow plate.

Dredge each fish fillet in flour, shaking off excess, then dip in egg white mixture. Gently press fillet into panko, coating all sides evenly, and transfer to prepared baking sheet.

Heat a large non-stick skillet over medium-high heat; mist with cooking spray. Working in batches if necessary, sear fillets for 1 to 2 minutes per side, until golden brown, misting tops with cooking spray before flipping. Place fillets on baking sheet and bake for about 5 minutes, until cooked through.

To assemble sandwiches, split buns and spread with tartar sauce. Layer bottom halves of buns with lettuce, fillets and cheese. Cover with top halves of buns.

PER SERVING
BEFORE: 1100 CALORIES, 54 G TOTAL FAT
DISH DO-OVER: 487 CALORIES, 5.5 G TOTAL FAT
NUTRITIONAL INFORMATION: 1.8 G SATURATED FAT,
54.3 G CARBOHYDRATES, 6.6 G FIBRE, 6.3 G SUGAR,
51.6 G PROTEIN, 990 MG SODIUM, 80 MG CHOLESTEROL

Tuna Melts

Tuna salad seems like a great, healthy choice, but full-fat mayonnaise adds an incredible amount of fat per serving. Because tuna is so lean, I used a combo of low-fat mayonnaise and non-fat Greek yogurt to keep the creamy texture. Use this tuna mixture for regular sandwiches, mix it with whole-wheat pasta to make a salad or just enjoy it with some veggies.

2 cans (6 oz/170 g each) low-sodium, water-packed chunk albacore tuna, drained

2 green onions, thinly sliced

1 celery rib, finely chopped

3 tbsp finely chopped dill pickle

3 tbsp non-fat plain Greek yogurt

2 tbsp low-fat olive oil mayonnaise

1/2 tsp dry powder mustard or 1 1/2 tsp Dijon mustard

Pinch cayenne pepper or a few dashes hot sauce

Sea salt and freshly ground black pepper

4 slices whole-grain or rye bread, lightly toasted

2 vine-ripened tomatoes, sliced 1/4 inch thick

1 1/3 cups shredded low-fat aged cheddar cheese

1/4 tsp smoked paprika

SERVES 4
HANDS-ON TIME: 12 MINUTES
TOTAL TIME: 15 MINUTES

Position rack in top third of oven and preheat broiler to high. Line a large baking sheet with parchment paper.

In a large bowl, flake tuna with a fork. Stir in green onions, celery, pickle, yogurt, mayonnaise, mustard and cayenne. Season with salt and pepper.

Top each bread slice with tuna mixture and arrange on prepared baking sheet. Top tuna with tomato slices and cheese. Broil until cheese is melted. Sprinkle with paprika.

PER SERVING
BEFORE: 537 CALORIES, 17.8 G TOTAL FAT
DISH DO-OVER: 303 CALORIES, 8.3 G TOTAL FAT
NUTRITIONAL INFORMATION: 2.6 G SATURATED FAT, 25 G CARBOHYDRATES, 4.5 G FIBRE, 5.4 G SUGAR, 33.2 G PROTEIN, 647 MG SODIUM, 41 MG CHOLESTEROL

Chicken Salad Sandwiches

Simple, classic chicken salad is perfect in so many ways: it's a great way to repurpose leftover chicken, a quick and easy lunch and, best of all, just pure comfort food when tucked between soft fresh bread with crisp lettuce. For this do-over, I cut down significantly on the mayonnaise and swap half of it for non-fat Greek yogurt. I've also opted for whole-grain bread. To lower the calories even further, omit the bread, leave the romaine leaves whole and scoop the chicken salad into the lettuce, like tacos.

2 cups shredded or chopped cooked
    and cooled boneless, skinless
    chicken breast
2/3 cup finely diced celery
2 green onions, thinly sliced
2 tbsp finely chopped dill pickle
1 tbsp chopped fresh tarragon
3 tbsp non-fat plain Greek yogurt
2 tbsp low-fat olive oil mayonnaise
1 tbsp fresh lemon juice
2 tsp Dijon mustard
Pinch cayenne pepper
Sea salt and freshly ground
    black pepper
8 slices whole-grain bread or 4 medium
    whole-grain buns
4 leaves romaine lettuce, thinly sliced

SERVES 4
HANDS-ON TIME: 15 MINUTES
TOTAL TIME: 15 MINUTES

In a large bowl, mix together chicken, celery, green onions, pickle, tarragon, yogurt, mayonnaise, lemon juice, Dijon and cayenne. Season with salt and pepper.

Top 4 bread slices with chicken salad and lettuce. Sandwich with remaining bread slice.

PER SERVING
BEFORE: 510 CALORIES, 19 G TOTAL FAT
DISH DO-OVER: 394 CALORIES, 8 G TOTAL FAT
NUTRITIONAL INFORMATION: 1.4 G SATURATED FAT, 42.6 G CARBOHYDRATES, 7.6 G FIBRE, 7 G SUGAR, 36.9 G PROTEIN, 598 MG SODIUM, 63 MG CHOLESTEROL

Sloppy Joes

Wanna make a group of adults feel like kids again? Make 'em some sloppy joes! I added mashed white beans to replace some of the ground beef, to cut the calories and add fibre. Bring on the napkins!

1 lb extra-lean ground beef, sirloin
   or bison
3 garlic cloves, minced
1 medium yellow onion, diced
1 red or green bell pepper, diced
2 tbsp tomato paste
1 tbsp Montreal steak spice
1 tbsp chili powder
1 tsp dry mustard
1/4 tsp cayenne pepper
1 1/2 cups canned white beans,
   drained and rinsed, coarsely
   mashed with a fork
1 1/2 cups jarred all-natural tomato
   sauce
3 tbsp apple cider vinegar
1 tbsp Worcestershire sauce
1 tbsp molasses
Sea salt and freshly ground
   black pepper
6 whole-wheat hamburger buns, split

SERVES 6
HANDS-ON TIME: 25 MINUTES
TOTAL TIME: 30 MINUTES

Heat a large non-stick skillet over medium-high heat; mist with cooking spray. Add beef to pan and cook until browned, about 6 minutes, breaking up with a wooden spoon. Add garlic, onion and bell pepper and cook, stirring frequently, until softened, about 4 minutes. Add tomato paste, steak spice, chili powder, mustard and cayenne and cook, stirring constantly, until fragrant, about 1 minute. Stir in beans, tomato sauce, vinegar, Worcestershire sauce and molasses and bring to a boil. Reduce heat to medium-low and simmer, stirring occasionally, for 5 minutes, until thickened.

To serve, scoop filling into buns.

PER SERVING
BEFORE: 555 CALORIES, 20 G TOTAL FAT
DISH DO-OVER: 409 CALORIES, 10.4 G TOTAL FAT
NUTRITIONAL INFORMATION: 2.9 G SATURATED FAT,
53.9 G CARBOHYDRATES, 11.1 G FIBRE, 11 G SUGAR,
26.9 G PROTEIN, 622 MG SODIUM, 42 MG CHOLESTEROL

Caramelized Onion & Cheddar Pub Burgers

Burgers will always top the list of favourite comfort foods, but a greasy burger topped with cheese and mayonnaise tips the scales at over 50 grams of fat! To cut the fat, I swap regular ground beef with extra-lean ground beef or sirloin, but the big trick to cut even more fat and still keep the burger moist is to use cremini mushrooms to replace half the meat in the patty. A smoky, tangy spread with a non-fat Greek yogurt base replaces the mayonnaise, and sweet caramelized onions top everything off with a big punch of flavour and virtually no fat.

8 medium cremini mushrooms, coarsely chopped

1/2 small yellow onion, coarsely chopped

2 garlic cloves, minced

3 tsp smoked paprika

2 tsp dry mustard

4 tsp Worcestershire sauce

2 tsp low-sodium tamari or soy sauce

1 tsp sea salt

1/4 tsp freshly ground black pepper

1 lb extra-lean ground beef or sirloin

1 batch Caramelized Onions (page 18)

1/2 cup non-fat plain Greek yogurt

1 green onion, thinly sliced

1 tbsp Dijon mustard

1 tbsp honey

1/4 tsp cayenne pepper

1 cup shredded low-fat aged cheddar cheese

4 whole-grain or gluten-free burger buns

2 cups lightly packed arugula, sprouts or roughly chopped iceberg lettuce

2 vine-ripened tomatoes, sliced

2 dill pickles, sliced

SERVES 4
HANDS-ON TIME: 40 MINUTES
TOTAL TIME: 1 HOUR, 10 MINUTES
+ 1 HOUR MINIMUM CHILLING TIME

In a food processor, finely chop mushrooms, onion and garlic. Transfer to a large bowl and add 2 tsp paprika, mustard, 2 tsp Worcestershire sauce, tamari, 1/2 tsp salt and black pepper, mixing well to combine. Mix in beef, then shape into patties that are 4 1/2 inches thick. Transfer patties to a baking sheet, cover and refrigerate for at least 1 hour, or overnight.

While burgers are chilling, prepare caramelized onions.

For burger sauce, in a bowl, combine yogurt, remaining 1 tsp paprika, remaining 2 tsp Worcestershire sauce, green onion, Dijon, honey, remaining 1/2 tsp salt and cayenne. Cover and refrigerate.

Preheat oven to 400°F.

Preheat non-stick skillet or cast-iron pan to medium-high heat. Mist patties with cooking spray and cook, turning once, until juices run clear, 6 to 8 minutes for medium-well doneness. If desired, after flipping, sprinkle cheese on top of each burger during the last 2 minutes of cooking time, to melt.

While burgers are cooking, toast buns in oven cut side up on a baking sheet, until golden brown.

To assemble burgers, divide arugula, tomatoes and pickles over bottoms of buns. Top with burgers, caramelized onions and sauce; sandwich with tops of buns.

PER SERVING
BEFORE: 890 CALORIES, 53 G TOTAL FAT
DISH DO-OVER: 555 CALORIES, 18.5 G TOTAL FAT
NUTRITIONAL INFORMATION: 6.7 G SATURATED FAT, 60 G CARBOHYDRATES, 10 G FIBRE, 22 G SUGAR, 41.4 G PROTEIN, 1527 MG SODIUM, 68 MG CHOLESTEROL

Pizza Burgers

Many put pizza toppings on their burgers, and a few restaurants have put this Frankenstein-esque creation on their menus. I've put a bacon double-cheeseburger pizza through a delicious do-over (see page 191), so I couldn't resist giving this one a whirl. The results? A do-over rendition with less than half the calories, fat and sodium. I've stolen elements from other recipes to put this together, all of which should be made at least 1 hour ahead of time, and preferably the day before. Once the burgers and dough are made, this recipe is easy-peasy.

4 beef patties from Caramelized Onion & Cheddar Pub Burgers (page 129), covered and refrigerated for at least 1 hour

1 ball Whole-Wheat Pizza Dough (page 23) or 1 lb prepared whole-wheat pizza dough

3/4 cup jarred pizza sauce

1 cup shredded low-fat mozzarella cheese

2 slices Perfect Crispy Bacon (page 17), coarsely chopped

12 pieces turkey pepperoni

1 large egg, whisked with 2 tbsp water

2 tbsp cornmeal

1 tbsp sesame seeds

2 medium pieces leaf lettuce, torn in half

1 plum tomato, sliced 1/4 inch thick

1 medium dill pickle, sliced at a 45-degree angle into 8 pieces

SERVES 4
HANDS-ON TIME: 40 MINUTES
TOTAL TIME: 1 HOUR +
1 HOUR CHILLING TIME
(SUBRECIPES NOT INCLUDED)

Preheat oven to 500°F. Line a large baking sheet with parchment paper.

Heat a non-stick skillet or cast-iron pan over medium-high heat. Mist patties with cooking spray and cook, turning once, for 2 to 4 minutes, until seared on the outside and cooked to medium-rare doneness. Transfer to a paper towel–lined plate to drain excess fat.

Divide dough into 4 pieces. Stretch each piece of pizza dough into an 8- or 9-inch circle. Spread 3 tbsp pizza sauce over each circle, spreading so that sauce is the same diameter as the burger. Top sauce with cheese, bacon and pepperoni. Place one patty into the centre of each pizza, on top of filling. Brush edges of each pizza with egg wash. Gently stretch sides of pizza dough over burger, pinching to enclose burger completely.

Dust prepared baking sheet with half of the cornmeal. Place pizza burgers on baking sheet, seam sides down. Lightly brush with egg wash and sprinkle with remaining cornmeal. Top with sesame seeds. Bake in centre of oven for 12 to 15 minutes, until crust is golden brown.

Remove from oven and top each pizza burger with lettuce, tomatoes and pickles, inserting a skewer through the centre to secure.

PER SERVING
BEFORE: 1170 CALORIES, 73 G TOTAL FAT
DISH DO-OVER: 595 CALORIES, 27.5 G TOTAL FAT
NUTRITIONAL INFORMATION: 9.9 G SATURATED FAT, 46.6 G CARBOHYDRATES, 8.6 G FIBRE, 6.4 G SUGAR, 43.2 G PROTEIN, 1416 MG SODIUM, 132 MG CHOLESTEROL

Crispy Shrimp Po' Boys

The shrimp could easily be lightly sautéed or grilled to make it healthier, but I love the combo of crunchy breaded shrimp, creamy rémoulade and crisp lettuce on a nice crusty bun. The sauce tastes best if you allow the flavours to blend for at least 1 hour. Be sure to choose rolls with a crusty exterior.

RÉMOULADE

3 tbsp non-fat plain Greek yogurt
2 tbsp low-fat olive oil mayonnaise
2 tbsp finely chopped dill pickle
1 tbsp Creole or deli-style mustard
1 tsp Cajun seasoning
1 small shallot, minced
1 green onion, minced
2 to 3 dashes hot sauce
Sea salt or freshly ground
    black pepper

SANDWICHES

1 large egg, whisked
3 tbsp 1% buttermilk or skim milk
2 tbsp Cajun seasoning
1 1/2 lb peeled and deveined
    extra-large raw shrimp
4 whole-grain hoagie rolls or
    1 16-inch whole-grain baguette,
    cut into 4 pieces
1/4 cup cornmeal
2 tbsp whole-wheat flour
Sea salt and freshly ground
    black pepper
2 cups thinly sliced iceberg lettuce
2 vine-ripened tomatoes, sliced
    1/4 inch thick

SERVES 4
HANDS-ON TIME: 15 MINUTES
TOTAL TIME: 25 MINUTES

Prepare rémoulade: In a bowl, combine yogurt, mayonnaise, pickle, mustard, Cajun seasoning, shallot, green onion and hot sauce. Season with salt and pepper, cover and refrigerate. [*Make-ahead:* Sauce can be prepared up to 48 hours in advance.]

Preheat oven to 425°F. Line a large baking sheet with parchment paper.

Prepare sandwiches: In a large bowl, whisk together egg, buttermilk and Cajun seasoning. Add shrimp; toss to coat.

Cut bread in half lengthwise, leaving one side attached. Hollow out buns, leaving a 1-inch crust. In a food processor, pulse torn bread until fine crumbs form. Transfer to a bowl and stir in cornmeal, flour and remaining Cajun seasoning.

Working with a few shrimp at a time, dredge shrimp in bread crumb mixture, gently tossing to coat. Arrange in a single layer on prepared baking sheet. Repeat until all shrimp are coated. Bake for 6 to 8 minutes, until golden brown. Season with salt and pepper.

To serve, spread rémoulade onto cut sides of bread. Layer lettuce, shrimp and tomatoes over bottom half of bread and sandwich with bread tops.

PER SERVING
BEFORE: 929 CALORIES, 49.2 G TOTAL FAT
DISH DO-OVER: 483 CALORIES, 10.6 G TOTAL FAT
NUTRITIONAL INFORMATION: 2 G SATURATED FAT,
46.7 G CARBOHYDRATES, 8.3 G FIBRE, 8 G SUGAR,
49.3 G PROTEIN, 901 MG SODIUM, 308 MG CHOLESTEROL

Tip: Creole mustard is a spicy mustard traditionally used in Louisiana cooking. The brown mustard seeds are marinated in white vinegar, then often blended with fiery horseradish for extra heat. Deli-style mustard is made from pungent brown mustard seeds rather than from the more mellow yellow seeds used in regular yellow mustard. Find either in the gourmet section of major supermarkets or in gourmet grocery stores.

Chicken Tostadas

Tostadas are Mexican open-faced sandwiches using deep-fried tortillas. When tortillas are not fresh enough to be made into tacos, they are fried until golden and crunchy. Deep-fried tortillas, refried beans, avocado, full-fat cheese and sour cream take the fat content of this simple street food through the roof. I bake the tortillas instead, use low-fat feta cheese and non-fat Greek yogurt, and mix the avocado into a tangy salsa verde. While the ingredient list may look extensive, the recipe is simple and all the ingredients can be prepared at least a day ahead.

1/2 large red onion, thinly sliced

Juice of 3 limes (about 1/4 cup)

1/2 tsp sea salt, plus more to taste

2/3 cup jarred all-natural salsa verde

1/2 ripe medium avocado, coarsely mashed

8 6-inch corn tortillas

1/2 large white onion, diced

2 garlic cloves, minced

1 tsp smoked paprika

1 tsp chili powder

1 tsp ground cumin

8 oz Perfect Marinated Chicken Breast (page 21), cooled and shredded

1/4 batch Black Bean Dip (page 39)

2 ripe plum tomatoes, sliced 1/4 inch thick

1 cup crumbled low-fat feta cheese

8 sprigs cilantro

1/2 cup non-fat plain Greek yogurt (optional)

4 leaves romaine lettuce, shredded (optional)

SERVES 4
HANDS-ON TIME: 35 MINUTES
TOTAL TIME: 50 MINUTES + 1 HOUR
MARINATING TIME

Combine red onion, lime juice and 1/2 tsp salt in a small resealable bag or container. Cover and refrigerate for at least 1 hour, mixing occasionally to marinate evenly. [*Make-ahead:* Marinated onions will last 1 week in the fridge.]

In a small bowl, combine 1/3 cup salsa verde and avocado.

Position racks in top and bottom thirds of oven and preheat oven to 400°F. Line two large baking sheets with parchment paper.

Arrange tortillas in a single layer on prepared baking sheets. Mist with cooking spray and bake for 6 minutes, until starting to turn golden brown. Remove from oven, flip tortillas over, mist again, season with salt and return to oven, switching racks and rotating baking sheets so tortillas bake evenly. Bake for about 8 minutes, until golden brown and crispy.

Meanwhile, heat a large non-stick skillet over medium-high heat; mist with cooking spray. Add white onion and garlic and cook, stirring frequently, until onion is softened, about 3 minutes. Add paprika, chili powder and cumin and cook, stirring constantly, until fragrant, about 1 minute. Deglaze pan with 3 tbsp water, stirring and scraping up any brown bits from bottom of pan with a wooden spoon. Stir in chicken and remaining 1/3 cup salsa verde and cook, stirring frequently, until heated through, about 2 minutes. Remove from heat and cover to keep warm.

To assemble tostadas, evenly spread black bean dip on baked tortillas. Top with tomatoes, avocado, chicken, feta, pickled onion, cilantro, and yogurt and lettuce (if using).

PER SERVING
BEFORE: 584 CALORIES, 46 G TOTAL FAT
DISH DO-OVER: 472 CALORIES, 19.9 G TOTAL FAT
NUTRITIONAL INFORMATION: 6.2 G SATURATED FAT, 44.2 G CARBOHYDRATES, 10.5 G FIBRE, 9.3 G SUGAR, 32.5 G PROTEIN, 1177 MG SODIUM, 60 MG CHOLESTEROL

Pastas & Noodles

Chicken Fettuccine Alfredo

Given the "Dish Do-Over" requests I received, it seems many of you love creamy pasta dishes but want to know how to make healthier versions. Although you may think all that butter and cream are what make fettuccine Alfredo delicious, my version has half the calories and one-third of the fat, and tastes even better!

ALFREDO SAUCE

3 tbsp olive oil
1 medium onion, finely diced
4 garlic cloves, minced
3 tbsp rice or whole-wheat flour
1 bay leaf
2 sprigs fresh thyme
2 small yellow zucchini, shredded
   (about 2 cups lightly packed)
1 cup low-sodium chicken stock
1 cup 1% milk
1 1/2 cups grated Parmesan cheese
1/4 cup non-fat plain Greek yogurt
Sea salt and freshly ground
   black pepper
Pinch freshly grated nutmeg
Pinch cayenne pepper

PASTA

Extra-virgin olive oil, for tossing
1 lb whole-wheat or brown rice
   fettuccine noodles
2 boneless, skinless chicken breasts
   (5 oz each), thinly sliced
2 cups broccoli florets
2 cups sliced cremini mushrooms
1 red bell pepper, thinly sliced

SERVES 8
HANDS-ON TIME: 30 MINUTES
TOTAL TIME: 30 MINUTES

Prepare sauce: In a medium saucepan over medium-high heat, heat 2 tbsp oil. Add onion and half the garlic; cook for 3 minutes, stirring constantly, until translucent. Stir in flour and continue to cook, stirring for about 1 minute, until flour is light brown. Stir in bay leaf, thyme, zucchini, stock and milk. Bring to a boil, reduce heat to medium and simmer for 10 minutes. Remove from heat, and discard bay leaf and thyme. Stir in Parmesan and yogurt. Purée in a blender or directly in saucepan with an immersion blender until smooth. Season with salt, pepper, nutmeg and cayenne. Cover and keep warm.

Prepare pasta: While sauce is cooking, bring a large pot of salted water to a boil and cook pasta according to package instructions. Drain, rinse and toss with oil. Spread on a baking sheet to cool. Set aside pasta pot for reheating pasta later.

Meanwhile, in a large non-stick skillet over medium-high heat, season chicken with remaining 1 tbsp oil, remaining garlic, salt and pepper. Cook chicken for about 2 minutes, until golden. Stir in broccoli, mushrooms and bell pepper and cook for another 4 minutes, stirring frequently, until vegetables are al dente. Stir in 1 cup sauce.

Return pasta to pot and stir in remaining sauce. Gently stir pasta and cook over medium-high heat until pasta is heated through. Transfer to a bowl for serving and top with chicken and vegetables.

PER SERVING
BEFORE: 910 CALORIES, 52 G TOTAL FAT
DISH DO-OVER: 406 CALORIES, 11.7 G TOTAL FAT
NUTRITIONAL INFORMATION: 4.1 G SATURATED FAT,
55.4 G CARBOHYDRATES, 2.8 G FIBRE, 4.1 G SUGAR,
21.7 G PROTEIN, 397 MG SODIUM, 33 MG CHOLESTEROL

Tip: Salted cooking water is essential for infusing pastas and boiled vegetables with flavour. While it might sound straightforward, most home cooks under-salt the water and end up with a flavourless product. For maximum flavour, cooking water should taste as salty as the ocean. Use about 1 tbsp salt for every 4 quarts of water.

Macaroni & Cheese

Macaroni and cheese is quite possibly the most perfect food on the planet. The original version uses full-fat cheese, cream and white pasta; the whole dish is pretty much fat and carbs. My version uses creamy sweet potato to thicken the sauce and add nutrients and flavour, evaporated milk so the sauce doesn't separate during baking and brown rice pasta.

2 1/2 cups sweet potato, peeled and chopped (1 medium)

3 tbsp olive oil

1 medium yellow onion, finely diced

2 garlic cloves, minced

1/4 cup whole-wheat or brown rice flour

2 tsp dry mustard

1 can (13 oz/370 mL) non-fat evaporated milk

1 cup low-sodium chicken or vegetable stock

2 cups shredded low-fat aged cheddar cheese

3/4 cup freshly grated Parmesan cheese

1/4 tsp freshly grated nutmeg

Dash hot sauce

Sea salt and freshly ground black pepper

1 cup non-fat plain Greek yogurt

4 cups whole-wheat or brown rice macaroni (1 lb/454 g)

1 cup panko bread crumbs (gluten-free, if desired) or fresh whole-wheat bread crumbs

1 tbsp chopped fresh flat-leaf parsley

SERVES 8
HANDS-ON TIME: 30 MINUTES
TOTAL TIME: 1 HOUR

Place sweet potato in a steamer basket set over a saucepan of boiling water. Steam potato until fork-tender, about 15 minutes. Mash until smooth.

In a medium saucepan, heat oil over medium heat. Add onion and garlic and cook, stirring frequently, until onion is softened and translucent, about 4 minutes. Add flour and cook, stirring constantly, for about 1 minute, until golden brown. Stir in mustard and sweet potato.

Whisk in evaporated milk and stock until smooth. Bring to a gentle simmer and cook, stirring frequently, until thickened, about 5 minutes. Remove from heat and gradually stir in cheddar and 1/2 cup Parmesan until smooth. Season with nutmeg, hot sauce, salt and pepper. Whisk in yogurt until mixture is smooth.

Preheat oven to 375°F.

Meanwhile, bring a large pot of salted water to a boil and cook pasta according to package instructions for al dente (if given a range of cooking time, choose shorter time, otherwise cook for 2 minutes less). Drain, reserving 1/3 cup pasta cooking water. Return pasta to pot and stir in sauce, adding as much reserved pasta cooking water as needed to loosen sauce. Season with salt and pepper. Transfer to a 9- × 13-inch baking pan misted with cooking spray.

In a small bowl, combine panko, parsley and remaining 1/4 cup Parmesan. Sprinkle mixture over pasta and mist with cooking spray. Bake for about 30 minutes, until sauce is bubbling and topping is golden brown and crispy

PER SERVING
BEFORE: 836 CALORIES, 52.6 G TOTAL FAT
DISH DO-OVER: 480 CALORIES, 11.2 G TOTAL FAT
NUTRITIONAL INFORMATION: 3.7 G SATURATED FAT,
73.4 G CARBOHYDRATES, 3.1 G FIBRE, 9.8 G SUGAR,
22.5 G PROTEIN, 704 MG SODIUM, 15 MG CHOLESTEROL

Spaghetti & Meatballs

I've cut the fat of traditional meatballs by using extra-lean meats and added mushrooms for bulk and moisture. If you're rushed, skip the sauce-making and use your favourite jarred sauce instead.

1 large yellow onion, coarsely chopped

3 cups cremini mushrooms, coarsely chopped

4 garlic cloves, minced

1 medium carrot, peeled and coarsely chopped

1 celery rib, coarsely chopped

Pinch chili flakes

3 tbsp coarsely chopped fresh basil (or 1 tbsp dried)

1/4 cup tomato paste

1 can (28 oz/796 mL) unsalted diced tomatoes

1 cup passata

2 tbsp honey or organic sugar

1/2 tsp sea salt, plus more to taste

1/4 tsp freshly ground black pepper, plus more to taste

1/3 cup egg whites (about 3 large)

1/3 cup fresh whole-wheat or regular panko bread crumbs

1/4 cup freshly grated Parmesan cheese

3 tbsp chopped fresh flat-leaf parsley

8 oz extra-lean ground beef

4 oz extra-lean ground pork

12 oz whole-wheat, brown rice or corn spaghetti

SERVES 6 (MAKES 18 MEATBALLS
+ 3.5 CUPS SAUCE)
HANDS-ON TIME: 50 MINUTES
TOTAL TIME: 1 HOUR, 25 MINUTES

PER SERVING
BEFORE: 778 CALORIES,
23.9 G TOTAL FAT
DISH DO-OVER: 429 CALORIES,
8 G TOTAL FAT
NUTRITIONAL INFORMATION:
3 G SATURATED FAT, 69.5 G
CARBOHYDRATES, 4.7 G FIBRE,
15.6 G SUGAR, 22 G PROTEIN, 586
MG SODIUM, 35 MG CHOLESTEROL

In a food processor, finely chop onion and mushrooms. Divide mixture evenly between two bowls (one bowl is for the sauce; the other is for the meatballs). Divide garlic evenly between the two bowls. Add carrot and celery to food processor and finely chop; transfer to bowl containing onion and mushrooms (for sauce).

Heat a large saucepan over medium-high heat; mist with cooking spray. Add carrot and mushroom mixture, chili flakes and basil and cook, stirring frequently, until vegetables are soft and fragrant, about 5 minutes. Stir in tomato paste and sauté until brown, about 3 minutes. Stir in diced tomatoes and passata and bring to a boil. Reduce heat to medium-low and simmer uncovered for 30 minutes. Stir in honey and season with salt and pepper.

Preheat oven to 425°F. Line a large baking sheet with parchment paper.

While sauce is simmering, prepare meatballs: Add egg whites, panko, Parmesan and parsley to reserved mushroom and onion mixture, stirring to incorporate. Add beef, pork, 1/2 tsp salt and 1/4 tsp pepper and mix by hand to combine.

With wet hands, roll meat mixture into 2-tbsp balls. Transfer to prepared baking sheet and mist all over with cooking spray. Bake until browned on top, about 15 minutes. Remove from oven and transfer to a paper towel–lined plate to drain excess fat; discard pan juices. Gently add meatballs to sauce and cook uncovered for 25 minutes, stirring occasionally. [*Make-ahead:* Meatballs can be refrigerated for up to 3 days or frozen for up to 1 month. Thaw completely in the fridge and warm over medium heat until heated through.]

While meatballs are simmering, bring a large pot of salted water to a boil and cook pasta according to package instructions. Drain, reserving 1/2 cup cooking water. Transfer pasta to a large bowl and gently stir in 1 cup sauce, adding reserved cooking water 3 tbsp at a time until desired consistency is reached. Season with salt and pepper. Place pasta in serving bowls and top with meatballs and remaining sauce.

Spaghetti Carbonara

There are two versions of this decadent creamy dish, American and Italian. The American version uses cream, the Italian doesn't, and most agree that true carbonara uses guanciale rather than bacon. I use a combo of pancetta and ham to help cut the fat, and also reduce the sheer number of egg yolks by using extra whites and some evaporated milk to keep it creamy. With this dish, hot pasta is the key to success — and it also helps cook the egg yolks slightly, making them creamy too. This is a dish that you must serve immediately — it's not a make-ahead.

2 oz pancetta, diced (about 1/2 cup)

2 oz Canadian bacon or ham (about 1/2 cup)

3 garlic cloves

2 large eggs

1/3 cup egg whites (about 3 large)

1/4 cup non-fat evaporated milk

1/2 cup freshly grated pecorino or Parmesan cheese

12 oz brown rice, whole-wheat or corn spaghetti

2 tsp extra-virgin olive oil

3 tbsp chopped fresh flat-leaf parsley

Sea salt and freshly ground black pepper

SERVES 4
HANDS-ON TIME: 25 MINUTES
TOTAL TIME: 25 MINUTES

Heat a small non-stick skillet over medium heat; mist with cooking spray. Add pancetta and bacon and cook, stirring frequently, until golden brown and crispy, about 3 minutes. Add garlic and cook, stirring frequently, until just golden, about 30 seconds. Transfer to a paper towel–lined plate to drain excess fat.

Whisk together eggs, egg whites, evaporated milk and cheese until smooth.

Bring a large pot of salted water to a boil and cook pasta according to package instructions. Drain, reserving 1/2 cup pasta cooking water. Return pasta to pot off the heat. Add oil to pasta and gently stir to coat. Add egg mixture and stir well to coat pasta, adding reserved pasta cooking water 2 to 3 tbsp at a time until sauce reaches desired consistency. Stir in pancetta, bacon and parsley and season with salt and lots of pepper.

Note: Raw egg warning! Use pasteurized eggs if you're concerned. Don't try to pasteurize eggs at home; it does not work.

Note: This dish is said to have come about after World War Two, when eggs and bacon were abundant in Italy. The name comes from the Italian word for coal, *carbone*, and refers to the little specks of pepper throughout.

PER SERVING
BEFORE: 937 CALORIES, 55.1 G TOTAL FAT
DISH DO-OVER: 478 CALORIES, 12.3 G TOTAL FAT
NUTRITIONAL INFORMATION: 4.3 G SATURATED FAT, 70.6 G CARBOHYDRATES, 1.7 G FIBRE, 2.7 G SUGAR, 22.7 G PROTEIN, 912 MG SODIUM, 122 MG CHOLESTEROL

Tuna Noodle Casserole

This one-dish wonder is a retro favourite that's designed to be quick, easy and inexpensive. With a few swaps, it can be a healthy choice too. Look for egg noodles made without yolks — you'll save fat and won't notice the difference in taste. True to tuna noodle casserole form, it was the first dish empty at the potluck I took this baby to, with everyone asking for the recipe. Well, here it is, ladies!

8 oz no-yolk extra-broad egg noodles (about 3 cups)

1 batch mushroom Creamy Condensed Soup Substitute (page 21)

3/4 cup low-sodium chicken stock

3/4 cup non-fat plain Greek yogurt

2 tbsp Dijon mustard

1 tsp low-sodium tamari or soy sauce

2 cans (6 oz/170 g each) non-sodium, water-packed chunk albacore tuna, drained

1 1/2 cups frozen peas, thawed and drained

1/4 tsp cayenne pepper or a few dashes hot sauce

Sea salt and freshly ground black pepper

1 cup whole-wheat or regular panko bread crumbs (gluten-free, if desired) or fresh bread crumbs

1/4 cup freshly grated Parmesan cheese

SERVES 6
HANDS-ON TIME: 30 MINUTES
TOTAL TIME: 1 HOUR, 10 MINUTES

Preheat oven to 400°F.

Bring a large pot of salted water to a boil and cook noodles according to package instructions until al dente (if given a range of cooking time, choose shorter time, otherwise cook for 2 minutes less). Drain and lightly mist with cooking spray to prevent noodles from sticking.

In a large saucepan, whisk together mushroom soup, stock, yogurt, Dijon and tamari until smooth. Warm over medium heat, stirring frequently, until steaming, about 5 minutes. Remove from heat and stir in tuna, peas and cayenne. Season with salt and pepper. Lightly mist a 9- × 13-inch baking dish with cooking spray; transfer mixture to dish.

In a small bowl, combine panko and Parmesan. Sprinkle over casserole and mist with cooking spray. Bake for 25 minutes, until crust is golden and sauce is bubbling.

PER SERVING
BEFORE: 697 CALORIES, 34.2 G TOTAL FAT
DISH DO-OVER: 396 CALORIES, 5.3 G TOTAL FAT
NUTRITIONAL INFORMATION: 1.2 G SATURATED FAT, 54.5 G CARBOHYDRATES, 5.6 G FIBRE, 11.1 G SUGAR, 29.9 G PROTEIN, 638 MG SODIUM, 24 MG CHOLESTEROL

Pad Thai

Possibly one of the worst takeout dishes from a health perspective, pad Thai is loaded with fat, sugar and salt. Fish sauce is the culprit for the huge sodium number. In this dish do-over, bumping up the tanginess allows you to cut back on the fish sauce. Not boiling the noodles in this recipe is key, so that you have the right texture and the sauce sticks to the noodles better. For a vegetarian version, you can replace the fish sauce with rice vinegar or lime juice and use tofu instead of shrimp.

8 oz medium dried rice noodles

2 tbsp fresh lime juice or
   tamarind paste

2 tbsp Homemade Ketchup (page 19)
   or organic ketchup

2 tbsp honey

2 tbsp low-sodium soy sauce

1 tbsp rice vinegar

1 tbsp fish sauce

1 tbsp Sriracha or sambal oelek sauce,
   or 1 red Thai chili pepper, plus
   more to taste

3 garlic cloves, minced

8 oz peeled and deveined medium
   raw shrimp

1 red bell pepper, thinly sliced

1 large egg, plus 5 egg whites,
   whisked together

3 cups bean sprouts

3 green onions, thinly sliced

1/3 cup coarsely chopped fresh
   cilantro

4 tbsp coarsely chopped toasted
   unsalted peanuts (page 17)

SERVES 4
HANDS-ON TIME: 30 MINUTES
TOTAL TIME: 30 MINUTES
(KETCHUP NOT INCLUDED)

Soak rice noodles in a large bowl of hot water for about 15 minutes, until pliable but not quite al dente; drain.

While noodles are soaking, prepare sauce: In a medium bowl, whisk together lime juice, ketchup, honey, soy sauce, vinegar, fish sauce, Sriracha and 3 tbsp water.

Heat a large non-stick wok or skillet over medium-high heat; mist with cooking spray. Add garlic and shrimp and cook, stirring frequently, for about 3 minutes, until shrimp are bright pink and cooked through. Transfer shrimp to a bowl and cover to keep warm.

Return wok to heat and mist with cooking spray. Add bell pepper and cook, stirring frequently, until softened, about 1 minute. Add egg mixture and cook, stirring frequently, for 30 seconds or until eggs are just partially set. Add noodles and cook, gently tossing, until noodles are softened and fully coated with egg.

Add sauce and shrimp to pan and cook, gently tossing, until shrimp is warmed and sauce is slightly thickened and sticky, about 2 minutes. Add bean sprouts and green onions and cook for 1 minute, gently tossing to mix. Transfer to serving plates and top with cilantro and peanuts.

PER SERVING
BEFORE: 643 CALORIES, 29.3 G TOTAL FAT
DISH DO-OVER: 455 CALORIES, 7.9 G TOTAL FAT
NUTRITIONAL INFORMATION: 1.3 G SATURATED FAT,
71.8 G CARBOHYDRATES, 4.3 G FIBRE, 18.2 G SUGAR,
24.9 G PROTEIN, 943 MG SODIUM, 132 MG CHOLESTEROL

Beef Stroganoff

This has been a family favourite for decades and makes a quick weeknight dinner. You can lose the fat and sodium by adding cremini mushrooms to a leaner beef and using your own condensed soup substitute.

1 lb chuck shoulder or eye of round beef, trimmed of visible fat and sliced into 1/4-inch strips

1/4 tsp each sea salt and freshly ground black pepper, plus more to taste

1/4 cup whole-wheat or brown rice flour

1 tbsp grapeseed oil

1 medium onion, thinly sliced

2 garlic cloves, minced

2 cups sliced cremini mushrooms

1 1/2 cups low-sodium beef stock

2 tbsp Dijon mustard

1 tbsp Worcestershire sauce

1 batch mushroom Creamy Condensed Soup Substitute (page 21)

8 oz no-yolk extra-broad egg noodles (about 3 cups)

2 tbsp chopped fresh dill

3/4 cup non-fat plain Greek yogurt

SERVES 4
HANDS-ON TIME: 35 MINUTES
TOTAL TIME: 1 HOUR

Pat beef dry with paper towel, season with 1/4 tsp salt and 1/4 tsp pepper, then toss in 2 tbsp flour to coat on all sides.

In a large non-stick, high-sided skillet, heat oil over medium-high heat. Working in batches if necessary, sear beef on all sides until browned, about 8 minutes. Transfer to a paper towel–lined baking sheet to drain excess fat.

Add onion, garlic and mushrooms to pan and cook, stirring occasionally, until onion is softened and mushrooms are golden brown, about 6 minutes. Stir in remaining flour and cook for 30 seconds, stirring constantly. Add beef and stock, scraping up any brown bits from bottom of pan with a wooden spoon. Stir in Dijon, Worcestershire sauce and mushroom soup. Bring to a gentle boil, reduce heat to low and simmer uncovered for 30 minutes or until beef is tender and pulls apart easily with a fork.

Meanwhile, bring a large pot of salted water to a boil and cook noodles according to package instructions. Drain and lightly mist noodles with cooking spray. Stir noodles and dill into beef mixture until noodles are evenly coated and warmed. Serve topped with a dollop of yogurt.

PER SERVING
BEFORE: 582 CALORIES, 32.1 G TOTAL FAT
DISH DO-OVER: 638 CALORIES, 16.5 G TOTAL FAT
*NUTRITIONAL INFORMATION: 4 G SATURATED FAT,
73.7 G CARBOHYDRATES, 7.1 G FIBRE, 15.7 G SUGAR,
47.3 G PROTEIN, 920 MG SODIUM, 70 MG CHOLESTEROL*

Lasagna

Lasagna is a calorie-dense disaster typically loaded with full-fat ground beef and ooey-gooey cheeses, like creamy ricotta and mozzarella, layered between white-flour pasta. I've replaced some of the ground meat with ground mushrooms, and opted for extra-lean for the rest. Dry-pressed cottage cheese helps keep the fat super low and keeps the lasagna from being too runny in the centre.

SAUCE

1 yellow onion, diced

4 garlic cloves, minced

1 medium carrot, peeled and diced

1 celery rib, diced

1 tsp dried oregano

1/4 tsp chili flakes

1 lb extra-lean ground beef

2 cups cremini mushrooms, chopped
    in a food processor

1/4 cup packed fresh basil, coarsely
    chopped

1/4 cup tomato paste

2 cans (28 oz/796 mL each) unsalted
    diced tomatoes

1/4 tsp each sea salt and freshly ground
    black pepper, plus more to taste

2 cups low-fat dry-pressed
    cottage cheese

3 cups shredded low-fat mozzarella
    cheese

3/4 cup freshly grated Parmesan cheese

1 large egg, lightly beaten

Pinch freshly grated nutmeg

6 fresh whole-wheat lasagna sheets
    (12 oz/360 g)

SERVES 12
HANDS-ON TIME: 40 MINUTES
TOTAL TIME: 2 HOURS +
10 MINUTES RESTING TIME

Tip: Spray the underside of foil with cooking spray before covering baking dish, to prevent cheese from sticking.

For sauce, heat a medium Dutch oven or heavy-bottomed saucepan over medium heat; mist with cooking spray. Add onion, garlic, carrot, celery, oregano and chili flakes and cook, stirring frequently, until softened, about 6 minutes. Add beef, mushrooms and basil and cook, breaking up meat with a wooden spoon, until no liquid remains, about 8 minutes. Add tomato paste and cook, stirring constantly, until fragrant, about 1 minute. Stir in diced tomatoes and bring to a boil. Reduce heat to medium-low and simmer, uncovered and stirring occasionally, for about 40 minutes, until sauce is thickened. Season with salt and pepper. [*Make-ahead:* Cool to room temperature, cover and refrigerate for up to 3 days.]

While sauce is simmering, prepare cheese mixture: In a medium bowl, combine cottage cheese, 2 cups mozzarella, 1/2 cup Parmesan, egg, 1/4 tsp salt, 1/4 tsp pepper and nutmeg.

Preheat oven to 375°F.

Lightly mist a 9- × 13-inch baking dish with cooking spray. Evenly spread 1 cup sauce in dish. Layer 2 lasagna sheets over sauce, overlapping slightly to fit. Top with one-third of cheese mixture, then one-third of sauce. Repeat with remaining lasagna sheets, cheese mixture and sauce, then top with remaining mozzarella and Parmesan.

Cover with foil and bake for 40 minutes, until hot throughout. Uncover and bake for another 10 to 15 minutes, until cheese is golden brown. Cover loosely with foil and let stand for 10 minutes before serving.

PER SERVING
BEFORE: 528 CALORIES, 29 G TOTAL FAT
DISH DO-OVER: 311 CALORIES, 10.7 G TOTAL FAT
NUTRITIONAL INFORMATION: 5.6 G SATURATED FAT, 28.5 G CARBOHYDRATES, 4 G FIBRE, 6.4 G SUGAR, 26.9 G PROTEIN, 467 MG SODIUM, 71 MG CHOLESTEROL

Penne with Pesto

Pesto pasta is a simple, fresh dish that you can whip up in a flash. However, the quantity of nuts, cheese and olive oil involved make this one of the most calorie-dense sauces in the kitchen. For this delicious do-over, I've reduced the amount of olive oil and added chicken or vegetable stock, replaced some of the nuts and cheese with low-fat ricotta to retain the creamy texture but cut fat, and used brown rice pasta. I suggest pecorino cheese here because it has a stronger flavour than Parmesan, allowing even less to be used. In a pinch, though, Parmesan makes a great substitute.

2 1/2 cups packed fresh basil
2 tbsp pine nuts
1 garlic clove, minced
1/3 cup low-fat ricotta cheese
1/4 cup freshly grated pecorino cheese
1/4 cup low-sodium chicken or
    vegetable stock
2 tbsp extra-virgin olive oil
12 oz whole-wheat, brown rice or
    corn penne
Sea salt and freshly ground
    black pepper

SERVES 6
HANDS-ON TIME: 10 MINUTES
TOTAL TIME: 15 MINUTES

Tip: I find that whole or just smashed garlic, when added to pesto or other dips and dressings in the food processor, often doesn't purée into the mixture. Although it's an extra step, mincing or rasping garlic before adding is essential — not many people will enjoy chomping down on a big hunk of raw garlic!

In a food processor, coarsely chop basil, nuts and garlic. Add ricotta and pecorino; pulse to combine. In a steady stream with motor running, add stock and then oil, processing until smooth, scraping down sides of the bowl as needed. Transfer pesto to a large bowl.

Bring a large pot of salted water to a boil and cook pasta according to package instructions. Drain, reserving 1/2 cup pasta cooking water. Transfer pasta to bowl with pesto, mix to coat, adding 2 tbsp pasta cooking water at a time until creamy. Season with salt and pepper.

PER SERVING
BEFORE: 492 CALORIES, 13.9 G TOTAL FAT
DISH DO-OVER: 301 CALORIES, 10.1 G TOTAL FAT
NUTRITIONAL INFORMATION: 2.8 G SATURATED FAT, 46.6 G CARBOHYDRATES, 1.8 G FIBRE, 0.2 G SUGAR, 7.8 G PROTEIN, 910 MG SODIUM, 9 MG CHOLESTEROL

Chicken, Spinach & Ricotta Cannelloni

A simple, impressive dish that's low in fat and big on flavour. With low-fat ricotta, you won't notice the difference or miss the fat. And using fresh lasagna sheets, which don't need to be parboiled, is the secret to making this crowd-pleaser quickly and without much fuss.

1 small yellow onion, diced
2 garlic cloves, minced
2 tsp chopped fresh thyme
    (or 1/2 tsp dried)
1 lb extra-lean ground turkey
    or chicken
1 package (10 oz/300 g) frozen
    chopped spinach, thawed and
    squeezed of excess water
1 1/2 cups low-fat ricotta cheese
1/4 cup freshly grated Parmesan cheese
1 large egg, lightly beaten
1/3 cup chopped fresh basil
1/4 tsp each sea salt and freshly
    ground black pepper
Pinch freshly grated nutmeg
2 1/2 cups jarred all-natural tomato
    sauce
6 fresh whole-wheat lasagna sheets
    (12 oz/360 g)
1 cup shredded low-fat mozzarella
    cheese

SERVES 6
HANDS-ON TIME: 30 MINUTES
TOTAL TIME: 1 HOUR

Preheat oven to 400°F.

Heat a large non-stick skillet over medium-high heat; mist with cooking spray. Add onion, garlic and thyme and cook, stirring frequently, until softened, about 3 minutes. Add turkey and cook, breaking up with a wooden spoon, until lightly browned and no liquid remains in pan. Transfer to a large bowl and cool to room temperature, then stir in spinach, ricotta, Parmesan, egg, 3 tbsp basil, salt, pepper and nutmeg.

Lightly mist a 9- × 13-inch baking dish with cooking spray. Evenly spread 1 cup sauce in dish.

Cut lasagna sheets in half to form 12 squares. Arrange pasta in a single layer on a clean work surface. Spread about 1/4 cup filling onto the bottom of each noodle and roll into a cylinder. Place, seam side down, in baking dish. Cover with remaining sauce and sprinkle with mozzarella.

Cover with foil and bake for about 20 minutes, until sauce is bubbling and filling is hot. Uncover and bake for another 10 minutes, until cheese is browned. Garnish with remaining basil.

PER SERVING
BEFORE: 686 CALORIES, 76 G TOTAL FAT
DISH DO-OVER: 486 CALORIES, 17.9 G TOTAL FAT
NUTRITIONAL INFORMATION: 6.7 G SATURATED FAT, 45.7 G CARBOHYDRATES, 9.8 G FIBRE, 7.5 G SUGAR, 36.4 G PROTEIN, 417 MG SODIUM, 142 MG CHOLESTEROL

Tip: Spray the underside of foil with cooking spray before covering baking dish, to prevent cheese from sticking.

Beef Lo Mein

Skip the delivery menu and whip up a much better version of beef lo mein, one that's not soaking in grease and loaded with sodium and sugar. I've reduced the sodium with low-sodium stock and soy sauce, used honey instead of refined white sugar and bumped up the veggies for a much fresher version that the whole family will love.

1/2 cup pre-sliced and stemmed dried
   shiitake mushrooms
12 oz Chinese-style egg noodles
2 tbsp low-sodium soy sauce
2 tbsp oyster sauce
2 tsp honey
1/4 cup low-sodium beef stock
2 tsp cornstarch
12 oz beef flank steak, thinly sliced
   across the grain into 2-inch pieces
2 tsp grapeseed oil
2 garlic cloves, minced
1 tbsp minced fresh ginger
Sea salt and freshly ground
   black pepper
1 carrot, peeled and thinly sliced
1 red bell pepper, thinly sliced
2 cups thinly sliced napa cabbage
1 tsp sesame oil
2 green onions, thinly sliced

SERVES 4
HANDS-ON TIME: 20 MINUTES
TOTAL TIME: 40 MINUTES

Tip: You can substitute fresh shiitake mushrooms for the dried variety called for in the recipe. Using scissors, trim and discard stems. Thinly slice mushroom caps until you have about 1 cup. Use 1/4 cup more beef stock in place of the soaking liquid.

In a small bowl, soak dried mushrooms in warm water for 30 minutes. Drain, reserving 1/4 cup soaking liquid. (You should have about 1 cup hydrated mushrooms.)

Meanwhile, bring a large pot of salted water to a boil and cook noodles according to package instructions; drain.

In a medium bowl, whisk together mushroom soaking liquid, soy sauce, oyster sauce, honey, stock and cornstarch.

In another medium bowl, toss beef with 1 tsp grapeseed oil, garlic, ginger, salt and pepper. In a large non-stick wok or skillet, heat remaining 1 tsp grapeseed oil over medium-high heat. Add beef and cook, stirring frequently, until browned on all sides, about 1 1/2 minutes. Transfer to a large bowl.

Return wok to heat and add carrot and bell pepper. Sauté, stirring frequently, for about 30 seconds, until softened. Transfer to a bowl. Add mushrooms and cabbage to pan and cook, stirring frequently, until cabbage is wilted, about 1 minute. Transfer to bowl with carrot and pepper.

Add prepared noodles to wok and cook, stirring, for about 30 seconds. Return beef, along with any juices in bowl, and vegetables to pan. Add broth mixture. Cook for about 1 minute, stirring frequently, until sauce is thickened and coats noodles. Season with sesame oil, salt and pepper. Transfer to a platter and garnish with green onions.

PER SERVING
BEFORE: 570 CALORIES, 21 G TOTAL FAT
DISH DO-OVER: 478 CALORIES, 12.3 G TOTAL FAT
*NUTRITIONAL INFORMATION: 3.6 G SATURATED FAT,
61.4 G CARBOHYDRATES, 4 G FIBRE, 7.4 G SUGAR,
30.3 G PROTEIN, 850 MG SODIUM, 102 MG CHOLESTEROL*

ONTARIO
RED
BEETS
99¢
lb

ONT HEIRLOOM
YELLOW
BEETS
$/ T

HEIRLOOM
CARROT'S CANDY
$.99
lb

U.S
NO 1
BRUSSEL
SPROUTS
$2.49
lb

ONTAR
PARSNIPS
$
.99
lb

Mains

Turkey Pot Pie

The key here is replacing the traditional buttery pastry top with flakey, crispy phyllo. Scrunching up small pieces of phyllo and piling them on top gives the pot pie a beautiful golden crust and is super easy to do — the kids will love giving you a hand with this. I also use milk instead of cream in the filling to cut the fat and, of course, load it up with extra veggies.

1 1/2 lb boneless, skinless turkey breast, cut into 6 even pieces

2 garlic cloves, minced

1 cup thinly sliced leek, white and light green parts only

1 cup diced peeled celery

1 cup diced carrot

2 cups thinly sliced cremini mushrooms

2 tsp coarsely chopped fresh thyme

3 tbsp whole-wheat flour

1 small butternut squash, peeled, seeded and finely diced (about 2 cups)

2 cups low-sodium chicken stock

1 cup 1% or skim milk

1 cup frozen peas, thawed and drained

Sea salt and freshly ground black pepper

6 sheets frozen regular, whole-wheat or spelt phyllo dough, thawed

SERVES 6
HANDS-ON TIME: 50 MINUTES
TOTAL TIME: 1 HOUR, 15 MINUTES

Preheat oven to 400°F. Line a large baking sheet with parchment paper.

Mist turkey with cooking spray, rub on garlic and season with salt and pepper. Arrange in a single layer on prepared baking sheet. Roast in oven for about 20 minutes, until cooked through (when an instant-read thermometer inserted into thickest part reads 160°F). Set aside until cool enough to handle, then dice into 1/2-inch chunks.

While turkey is roasting, heat a large non-stick skillet over medium-high heat. Add leek, celery and carrot and cook, stirring frequently, for 5 minutes or until leeks are softened. Add mushrooms and thyme, and cook for another 6 minutes, until mushrooms are softened. Add flour and cook, stirring constantly, until vegetables are coated, about 1 minute.

Stir in cooked turkey, squash, stock and milk. Bring to a boil, reduce heat to medium-low and simmer for about 10 minutes, until liquid is thickened and reduced slightly. Remove from heat, stir in peas and season with salt and pepper. Transfer to a deep 9- × 13-inch baking dish.

Unroll phyllo and mist top sheet with cooking spray. Scrunch 1 phyllo sheet with your hand and place on top of casserole. Repeat with remaining phyllo sheets, misting each before scrunching and overlapping slightly, until pie is covered. Mist top of pie once more with oil and season with salt and pepper.

Bake for 25 to 30 minutes or until phyllo is crispy and golden and pie is bubbling. Let rest at room temperature for 5 minutes before serving, to allow filling to set.

PER SERVING
BEFORE: 570 CALORIES, 34 G TOTAL FAT
DISH DO-OVER: 322 CALORIES, 6.5 G TOTAL FAT
NUTRITIONAL INFORMATION: 1.6 G SATURATED FAT,
32.2 G CARBOHYDRATES, 4.5 G FIBRE, 6.6 G SUGAR,
33.5 G PROTEIN, 420 MG SODIUM, 70 MG CHOLESTEROL

Shepherd's Pie

The ultimate comfort food, shepherd's pie is chock full of delicious ingredients that can really add up. Thankfully, with my dish do-over version, you get all the amazing flavour with only a fraction of the fat and calories. Cauliflower instead of potatoes = low carb.

1 large cauliflower, cut into florets (about 5 cups)

1 1/2 cups low-sodium beef stock

1/2 tsp onion powder

Sea salt and freshly ground black pepper

1 lb lean ground lamb or extra-lean ground beef

1 large Spanish onion, diced

2 garlic cloves, minced

2 medium carrots, peeled and diced

2 celery ribs, diced

1 tsp chopped fresh thyme (or 1/4 tsp dried)

4 cups sliced cremini mushrooms

2 tbsp brown rice flour

1 cup unsalted diced tomatoes

1 tbsp Worcestershire sauce

1 tbsp Dijon mustard

1 cup frozen peas, thawed and drained

1/3 cup freshly grated Parmesan cheese

SERVES 8
HANDS-ON TIME: 40 MINUTES
TOTAL TIME: 1 HOUR, 10 MINUTES

Preheat oven to 400°F. Line a large baking sheet with parchment paper.

Spread cauliflower in a single layer on prepared baking sheet and mist with cooking spray. Roast for 30 minutes, until soft. Cool slightly, then place in a food processor. Add 1/2 cup stock and onion powder and purée until smooth. Transfer to a bowl and season with salt and pepper.

Meanwhile, heat a large non-stick skillet over medium-high heat; mist with cooking spray. Add lamb and cook, breaking up with a wooden spoon, for 8 minutes, until browned. Transfer to a paper towel–lined baking sheet.

To skillet, add onion, garlic, carrots, celery and thyme. Cook, stirring frequently, for 3 minutes, until softened. Add mushrooms and cook, stirring frequently, until golden brown and softened, about 6 minutes. Return lamb to skillet and stir in flour. Cook, stirring for 2 minutes. Add remaining 1 cup stock, tomatoes, Worcestershire sauce and Dijon. Cook for about 6 minutes, until thickened slightly and reduced by half. Stir in peas, season with salt and pepper and transfer to a 10- × 10-inch non-stick baking dish, smoothing out with a spatula. Spoon cauliflower purée over top. Using your fingers, gently spread to cover meat and smooth out.

Sprinkle with Parmesan, cover with foil and bake for 20 to 25 minutes, until hot throughout and bubbling. Remove foil and bake for another 10 minutes until golden brown or until an instant-read thermometer inserted into centre reads 160°F.

PER SERVING
BEFORE: 570 CALORIES, 32 G TOTAL FAT
DISH DO-OVER: 209 CALORIES, 8.7 G TOTAL FAT
NUTRITIONAL INFORMATION: 3.8 G SATURATED FAT, 17.8 G CARBOHYDRATES, 4.9 G FIBRE, 6.7 G SUGAR, 16.4 G PROTEIN, 333 MG SODIUM, 36 MG CHOLESTEROL

Chicken Parmesan

Perfectly innocent chicken breast, breaded, fried and blanketed with cheese. Use toasted panko to give it that crispy-fried feeling, egg whites and tangy buttermilk to coat, whole-wheat flour and pasta for added fibre. I love arugula tossed with my pasta for a nice peppery bite.

1 1/2 cups toasted whole-wheat panko
    bread crumbs (page 17)
    (gluten-free, if desired)
1/2 cup freshly grated Parmesan cheese
1 tsp Italian herb seasoning
1/4 tsp freshly ground black pepper,
    plus more to taste
1/2 cup egg whites (about 4 large)
1/2 cup 1% buttermilk
1/2 cup whole-wheat or brown rice flour
4 boneless, skinless chicken breasts
    (5 oz each), pounded to 1/2-inch
    thickness
4 cups jarred all-natural tomato sauce
1 cup shredded low-fat mozzarella
    cheese
10 oz whole-wheat or brown rice
    spaghetti
2 cups lightly packed arugula
Sea salt
2 tbsp chopped fresh basil

SERVES 4
HANDS-ON TIME: 20 MINUTES
TOTAL TIME: 40 MINUTES

Serving Suggestion: Turn this main into sandwiches by cutting each chicken breast in half after melting cheese and piling 2 pieces onto a whole-grain bun. Top with a handful of fresh arugula or leftover grilled vegetables.

Preheat oven to 425°F. Place a baking rack on a parchment-lined baking sheet and mist with cooking spray.

Prepare breading station: In a shallow bowl, combine panko with 1/4 cup Parmesan, Italian herbs and 1/4 tsp pepper. In a separate shallow bowl, whisk together egg whites and buttermilk. Place flour in a shallow dish.

Dredge 1 piece of chicken in flour, shaking off excess. Dip in egg wash, turning to coat both sides, then into panko mixture, gently pressing to adhere. Transfer to baking rack and repeat with remaining chicken. Bake for 16 to 18 minutes or until chicken is cooked through (when an instant-read thermometer inserted into thickest part reads 160°F).

While chicken is baking, bring a large pot of salted water to a boil and cook pasta according to package instructions. Drain, reserving 1/2 cup pasta cooking water. Transfer pasta to a baking sheet, mist with cooking spray, gently tossing to coat.

In a medium saucepan over medium heat, warm sauce, stirring frequently, until gently bubbling. Reduce heat to low, cover and simmer, stirring occasionally.

When chicken is cooked, ladle 1/3 cup sauce over each chicken breast. Top with mozzarella and remaining 1/4 cup Parmesan. Return to oven and bake until cheese is melted and golden, about 5 minutes.

While chicken is baking, add pasta and arugula to remaining sauce, stirring to coat. Add reserved pasta cooking water 3 tbsp at a time as needed to loosen the sauce. Season with salt and pepper.

Transfer pasta and chicken to serving plates and garnish with basil.

PER SERVING
BEFORE: 1090 CALORIES, 49 G TOTAL FAT
DISH DO-OVER: 805 CALORIES, 17.3 G TOTAL FAT
*NUTRITIONAL INFORMATION: 5.6 G SATURATED FAT,
97 G CARBOHYDRATES, 19.3 G FIBRE, 13.2 G SUGAR,
64.6 G PROTEIN, 743 MG SODIUM, 106 MG CHOLESTEROL*

Fried Chicken

Okay, so the recipe title is a little white lie, but the only thing you'll miss from the original is the slick coating of oil on your hands. The signature of perfect fried chicken is the über-crispy coating encasing a plump, juicy piece of chicken. To achieve that same texture without a greasy deep fryer, I used corn flake–style cereal for the crispy crust and marinate the chicken in buttermilk to help tenderize the meat. Although you could easily use boneless chicken for this recipe, the simple act of tucking into a juicy piece of chicken on the bone has a distinctly different appeal. It also gives you a perfect excuse to eat with your hands — not that you need one. As my mom always said, fingers were invented before forks.

4 bone-in, skinless chicken breast
   halves (6 oz each), halved
   through centre crosswise
4 bone-in, skinless chicken thighs or
   skinless drumsticks (3 oz each)
1 1/2 cups 1% buttermilk
1 tbsp smoked paprika
1 tsp cayenne pepper
1 tsp garlic powder
1 tsp onion powder
1 tsp dried thyme
1 tsp sea salt
1/4 tsp freshly ground black pepper
3 cups corn flake–style cereal,
   finely crushed
1/4 cup freshly grated Parmesan cheese

SERVES 8
HANDS-ON TIME: 20 MINUTES
TOTAL TIME: 1 HOUR + 2 HOURS
MARINATING TIME

Tip: Make this recipe gluten-free by choosing your favourite gluten-free corn flake–style or crisp brown rice cereal.

Tip: Cutting the breasts in half makes them similar in size to the thighs and drumsticks, allowing for even cooking. Or use 2 whole chickens instead of pieces: remove backbone, cut chicken into 10 pieces and trim off wings, saving wings and backbone for stock. (To save time, have your butcher do this for you.)

Pat chicken pieces dry with paper towel.

In a large bowl, whisk together buttermilk, paprika, cayenne, garlic powder, onion powder, thyme, 1/2 tsp sea salt and pepper. Add chicken to marinade, turning to coat completely. Transfer chicken and marinade to a large resealable container or bag and refrigerate for at least 2 hours or overnight, and up to 24 hours, turning occasionally to marinate evenly.

Preheat oven to 425°F. Place a baking rack on a parchment- or foil-lined baking sheet.

In a bowl, combine crushed cereal, Parmesan and remaining 1/2 tsp salt. Spread in shallow dish.

Mist baking rack with cooking spray. Working with 1 piece at a time, remove chicken from marinade, allowing excess to drip off (discard marinade), and dredge in breading mixture, gently pressing to adhere. Place breaded chicken on baking rack. Repeat with remaining chicken pieces.

Mist tops of chicken with cooking spray and bake for 40 to 45 minutes or until chicken is cooked through (when an instant-read thermometer inserted into thickest part reads 160°F).

Serving Suggestion: If you'd like to make fried chicken sandwiches — and you should — simply use boneless, skinless chicken breasts and thighs in place of the bone-in pieces. Reduce cooking time to 25 to 30 minutes. Serve on whole-grain or gluten-free rolls with Spicy Yogurt Aioli (page 189), sliced vine-ripened tomato, crispy lettuce and a slice of dill pickle.

PER SERVING
BEFORE: 360 CALORIES, 21 G TOTAL FAT
DISH DO-OVER: 224 CALORIES, 6 G TOTAL FAT
*NUTRITIONAL INFORMATION: 1.7 G SATURATED FAT,
9.5 G CARBOHYDRATES, 0.5 G FIBRE, 2 G SUGAR,
31.6 G PROTEIN, 354 MG SODIUM, 97 MG CHOLESTEROL*

Butter Chicken

This popular Indian-restaurant favourite is a crowd-pleaser but full of fat and calories thanks to oil, butter and cream. Indian cuisine is all about building layers of flavour with fragrant spices. Don't be put off by the number of ingredients in this recipe; it is really simple to make. Most of it can also be prepared in advance for a quick and easy weeknight dinner

2 lb boneless, skinless chicken breasts, cut into 1 1/2–inch cubes
1/4 tsp salt

MARINADE

5 garlic cloves, minced
3 tbsp fresh lemon juice
3 tbsp non-fat plain Greek yogurt
2 tbsp grated fresh ginger
2 tsp garam masala
1 tsp ground cumin
1/2 tsp chili powder
1/2 tsp turmeric

SAUCE

1 tbsp grapeseed oil
1 medium yellow onion, diced
4 garlic cloves, minced
2 tbsp grated fresh ginger
2 tsp garam masala
1 tsp ground coriander
1 tsp chili powder
1 tsp turmeric
2 tbsp almond butter
1 1/2 cups passata
1/2 cup low-sodium chicken stock
1 tbsp honey
1/2 cup non-fat evaporated milk
1/2 cup non-fat plain Greek yogurt
1 tsp dried fenugreek
Sea salt and freshly ground black pepper
1/4 cup coarsely chopped fresh cilantro
2 tbsp sliced almonds, toasted

SERVES 8
HANDS-ON TIME: 45 MINUTES
TOTAL TIME: 45 MINUTES + 1 HOUR MARINATING TIME

Prepare marinade: In a large bowl, combine garlic, lemon juice, yogurt, ginger, garam masala, cumin, chili powder and turmeric to form a paste. Add chicken and mix well, gently rubbing marinade into meat. Cover and refrigerate for at least 1 hour and up to 24 hours.

Meanwhile, prepare sauce: In a large non-stick skillet, heat oil over medium-high heat. Add onion, garlic and ginger and cook, stirring frequently, until medium golden brown, about 3 minutes. Add garam masala, coriander, chili powder and turmeric and cook, stirring constantly, until fragrant, about 1 minute. Stir in almond butter, passata, stock and honey and bring to a simmer. Reduce heat to medium-low and simmer for 10 minutes, until thickened. [*Make-ahead:* Marinate chicken and prepare sauce to this point up to 24 hours in advance. Bring sauce to a simmer over medium-low heat before proceeding with recipe.]

Preheat oven to 450°F. Line a large baking sheet with parchment paper.

Place marinated chicken on prepared baking sheet (discard marinade), season with 1/4 tsp salt and mist with cooking spray. Bake in oven for about 10 minutes, until just browned.

Stir evaporated milk, yogurt and fenugreek into sauce until smooth. Add cooked chicken and pan juices, stirring to coat chicken. Cover and simmer for about 5 minutes, until chicken is heated through. Season with salt and pepper.

Serve over brown basmati rice and top with cilantro and toasted almonds, with warm whole-wheat naan on the side.

PER SERVING
BEFORE: 592 CALORIES, 33.6 G TOTAL FAT
DISH DO-OVER: 248 CALORIES, 7.2 G TOTAL FAT
NUTRITIONAL INFORMATION: 1 G SATURATED FAT, 14.2 G CARBOHYDRATES, 1.7 G FIBRE, 7.5 G SUGAR, 31.1 G PROTEIN, 296 MG SODIUM, 68 MG CHOLESTEROL

Steak Béarnaise

I like my steaks straight up, with a little salt and pepper, but sometimes a steakhouse classic is hard to resist. Tangy béarnaise sauce gets its velvety texture from egg yolks and lots of butter, but my version uses a little low-fat mayonnaise in place of all that, with the same vinegar, tarragon and shallot seasonings.

4 beef tenderloin filets
   (4 oz each and about 1 inch thick)
1 lb thin asparagus spears

BÉARNAISE SAUCE

1/3 cup white wine vinegar
1/3 cup dry white wine
2 medium shallots, minced
3 tbsp coarsely chopped fresh tarragon
1/2 tsp coarsely crushed black
   peppercorns
1/2 cup low-fat mayonnaise
1 tbsp Dijon mustard
1 tbsp fresh lemon juice
Pinch cayenne pepper
Sea salt and freshly ground
   black pepper

SERVES 4
HANDS-ON TIME: 30 MINUTES
TOTAL TIME: 45 MINUTES

In a small saucepan, combine vinegar, wine, shallots, 2 tbsp tarragon and peppercorns. Bring to a boil over high heat and boil until reduced by half. Remove from heat, strain and allow to cool to room temperature. Whisk in mayonnaise, Dijon, lemon juice, cayenne and remaining 1 tbsp tarragon. Season with salt and pepper, cover and set aside.

Preheat a lightly oiled grill or grill pan to medium-high heat.

Mist beef with cooking spray and season with salt and pepper. Mist asparagus with cooking spray and season with salt and pepper. Grill steaks, turning once, for about 4 minutes per side or until an instant-read thermometer inserted into centre of steak reads 145°F for medium-rare, 160°F for medium or 170°F for well done. Transfer steaks to a large plate or cutting board, cover loosely with foil and let rest for 5 minutes before serving. Meanwhile, grill asparagus, turning occasionally, for about 5 minutes, until lightly charred and tender-crisp.

Arrange asparagus on serving plates, top with steak and pour sauce over top.

PER SERVING
BEFORE: 1198 CALORIES, 104 G TOTAL FAT
DISH DO-OVER: 309 CALORIES, 17.5 G TOTAL FAT
NUTRITIONAL INFORMATION: 5.4 G SATURATED FAT,
8.7 G CARBOHYDRATES, 2.4 G FIBRE, 3.1 G SUGAR,
26.6 G PROTEIN, 319 MG SODIUM, 68 MG CHOLESTEROL

General Tsao Chicken

Invented in New York City, this favourite of restaurant-goers is deep-fried breaded dark chicken tossed in a slightly spicy, sticky sweet-and-sour sauce. This is possibly one of the biggest diet offenders of all the Westernized Asian favourites; the fat, sugar and sodium content is extraordinarily high. I've lightened up the sauce with low-sodium chicken stock and packed it with tons of flavour. The light batter is egg whites and cornstarch, and the chicken is pan seared instead of deep-fried.

1/2 lb boneless, skinless chicken breast, cut into 1/2-inch cubes
1/2 lb boneless, skinless thighs, cut into 1/2-inch cubes

MARINADE
2 tbsp low-sodium soy sauce
2 tbsp rice vinegar
2 garlic cloves, minced
2 tsp grated fresh ginger
1 tbsp honey

SAUCE
3 garlic cloves, minced
4 tsp grated fresh ginger
1 tsp chili flakes
1 cup low-sodium chicken stock
1/3 cup hoisin sauce
3 tbsp rice vinegar
2 tbsp honey
3 tbsp low-sodium soy sauce
1 tsp sesame oil
1 tbsp cornstarch mixed with
    2 tbsp water

CHICKEN COATING
1/2 cup egg whites (about 4 large)
1/2 cup cornstarch
3 tbsp whole-wheat or
    brown rice flour
1/4 tsp baking soda

GARNISH
2 tsp toasted sesame seeds
2 green onions, thinly sliced

SERVES 4
HANDS-ON TIME: 45 MINUTES
TOTAL TIME: 45 MINUTES +
1 HOUR MARINATING TIME

Prepare marinade: In a medium bowl, whisk together soy sauce, vinegar, garlic, ginger and honey. Add chicken, turning to coat completely. Cover and refrigerate for at least 1 hour and up to 24 hours.

Meanwhile, prepare sauce: Warm a medium non-stick skillet over medium heat; mist with cooking spray. Add garlic, ginger and chili flakes and cook, stirring constantly, until fragrant, about 1 minute. Stir in stock, then hoisin, vinegar, honey, soy sauce and sesame oil. Stir in cornstarch slurry, bring sauce to a simmer and cook, stirring frequently, until thickened, about 2 minutes. Remove from heat and cover to keep warm.

Prepare chicken coating: In a medium bowl, whisk egg whites until foamy. Whisk in cornstarch, flour and baking soda. Drain chicken from marinade, discarding marinade. Gently toss chicken in coating mixture, coating completely.

Preheat a large non-stick skillet over medium-high heat and mist with cooking spray. Working in batches if necessary, cook chicken pieces for 3 to 4 minutes per side, until golden brown and cooked through. Reduce heat to medium-low. Pour sauce over chicken, gently tossing to coat.

Serve over brown rice and garnish with sesame seeds and green onions.

PER SERVING
BEFORE: 844 CALORIES, 40 G TOTAL FAT
DISH DO-OVER: 376 CALORIES, 7.5 G TOTAL FAT
NUTRITIONAL INFORMATION: 1.5 G SATURATED FAT, 46.2 G CARBOHYDRATES, 2.2 G FIBRE, 19.4 G SUGAR, 30.8 G PROTEIN, 1395 MG SODIUM, 81 MG CHOLESTEROL

Jambalaya

There are worse comfort-food offenders than jambalaya, but with full-fat sausage, white rice and all the oil many restaurants sneak in, the calories and fat — not to mention the sodium — can really add up. With a few swaps, you can include this dish in your regular rotation at home; the leftovers make a perfect lunch. I use extra-lean turkey or chicken sausage, brown rice for added fibre and nutrients, very little oil and low-sodium stock to keep the salt in check.

2 extra-lean smoked turkey sausages
   (3 oz each)
8 oz boneless, skinless chicken breast,
   thinly sliced
1/2 tsp vegetable oil
2 garlic cloves, minced
1 medium onion, diced
2 celery ribs, diced
1 green bell pepper, diced
1 red bell pepper, diced
2 tbsp Cajun seasoning
2 tsp smoked paprika
1 cup brown rice, rinsed and
   drained well
2 bay leaves
2 cups canned unsalted diced tomatoes
3 cups low-sodium chicken stock
1 lb peeled and deveined extra-jumbo
   raw shrimp, tail-on
Sea salt and freshly ground
   black pepper
2 green onions, thinly sliced

SERVES 6
HANDS-ON TIME: 30 MINUTES
TOTAL TIME: 1 HOUR, 15 MINUTES

Preheat oven to 400°F. Line a large baking sheet with parchment paper.

Place sausages on prepared baking sheet and roast, turning once, for about 18 minutes, until cooked through. Cool at room temperature for 5 minutes and slice into 1/2-inch chunks.

Meanwhile, in a medium bowl, toss chicken with oil and garlic. Heat a large non-stick skillet over medium-high heat; mist with cooking spray. Cook chicken, stirring occasionally, until golden brown on all sides, about 3 minutes. Add onion, celery and bell peppers and cook, stirring frequently, until softened, about 3 minutes. Add Cajun seasoning and paprika and cook, stirring constantly, until fragrant, about 1 minute. Stir in cooked sausages, brown rice, bay leaves, tomatoes and stock. Bring to a boil, reduce heat to low, cover and simmer for 45 minutes or until rice is tender.

When rice is tender, stir in shrimp, cover and cook for 5 minutes or until shrimp is bright pink and cooked through. Season with salt and pepper. To serve, spoon into bowls and garnish with green onions.

PER SERVING
BEFORE: 848 CALORIES, 42 G TOTAL FAT
DISH DO-OVER: 338 CALORIES, 6.5 G TOTAL FAT,
*NUTRITIONAL INFORMATION: 1.7 G SATURATED FAT,
35.9 G CARBOHYDRATES, 4.5 G FIBRE, 6.7 G SUGAR,
34.2 G PROTEIN, 912 MG SODIUM, 152 MG CHOLESTEROL*

Black Bean Enchiladas

Don't be intimidated by the long ingredient list; you can make most of this vegetarian dish ahead of time. I've saved calories by not frying the tortillas, and by using low-fat cheddar, non-fat Greek yogurt and a healthier filling.

SAUCE

1 tbsp olive oil
1 medium yellow onion, finely diced
1 tbsp whole-wheat or brown rice flour
1 tbsp chili powder
2 tsp ground cumin
1 tsp dried oregano
1/2 tsp garlic powder
1 canned chipotle pepper, minced, plus
   2 tsp adobo sauce
2 cups low-sodium vegetable or
   chicken stock
2 cups passata
1 tbsp honey
Sea salt and freshly ground
   black pepper

BLACK BEAN FILLING

1 medium yellow onion, diced
1 medium jalapeño pepper, minced
2 tbsp chili powder
2 tsp ground cumin
1 can (15 oz/398 mL) black beans,
   drained and rinsed
2 cups canned unsalted diced tomatoes
1/4 cup passata
1 tbsp honey
1 red bell pepper, diced
1 cup frozen corn kernels, thawed
   and drained
Sea salt and freshly ground
   black pepper

FOR ASSEMBLY

12 6-inch whole-wheat flour tortillas
2 cups cooked brown rice
2 cups shredded low-fat aged cheddar
   cheese
3 green onions, thinly sliced
3 tbsp chopped fresh cilantro
1/2 cup non-fat plain Greek yogurt

Prepare sauce: In a medium saucepan, heat oil over medium-high heat. Add onion and cook, stirring frequently, until softened and light golden brown. Add flour, chili powder, cumin, oregano and garlic powder and cook, stirring constantly, until fragrant, about 1 minute. Add chipotle pepper and adobo sauce, stock, passata and honey, stirring until incorporated and smooth. Bring to a boil, reduce heat to medium-low and simmer for 10 to 12 minutes, until thickened slightly. Season with salt and pepper.

Meanwhile, prepare black bean filling: Heat a medium saucepan over medium-high heat. Add onion and jalapeño and cook, stirring occasionally, until softened and onion is light golden brown. Add chili powder and cumin and cook, stirring frequently, until fragrant, about 1 minute. Add beans, tomatoes, passata and honey and bring to a boil. Reduce heat to medium-low and cook for 5 minutes. Remove from heat and stir in bell pepper and corn. Season with salt and pepper.

Preheat oven to 400°F.

To assemble enchiladas, evenly spread one-third of prepared sauce in a 9- × 13-inch baking dish. On a clean work surface, arrange tortillas in a single layer. Place some rice, bean mixture and cheese (saving some for the topping) in the centre of each tortilla. Roll each tortilla over filling into a cylinder shape and arrange seam side down in baking dish. Pour remaining sauce over enchiladas, cover with a lid or foil and bake for 20 minutes until bubbling and hot throughout. Uncover, sprinkle with remaining cheese and bake uncovered for about 10 minutes, until cheese is melted and golden. To serve, garnish with green onions and cilantro and serve with yogurt on the side.

SERVES 6
HANDS ON TIME: 40 MINUTES
TOTAL TIME: 1 HOUR, 15 MINUTES

PER SERVING
BEFORE: 848 CALORIES, 42 G TOTAL FAT
DISH DO-OVER: 556 CALORIES, 12.4 G TOTAL FAT
*NUTRITIONAL INFORMATION: 3.3 G SATURATED FAT,
85.4 G CARBOHYDRATES, 0.5 G FIBRE, 2 G SUGAR,
31.3 G PROTEIN, 354 MG SODIUM, 97 MG CHOLESTEROL*

Chicken Nuggets with Honey Mustard Sauce

Kids big and small love chicken nuggets. They're the ultimate convenience food for busy families. Boxed versions, though, are highly processed and also pack a fat-laden punch. My version of nuggets will fool even the savviest of connoisseurs.

CHICKEN NUGGETS

2 1/2 cups toasted panko bread crumbs
   (page 17) (gluten-free, if desired)
3/4 cup egg whites (about 6 large)
3/4 cup 1% buttermilk
1/4 tsp cayenne pepper
3/4 cup whole-wheat or brown
   rice flour
1 lb boneless, skinless chicken breasts,
   chopped into 1- to 2-inch chunks
1/2 tsp onion powder
1/2 tsp Italian herb seasoning
1/2 tsp sea salt
1/4 tsp freshly ground black pepper

HONEY MUSTARD SAUCE

1 cup non-fat plain Greek yogurt
1/4 cup honey
1/4 cup yellow or Dijon mustard
2 tbsp finely chopped fresh chives or
   flat-leaf parsley (optional)
Sea salt and freshly ground
   black pepper

SERVES 8 (MAKES 22 TO 24 PIECES)
HANDS-ON TIME: 30 MINUTES
TOTAL TIME: 50 MINUTES

Place panko in a shallow dish. In a medium bowl, whisk together egg whites, buttermilk and cayenne. Place flour in a shallow bowl.

In a food processor, pulse chicken, onion powder, Italian herbs, salt and pepper until chicken is coarsely ground or minced; do not purée. Transfer to a bowl.

Preheat oven to 400°F. Line a large baking sheet with foil and place a baking rack on top. Spray rack with cooking spray.

Using a 1-tbsp measuring spoon or disher (a small ice cream scoop), scoop chicken into balls about 1 1/2 tbsp each. Drop 1 chicken ball into flour and coat completely. Shake off excess flour and gently flatten into a 1/2-inch-thick oval. Dip in egg wash, then panko. Gently press panko into nugget on all sides. Repeat egg wash and breading steps to double-coat nugget. Place nugget on baking rack. Repeat breading procedure, working with 2 or 3 nuggets at a time. Lightly mist nuggets with cooking spray.

Bake nuggets in centre of oven for 20 minutes until golden. Remove from oven and carefully flip each nugget, misting again with cooking spray. Return to oven and bake for another 5 minutes, until crispy on all sides.

While nuggets are baking, prepare sauce: Whisk together yogurt, honey, mustard, chives, salt and pepper. Cover and refrigerate until needed.

PER SERVING
BEFORE: 558 CALORIES, 26 G TOTAL FAT
DISH DO-OVER: 233 CALORIES, 2.7 G TOTAL FAT
*NUTRITIONAL INFORMATION: 0.5 G SATURATED FAT,
31.2 G CARBOHYDRATES, 1.8 G FIBRE, 27.4 G SUGAR,
21.6 G PROTEIN, 480 MG SODIUM, 35 MG CHOLESTEROL*

Chicken Piccata

The key to a simple recipe like chicken piccata is to use the best ingredients possible. Moist, juicy organic chicken and crisp, dry white wine with a hint of lemon make this dish worthy of any bistro menu. It is quick enough to make for a weeknight dinner but is also an elegant main that will impress dinner guests.

4 boneless, skinless chicken breasts
   (5 oz each), pounded to 1/4-inch
   thickness
Sea salt and freshly ground
   black pepper
1/3 cup chickpea or whole-wheat flour
1 tbsp olive oil
3 tbsp capers, rinsed
1/2 cup dry white wine
3/4 cup low-sodium chicken stock
2 tbsp fresh lemon juice
2 tbsp chopped fresh flat-leaf parsley
1 tbsp cold unsalted butter
Freshly grated Parmesan, to taste
   (optional)

SERVES 4
HANDS-ON TIME: 30 MINUTES
TOTAL TIME: 50 MINUTES

Season chicken on all sides with salt and pepper. Place flour in a shallow dish or plate. Dredge chicken in flour to coat completely and shake off excess.

In a large non-stick skillet, heat oil over medium-high heat. Working in batches if necessary, cook chicken for 2 to 3 minutes per side, until golden brown. Remove pan from heat and transfer chicken to a plate; cover to keep warm.

Return pan to heat, add capers, wine and stock. Bring to a boil over high heat, lower heat to medium-high and simmer for 1 minute, until reduced slightly. Return chicken to pan and continue to simmer for 2 minutes or until sauce is reduced by half. Remove chicken from pan and arrange on a platter. Remove pan from heat. Whisk lemon juice, parsley and butter into sauce. Season with salt and pepper. Pour sauce over chicken. Top with Parmesan, if using.

Serving Suggestion: Prepare double the amount of sauce. Toss half of the sauce with your favourite gluten-free pasta and freshly grated Parmesan. Plate pasta, top with chicken and drizzle remaining sauce on top.

PER SERVING
BEFORE: 870 CALORIES, 43 G TOTAL FAT
DISH DO-OVER: 249 CALORIES, 8.8 G TOTAL FAT
NUTRITIONAL INFORMATION: 2.9 G SATURATED FAT,
3.4 G CARBOHYDRATES, 0.7 G FIBRE, 0.1 G SUGAR,
33.9 G PROTEIN, 389 MG SODIUM, 90 MG CHOLESTEROL

Chicken Fried Rice

As the name implies, fried rice is usually cooked in a ton of oil, which contributes to most of the fat and calories. Using a large non-stick skillet allows you to use a fraction of the oil. I've also added more vegetables, used brown rice and opted for chicken breasts to lighten things up.

2 tbsp low-sodium soy sauce
2 tbsp fresh lime juice
1 tsp sesame oil
1 large egg
1/4 cup egg whites (about 2 large)
1 lb boneless, skinless chicken breast, thinly sliced
1 tbsp grapeseed or vegetable oil
3 garlic cloves, minced
1 tbsp minced fresh ginger
1/4 tsp chili flakes
1/2 medium red onion, diced
1 medium carrot, peeled and diced
1 red bell pepper, diced
1 cup frozen corn kernels, thawed and drained
3 cups cooked and cooled long-grain brown rice
1 cup frozen peas, thawed and drained, or 1 cup thinly sliced snow peas
2 green onions, thinly sliced
Sriracha or sambal oelek sauce

SERVES 4
HANDS-ON TIME: 35 MINUTES
TOTAL TIME: 1 HOUR

In a small bowl, whisk together soy sauce, lime juice and sesame oil. In another small bowl, whisk together egg and egg whites.

In a large bowl, toss chicken with 2 tsp oil, garlic, ginger and chili flakes to evenly coat.

Heat a large non-stick skillet over medium-high heat. Add chicken to pan and cook, stirring frequently, until golden brown and cooked through, about 3 to 4 minutes. Transfer to a bowl.

Add remaining 1 tsp oil to pan, then onion, carrot, bell pepper and corn. Cook, stirring frequently, for about 2 minutes, until onion is light golden brown.

Add rice and toss to mix with vegetables. Push rice mixture to one side of skillet. Add egg mixture to empty side of skillet and allow to cook without stirring for 30 seconds or until just beginning to set. Mix rice into egg and cook, stirring frequently, for 1 minute.

Stir in chicken, peas, green onions and soy sauce mixture, making sure rice is evenly and lightly coated with sauce. Serve with Sriracha sauce on the side.

PER SERVING
BEFORE: 658 CALORIES, 24 G TOTAL FAT
DISH DO-OVER: 461 CALORIES, 9.6 G TOTAL FAT
NUTRITIONAL INFORMATION: 1.7 G SATURATED FAT,
57.2 G CARBOHYDRATES, 6.3 G FIBRE, 7.3 G SUGAR,
37 G PROTEIN, 455 MG SODIUM, 112 MG CHOLESTEROL

BBQ Boneless Ribs

I used to work for a BBQ chef, so I've made many a rack of ribs over the years. There's no real way to make them lower in fat, because the cut of meat is the culprit. Ribs are laced with fat and connective tissue — that's what makes them so tender when you cook them low and slow. The obvious solution was to change the cut of meat. I chose pork loin over tenderloin because the loin is closer in texture to what ribs would be; I find the tenderloin too soft. Brining the pork loin keeps it juicy and tender. There's no gnawing meat off the bone, which is part of the whole sensory experience of eating ribs, but you are still encouraged to eat these with your hands and get a little messy. To save time, use a jar of your favourite all-natural BBQ sauce and make a big batch of the rub for your pantry.

2 lb boneless centre-cut pork loin,
    trimmed of excess fat

BRINE
6 cups water
1/4 cup apple cider vinegar
1/4 cup honey
1/4 cup kosher or sea salt
1/2 tsp cayenne pepper

BBQ SAUCE
1 medium yellow onion, diced
2 garlic cloves, minced
1 tbsp chili powder
1 tbsp smoked paprika
3 tbsp tomato paste
2 cups passata
1/3 cup apple cider vinegar
1/4 cup molasses
1/4 cup honey
Sea salt and freshly ground
    black pepper

RUB
2 tsp chili powder
2 tsp smoked paprika
2 tsp ground cumin
2 tsp sea salt
2 tsp organic brown sugar
1/2 tsp garlic powder
1/2 tsp onion powder
1/2 tsp freshly ground black pepper

Pat pork loin dry with paper towel. Cut loin in half lengthwise through centre, to make 2 "racks." Flip loins over so that the tops are face down on the cutting board. Leaving a 1-inch top layer of each "rack" intact (so it doesn't curl too much while cooking and is easier to flip on the grill), slice two-thirds of the way deep into the meat every 1 1/2 inches or so, to make "ribs." (See photo on page 183.)

Prepare brine: In a resealable container large enough to hold the pork, whisk together water, vinegar, honey, salt and cayenne. Immerse pork in liquid, ensuring meat is submerged completely, seal and refrigerate for 3 hours. If using a resealable bag, gently squeeze out excess air before sealing.

While ribs are brining, prepare sauce: Heat a large saucepan over medium-high heat; mist with cooking spray. Add onion and garlic to pan and cook, stirring frequently, until onion is softened, about 2 minutes. Add chili powder and paprika and cook, stirring frequently, until fragrant, about 1 minute. Stir in tomato paste, passata, vinegar, molasses and honey. Bring to a boil, partially cover pan, reduce heat to medium-low and simmer uncovered until reduced by half, about 15 minutes. Remove from heat. Add salt and pepper, to taste.

While sauce is cooking, prepare rub: In a small bowl, combine chili powder, paprika, cumin, salt, brown sugar, garlic powder, onion powder and pepper.

Preheat greased grill or grill pan to medium-high heat. Remove ribs from brine, discarding brine. Rinse ribs under cold water to remove excess salt; pat dry with paper towel. Gently rub spice mixture into meat on all sides and into the incisions. (*Continued overleaf*)

Tip: Use up any leftover BBQ sauce in the Bacon Double-Cheeseburger Pizza (page 191).

Grill ribs for 5 to 6 minutes per side, turning occasionally and liberally brushing ribs on all sides with sauce during the last quarter of cooking time. To serve, slice ribs into pieces using the incisions as a guide. Serve with remaining sauce on the side.

PER SERVING
BEFORE: 325 CALORIES, 21.5 G TOTAL FAT
DISH DO-OVER: 260 CALORIES, 4 G TOTAL FAT
NUTRITIONAL INFORMATION: 1.4 G SATURATED FAT, 27.9 G CARBOHYDRATES, 1.7 G FIBRE, 21.8 G SUGAR, 28.1 G PROTEIN, 1080 MG SODIUM, 57 MG CHOLESTEROL

Fish & Chips

Traditionally battered and deep-fried fish served with deep-fried potatoes and a mayonnaise-based sauce is not something you want to add to your weekly dinner rotation. But instead of batter, which would be virtually impossible to bake, I make a crispy golden coating with brown rice crisp cereal to help mimic the beer-battered fried texture. You'll never miss the mayo in the tangy tartar sauce either; I've loaded that with pickles, capers and shallots for tons of zing to go with the crispy fish.

1 batch baked french fries (page 83)
1 1/2 lb halibut fillets, cut into 8 pieces
   (2 to 3 oz each)

TARTAR SAUCE

3/4 cup non-fat plain Greek yogurt
2 medium shallots, minced
1/4 cup minced dill pickle
2 tbsp chopped capers
1 tbsp fresh lemon juice
1 tbsp Dijon mustard
Dash hot sauce
Sea salt and freshly ground
   black pepper

BREADING

1/2 cup egg whites (about 4 large)
1 large egg
Pinch cayenne pepper
1/4 cup brown rice flour
1/4 tsp each sea salt and freshly
   ground black pepper
2 cups brown rice crisp cereal,
   coarsely crushed

SERVES 4
HANDS-ON TIME: 50 MINUTES
TOTAL TIME: 55 MINUTES +
30 MINUTES SOAKING TIME

Prepare tartar sauce: In a small bowl, whisk together yogurt, shallots, dill pickle, capers, lemon juice, Dijon and hot sauce. Season with salt and pepper. Cover and refrigerate, ideally for at least 1 hour.

Meanwhile, preheat oven to 475°F and prepare french fries.

While fries are baking, prepare breading station: In a shallow dish, whisk together egg whites, egg and cayenne. Spread flour in a second shallow dish and whisk in salt and pepper. Spread crushed brown rice crisp cereal in a third shallow dish.

Working with 1 piece of fish at a time, dredge fish in flour, turning to coat both sides; shake off excess flour. Transfer to egg wash, turning to coat both sides, then gently press into crushed rice crisp cereal, coating fish completely. Place fillet on a baking sheet. Repeat with remaining fillets.

Heat a large non-stick skillet over medium-high heat; mist with cooking spray. Working in batches, sear fish until golden brown and crispy on both sides, about 4 minutes, flipping only once. Transfer to a parchment-lined baking sheet.

When fries have 5 minutes cooking time remaining, transfer them to a single baking sheet and return to oven on rack positioned in top third of oven. Place fish in oven on rack positioned in bottom third of oven and bake for 5 minutes or until cooked through.

Serve with tartar sauce on the side.

Note: Sauce is best prepared at least 1 hour and up to 24 hours in advance, to allow flavours to blend.

PER SERVING
BEFORE: 1021 CALORIES, 65 G TOTAL FAT
DISH DO-OVER: 417 CALORIES, 6.4 G TOTAL FAT
NUTRITIONAL INFORMATION: 1 G SATURATED FAT,
39.7 G CARBOHYDRATES, 2.8 G FIBRE, 3.3 G SUGAR,
48.1 G PROTEIN, 726 MG SODIUM, 95 MG CHOLESTEROL

Coconut Shrimp with Spicy Mango Sauce

Another deep-fried favourite that doesn't have to be! Coconut, panko and egg whites make the coating super crispy without sending these shrimp for a swim in hot oil. Serve with salad for a meal or as an appetizer.

COCONUT SHRIMP

1 cup unsweetened shredded coconut
1/2 cup toasted panko bread crumbs
　　(page 17)
1/2 tsp sea salt
1/2 cup egg whites (about 4 large)
Pinch cayenne pepper
1 lb peeled and deveined extra-large
　　raw shrimp, tail-on, patted dry
　　with paper towel

SPICY MANGO SAUCE

1 ripe medium mango, diced
　　(about 1 1/2 cups)
1 tbsp honey
1 tsp Sriracha or sambal oelek sauce
1 tbsp chopped fresh cilantro
Sea salt and freshly ground
　　black pepper

SERVES 6
HANDS-ON TIME: 25 MINUTES
TOTAL TIME: 25 MINUTES

Preheat oven to 450°F. Line a large baking sheet with parchment paper.

Prepare shrimp: In a large bowl, combine coconut, panko and salt. In a second large bowl, whisk egg whites until foamy; season with cayenne.

Toss shrimp with egg wash to coat. Working with a few at a time, lift shrimp from egg wash by the tail, allowing excess egg to drip off. Dredge shrimp in coconut mixture, gently pressing to adhere and turning to coat all sides. Transfer to prepared baking sheet. Repeat with remaining shrimp.

Mist shrimp with cooking spray and bake for about 10 minutes, until coating is golden brown and crispy and shrimp are cooked through.

While shrimp are baking, prepare sauce: In a blender or food processor, blend mango, honey, Sriracha and cilantro until smooth. Season with salt and pepper. Serve alongside shrimp for dipping.

PER SERVING
BEFORE: 530 CALORIES, 36 G TOTAL FAT
DISH DO-OVER: 228 CALORIES, 10.3 G TOTAL FAT
NUTRITIONAL INFORMATION: 7.9 G SATURATED FAT,
16.4 G CARBOHYDRATES, 2.9 G FIBRE, 13.5 G SUGAR,
18.6 G PROTEIN, 273 MG SODIUM, 115 MG CHOLESTEROL

Crab Cakes with Spicy Yogurt Aioli

My biggest problem with many crab cakes? Not enough crab! Good-quality crabmeat is essential here; this isn't the time to use the fake stuff (when is it, really, other than for California Roll?). Broiling these crab cakes in the oven saves calories and is a lot easier than flipping them in a pan. Because crab meat is lean, I used a little low-fat mayonnaise for some creaminess and egg whites to help bind it together. Spicy yogurt aioli makes a perfect dipping sauce and is a great alternative to the full-fat mayo-based dip that usually accompanies crab cakes.

1 1/2 cups panko bread crumbs
  (gluten-free, if desired)
1/2 red bell pepper, finely diced
3 green onions, thinly sliced
1 garlic clove, minced
2 tbsp chopped fresh dill
1/4 cup low-fat olive oil mayonnaise
1/2 cup egg whites (about 4 large),
  whisked until foamy
3 tbsp fresh lemon juice
1 tsp Worcestershire sauce
1/2 tsp smoked paprika
1/2 tsp dry mustard
1/2 tsp sea salt
1/4 tsp freshly ground black pepper
Pinch cayenne pepper
2 lb lump crabmeat, drained, picked
  over for shells and patted dry
  with paper towel

SPICY YOGURT AIOLI
3/4 cup non-fat plain Greek yogurt
1/4 cup low-fat olive oil mayonnaise
2 tbsp Sriracha sauce
1 tbsp fresh lemon juice
Sea salt and freshly ground
  black pepper

SERVES 6
HANDS-ON TIME: 20 MINUTES
TOTAL TIME: 35 MINUTES

Position rack in top third of oven and preheat broiler to high.

In a large bowl, combine 1 cup panko, bell pepper, green onions, garlic, dill, mayonnaise, egg whites, lemon juice, Worcestershire sauce, paprika, mustard, salt, pepper and cayenne, gently mixing with a spatula. Gently fold in crab meat. Place remaining 1/2 cup panko in a shallow dish.

Divide crab mixture into 1/4-cup portions. Dip each portion into reserved panko, lightly pressing to form rounded patties about 1 inch thick. Transfer to a parchment-lined baking sheet and mist tops of each cake with cooking spray.

Broil for 10 minutes, until golden brown. Using a spatula, gently flip cakes over, mist with cooking spray and broil for another 6 to 8 minutes, until golden and heated through.

Meanwhile, prepare aioli: In a small bowl, whisk together yogurt, mayonnaise, Sriracha and lemon juice. Season with salt and pepper.

Serve crab cakes with sauce on the side for dipping.

PER SERVING
BEFORE: 618 CALORIES, 43 G TOTAL FAT
DISH DO-OVER: 340 CALORIES, 9.5 G TOTAL FAT
NUTRITIONAL INFORMATION: 0.8 G SATURATED FAT,
18.4 G CARBOHYDRATES, 1 G FIBRE, 17.3 G SUGAR,
43.1 G PROTEIN, 1460 MG SODIUM, 116 MG CHOLESTEROL

Bacon Double-Cheeseburger Pizza

When a *Steven and Chris* viewer challenged me to create a healthy pizza, I wanted to make one that tasted like junk food but was actually good for you. Lots of pizza joints have bacon double-cheeseburger pizza, so that was the perfect choice! I cut some of the fat in the beef by swapping half of it for cremini mushrooms and using my mom's burger-enhancing secret ingredient, Worcestershire sauce, along with steak spice to amp up the beefy goodness. The Greek yogurt–mustard sauce brings the whole dish together. The result? The *S&C* crew gobbling it up faster than I've ever seen, and everyone exclaiming that it tasted like a fast-food burger, but better! Mission accomplished.

8 medium cremini mushrooms, coarsely chopped
1/2 small yellow onion, coarsely chopped
2 garlic cloves, minced
12 oz extra-lean ground beef or sirloin
1 tbsp Montreal steak spice
2 tbsp Worcestershire sauce
Sea salt and freshly ground black pepper
2 tbsp finely ground cornmeal
1 ball Whole-Wheat Pizza Dough (page 23) or 1 lb prepared whole-wheat pizza dough
3/4 cup jarred all-natural tomato sauce
1/4 cup jarred all-natural BBQ sauce (homemade version, page 181)
1 cup shredded low-fat aged cheddar cheese
1 cup shredded low-fat mozzarella cheese
1/2 large red onion, diced
2 medium plum tomatoes, diced
3 slices Perfect Crispy Bacon (page 17), crumbled
1/3 cup non-fat plain Greek yogurt
3 tbsp yellow or Dijon mustard (or combination of the two)
1 1/2 cups shredded iceberg lettuce

SERVES 12
HANDS-ON TIME: 60 MINUTES
TOTAL TIME: 1 HOUR, 10 MINUTES
+ 90 MINUTES RISING TIME

Position rack in bottom third of oven and preheat oven to 500°F.

In a food processor, finely chop mushrooms, yellow onion and garlic.

Heat a large non-stick skillet over medium-high heat. Add beef and steak spice and cook, stirring and breaking up meat with a wooden spoon, for 8 minutes or until meat is no longer pink and no liquid remains in bottom of pan. Add mushroom mixture and cook, stirring frequently, until mixture is fragrant and liquid is evaporated. Transfer to a large bowl. Stir in Worcestershire sauce and season with salt and pepper.

Line a large (about 11- × 16-inch) baking sheet with parchment paper, mist with cooking spray and sprinkle with cornmeal. Stretch dough to fit sheet.

Mix tomato and BBQ sauces together and spread in an even layer onto pizza dough. In a bowl, combine the cheddar and mozzarella, then sprinkle half the cheese mixture overtop the sauces. Spread beef mixture over cheese. Top with remaining cheeses, red onion, tomatoes and bacon.

Bake for 12 to 15 minutes, until crust is golden and cheese is golden brown.

While pizza is baking, combine yogurt and mustard. To serve, slice pizza, drizzle with yogurt sauce and top with shredded lettuce.

PER SERVING
BEFORE: 562 CALORIES, 31 G TOTAL FAT
DISH DO-OVER: 214 CALORIES, 9.7 G TOTAL FAT
*NUTRITIONAL INFORMATION: 3.6 G SATURATED FAT,
18.5 G CARBOHYDRATES, 2.9 G FIBRE, 4.4 G SUGAR,
14.8 G PROTEIN, 407 MG SODIUM, 27 MG CHOLESTEROL*

Loaded Deep Dish Pizza

There are so many styles of pizza out there: traditional Italian thin crust, New York style and, the big boy of the bunch, the Chicago-style deep dish—basically a giant pie-size slice of pizza stuffed with various meats and piles of cheese. I swapped the meat for low-fat versions and added a ton of veggies. Sautéing the vegetables lightly before assembling and putting a layer of cheese at the bottom helps keep the filling from making the crust soggy. You'll need a 10-inch deep dish pizza pan, non-stick cake or springform pan, or cast-iron skillet for this recipe.

2 low-fat turkey or chicken sausages
   (3 oz each), casings removed
1 medium yellow onion, thinly sliced
2 cups thinly sliced cremini mushrooms
1 red bell pepper, thinly sliced
Sea salt and freshly ground
   black pepper
1 tbsp finely ground cornmeal
1 ball Whole-Wheat Pizza Dough
   (page 23) or 1 lb prepared
   whole-wheat pizza dough
2 cups shredded low-fat mozzarella
   cheese
4 oz turkey pepperoni
1/2 cup sliced pimento-stuffed
   green olives
1 cup jarred all-natural tomato sauce
1 tsp Italian herb seasoning
3 tbsp freshly grated Parmesan cheese

SERVES 10
HANDS-ON TIME: 55 MINUTES
TOTAL TIME: 1 HOUR, 25 MINUTES
+ 90 MINUTES RISING TIME

Preheat oven to 450°F.

Heat a large non-stick skillet over medium-high heat; mist with cooking spray. Add sausages and cook, stirring frequently and breaking up with a wooden spoon, until cooked through and lightly browned, about 4 minutes. Transfer to a large paper towel–lined bowl to drain excess fat.

Return skillet to heat, mist with cooking spray and add onion and mushrooms. Cook, stirring frequently, until onion is translucent and mushrooms are softened and browned, about 4 minutes. Add bell pepper and cook, stirring frequently, until softened, about 3 minutes. Season with salt and pepper and add to bowl with sausage. Allow to drain for 5 minutes, then remove paper towel and mix together sausage and vegetables.

Mist pizza pan with cooking spray and sprinkle with cornmeal. Roll or stretch dough into a 14-inch circle and place in pan, gently pressing dough into the bottom and sides of pan and ensuring it extends about 2 inches up the sides.

Sprinkle half the mozzarella over crust. Add a layer of pepperoni slices and top with sausage and vegetable mixture, then olives. Pour tomato sauce over top and sprinkle with remaining mozzarella, Italian herbs and Parmesan.

Bake for 25 to 30 minutes, until crust is golden, cheese is bubbling and filling is heated through. Let rest at room temperature for 5 minutes before serving, to allow filling to set.

PER SERVING
BEFORE: 770 CALORIES, 55 G TOTAL FAT
DISH DO-OVER: 219 CALORIES, 10.2 G TOTAL FAT
*NUTRITIONAL INFORMATION: 3.8 G SATURATED FAT,
19 G CARBOHYDRATES, 4.1 G FIBRE, 3.4 G SUGAR,
14.8 G PROTEIN, 512 MG SODIUM, 31 MG CHOLESTEROL*

Chicken & Broccoli Calzone

Just because the name of a dish has the words "chicken" and "broccoli" in it doesn't mean that the dish is innocent. A lot of times, especially at restaurants, healthy items like this are usually accompanied by cream sauce and cheese; this calzone is a classic example. Instead of the creamy full-fat sauce, I use my condensed soup substitute as the base for the calzone filling.

3 cups broccoli florets

2 1/2 cups mushroom Creamy
  Condensed Soup Substitute (page 21)

2 cooked and cooled Perfect Marinated
  Chicken Breasts (page 21), diced
  or shredded

1 cup shredded low-fat mozzarella
  cheese

1/3 cup freshly grated Parmesan cheese

2 tsp chopped fresh oregano or
  1/2 tsp dried

1/4 tsp sea salt

Freshly ground black pepper

Pinch cayenne pepper

1 ball Whole-Wheat Pizza Dough
  (page 23) or 1 lb prepared
  whole-wheat pizza dough

1/3 cup whole-wheat flour

1/4 cup egg whites (about 2 large),
  lightly beaten

2 tbsp finely ground cornmeal

SERVES 4
HANDS-ON TIME: 45 MINUTES
TOTAL TIME: 1 HOUR +
5 MINUTES RESTING TIME
(PIZZA DOUGH NOT INCLUDED)

Preheat oven to 450°F. Line a large baking sheet with parchment paper.

Bring a medium pot of salted water to a boil and fill a bowl with ice water. Blanch broccoli for 1 minute in boiling water, refresh in ice water until chilled, drain and return to bowl.

Add mushroom soup, chicken, cheeses, oregano, salt, pepper and cayenne to broccoli, mixing well.

Divide dough evenly into 4 balls. On a floured work surface, roll each dough ball into a circle about 7 inches in diameter. Scoop filling into centre of each pizza round, leaving about a 1 1/2–inch border around the edges. Brush the edges of one pizza round with water. Fold dough over filling to form a half-circle, leaving about 1/2 inch of the bottom layer exposed. Press edges together to seal. Fold exposed layer of dough over the top edge, pinching and crimping to seal again. (Or fold the bottom edge up and crimp with a fork.)

Brush calzones all over with egg wash. Using a paring knife, cut two to three slits in top of each to release steam. Dust prepared baking sheet with cornmeal. Place calzones on baking sheet and bake for 12 to 15 minutes, until top is golden brown and bottom is golden brown and crispy. Let cool at room temperature for 5 minutes before serving.

PER SERVING
BEFORE: 832 CALORIES, 28 G TOTAL FAT
DISH DO-OVER: 574 CALORIES, 18.7 G TOTAL FAT
NUTRITIONAL INFORMATION: 5.8 G SATURATED FAT,
64.5 G CARBOHYDRATES, 9.4 G FIBRE, 12.8 G SUGAR,
41.4 G PROTEIN, 1094 MG SODIUM, 56 MG CHOLESTEROL

Eggplant Parmesan

Like Spaghetti Carbonara (page 143), this Italian classic has two versions. In the American version, the eggplant is breaded, deep-fried and layered; in the Italian version, it's simply fried in a ton of olive oil. To bread or not to bread? I struggled with this one for a while and decided that breaded anything tastes better than not, so the American version reigned supreme. Pressing and draining the water from the eggplant is important, as it gives the eggplant a beautiful texture and keeps it crispy on the outside.

2 large eggplants (about 2 lb each), sliced into 1/2-inch-thick rounds
3 1/2 tsp sea salt, divided
1/2 cup whole-wheat or brown rice flour
1/3 cup egg whites (about 3 large)
1 large egg
2 cups toasted panko bread crumbs (page 17) (gluten-free, if desired)
1/2 tsp garlic powder
1/4 tsp freshly ground black pepper
Pinch cayenne pepper
2 1/2 cups jarred all-natural tomato sauce
2 cups shredded low-fat mozzarella cheese
1/3 cup freshly grated Parmesan cheese
1/3 cup chopped fresh basil

SERVES 6
HANDS-ON TIME: 45 MINUTES
TOTAL TIME: 2 HOURS

> *Tip:* Eggplant Parmesan should not be swimming in sauce; just dollops over each eggplant slice does the trick.

Line a large baking sheet with a clean kitchen towel or three layers of paper towel. Arrange eggplant in a single layer on top and generously sprinkle with 3 tsp of salt. Top eggplant with a second kitchen towel or layer of paper towel and place a second baking sheet on top. Weigh baking sheet down with a few heavy cans from your pantry to press excess water from eggplant. Let stand for 30 minutes, then rinse eggplant well and pat dry.

Preheat oven to 425°F. Line a large baking sheet with parchment paper or foil and place a baking rack on top. Mist rack with cooking spray.

Prepare breading station: Place flour in a shallow dish. In a second shallow dish, whisk together egg whites and egg. In a third shallow dish, combine panko, garlic powder, pepper, cayenne and remaining 1/2 tsp of salt.

Working with 1 or 2 slices at a time, dredge eggplant in flour, turning to coat both sides and shaking off excess. Dip in egg wash, turning to coat both sides. Transfer to panko mixture, gently pressing panko onto both sides to adhere, and place on baking rack. Repeat with remaining eggplant slices. Roast for about 40 minutes, until eggplant is tender and coating is crispy and golden brown.

Lightly mist a 9- × 13-inch baking dish with cooking spray. Evenly spread 1 cup sauce in dish. Arrange one-third of the eggplant slices in a single layer in pan, gently pressing them down to fit. Top with one-third each remaining sauce, mozzarella, Parmesan and basil. Repeat two more times to form 3 layers. Bake uncovered for 25 to 30 minutes, until cheese is golden brown and eggplant is heated through.

PER SERVING
BEFORE: 832 CALORIES, 28 G TOTAL FAT
DISH DO-OVER: 382 CALORIES, 12.2 G TOTAL FAT
NUTRITIONAL INFORMATION: 5.1 G SATURATED FAT, 52.5 G CARBOHYDRATES, 12.8 G FIBRE, 30 G SUGAR, 19.8 G PROTEIN, 847 MG SODIUM, 49 MG CHOLESTEROL

Desserts

Mixed Berry Cheesecake

Is it possible to make a cheesecake with all the flavour but half the calories? Yes! I love serving this at dinner parties. It's a sure-fire crowd pleaser.

CRUST

1 cup rolled oats
1/2 cup raw almonds
1/4 cup whole-wheat flour
1/4 cup organic sugar
1/4 cup unsalted butter
1 tsp pure vanilla extract
1/2 tsp ground cinnamon
Pinch sea salt

FILLING

2 cups low-fat cream cheese
1/3 cup organic sugar
2 tbsp fresh lemon juice
1 tsp pure vanilla extract
1 cup non-fat plain Greek yogurt
1 large egg
1/2 cup egg whites (about 4 large)
Pinch sea salt

TOPPING

3 cups frozen mixed berries, thawed,
   or fresh berries in season
2 tbsp fresh lemon juice
1/4 cup organic sugar
1 tbsp tapioca starch, arrowroot powder
   or cornstarch

SERVES 12 (MAKES ONE 8-INCH
ROUND CHEESECAKE)
HANDS-ON TIME: 30 MINUTES
TOTAL TIME: 2 HOURS + 5 HOURS
COOLING AND CHILLING TIME

> *Tip:* If using fresh berries, reserve a few for garnish.

Preheat oven to 350°F. Spray an 8-inch springform pan with cooking spray.

Prepare crust: In a food processor, pulse oats, almonds and flour to a fine powder. Add sugar, butter, vanilla, cinnamon and salt. Pulse until combined and crumbly.

Gently press crust evenly into bottom of prepared pan. Bake for 30 minutes, until golden brown. Remove from oven and allow to cool at room temperature. Increase oven temperature to 500°F.

Prepare filling: In food processor, pulse cream cheese, sugar, lemon juice and vanilla until combined and smooth. Add yogurt, egg, egg whites and salt; pulse again until smooth. Pour filling into cooled crust.

Place cheesecake in the centre of a 14-inch-square piece of foil. Wrap bottom and sides of pan entirely with foil to prevent water from seeping in. Place in a bain-marie and bake for 10 minutes (see Note on page 200). Reduce oven temperature to 200°F and continue to bake for 1 hour, until cake is just slightly wobbly in the centre and an instant-read thermometer inserted into the centre reads 150°F.

Transfer pan to a wire rack and allow to cool for 5 minutes. Run a thin, sharp knife between cake and sides of pan, leaving cake in pan. Allow to cool at room temperature for 2 hours. Wrap with plastic wrap and refrigerate for at least 3 hours and up to 3 days.

While cake is cooling, prepare topping: Combine berries, lemon juice, sugar and 3/4 cup water in a medium saucepan. Bring to a boil over high heat, reduce heat to medium-low and simmer uncovered for 15 minutes. Transfer to a blender or food processor and purée until smooth. Return sauce to saucepan and heat over medium-low heat.

In a small bowl, stir tapioca starch with 1 tbsp water until smooth, to form a slurry. Stir into berry mixture and cook, stirring frequently, for 2 minutes. Remove from heat, allow to cool to room temperature, cover and refrigerate. (*Continued overleaf*)

To serve, release springform from cheesecake. Fill a pitcher or bowl with warm water. Using a sharp knife, slice cheesecake into 12 pieces, dipping knife into water and carefully wiping it clean with a kitchen towel after each slice. Place a dollop of berry topping on each serving and garnish with fresh berries. Serve immediately.

Note: A bain-marie is a culinary term for a hot water bath, which uses indirect heat to cook delicate foods, such as custards and cheesecakes. The heat from the oven is transferred to the food through water, which ensures a more even, gentle bake. To make a bain-marie, simply place the cheesecake or custards in a large roasting pan and fill the pan halfway full with boiling water; transfer to the oven and bake as directed.

PER SERVING
BEFORE: 500 CALORIES, 30 G TOTAL FAT
DISH DO-OVER: 309 CALORIES, 15.3 G TOTAL FAT
NUTRITIONAL INFORMATION: 7.5 G SATURATED FAT, 32.9 G CARBOHYDRATES, 3.8 G FIBRE, 18.5 G SUGAR, 11.1 G PROTEIN, 154 MG SODIUM, 50 MG CHOLESTEROL

Chocolate Cheesecake

Chocolate cheesecake is one of the most ubiquitous decadent treats. There is nothing guilt-free about it — until today! I've hidden a touch of ground oats in the crust for added fibre and use better-for-you chocolate wafers. For the filling, low-fat cream cheese, non-fat Greek yogurt and egg whites do the trick to lighten things up. For the ganache topping, I've replaced 35% cream with non-fat Greek yogurt and added a little cocoa powder to bump up the rich chocolate flavour and reduce fat.

CRUST

1/2 cup rolled oats

3 oz gluten-free or whole-grain chocolate wafer cookies

1/4 cup unsalted butter, softened

2 tbsp organic sugar

FILLING

8 oz dark chocolate (70% cocoa or greater), chopped

2 cups low-fat cream cheese

1/3 cup organic sugar

1/4 cup unsweetened cocoa powder (Dutch-process is best)

1 large egg

1/3 cup egg whites (about 3 large)

3/4 cup non-fat plain Greek yogurt

1 tsp pure vanilla extract

Pinch sea salt

TOPPING

4 oz dark chocolate (70% cocoa or greater), chopped

1 1/2 cups non-fat plain Greek yogurt

1/4 cup unsweetened cocoa powder (Dutch-process is best)

1/4 cup organic icing sugar

SERVES 12 (MAKES ONE 8-INCH ROUND CHEESECAKE)
HANDS-ON TIME: 30 MINUTES
TOTAL TIME: 2 HOURS + 5 HOURS COOLING AND CHILLING TIME

Preheat oven to 350°F. Spray an 8-inch springform pan with cooking spray.

Prepare crust: In a food processor, pulse oats and cookies to a fine powder. Add butter and sugar; pulse until combined and crumbly. Gently press crust evenly into bottom of prepared pan. Bake for 30 minutes, until golden brown. Remove from oven and allow to cool at room temperature. Increase oven temperature to 500°F.

Meanwhile, prepare filling: Melt chocolate in a heatproof bowl placed over a pot of barely simmering water. Make sure water does not touch bottom of the bowl. Pulse cream cheese in clean food processor until smooth and fluffy, about 1 minute. Add sugar, sift in cocoa powder and pulse until incorporated and smooth. Add melted chocolate and pulse until fully incorporated, scraping down sides of bowl as needed with a spatula. Add egg and egg whites, pulsing until incorporated and scraping down sides of bowl with a spatula as needed. Add yogurt, vanilla and salt; pulse until incorporated. Pour filling into cooled crust.

Place cheesecake in the centre of a 14-inch-square piece of foil. Wrap bottom and sides of pan entirely with foil to prevent water from seeping in. Place in a bain-marie and bake for 10 minutes (see Note on facing page). Reduce oven temperature to 200°F and continue to bake for 1 hour, until cake is just slightly wobbly in the centre and an instant-read thermometer inserted into the centre reads 150°F.

Transfer pan to a wire rack and allow to cool for 5 minutes. Run a thin, sharp knife between cake and sides of pan, leaving cake in pan. Allow to cool at room temperature for 2 hours. *(Continued overleaf)*

Meanwhile, prepare topping: Melt chocolate in a heatproof bowl placed over a pot of barely simmering water. Make sure water does not touch bottom of bowl. While chocolate is melting, sift cocoa powder into yogurt and add icing sugar, stirring to combine. Stir chocolate into yogurt until smooth. Pour chocolate mixture over centre of cooled cheesecake, spreading out evenly with the back of a spoon or spatula.

Wrap with plastic wrap and refrigerate for at least 3 hours and up to 3 days.

To serve, release cheesecake from springform. Fill a pitcher or bowl with warm water. Using a sharp knife, slice cheesecake into 12 pieces, dipping knife into water and carefully wiping it clean with a kitchen towel after each slice. If you wish, garnish with fresh berries. Serve immediately.

PER SERVING
BEFORE: 470 CALORIES, 32 G TOTAL FAT
DISH DO-OVER: 339 CALORIES, 10.3 G TOTAL FAT
NUTRITIONAL INFORMATION: 6 G SATURATED FAT, 53 G CARBOHYDRATES, 7.1 G FIBRE, 25.8 G SUGAR, 13.2 G PROTEIN, 236 MG SODIUM, 17 MG CHOLESTEROL

Peanut Butter Cookies

Better ingredients make this cookie a much healthier treat than the usual suspect, which is loaded with regular peanut butter, white and brown sugar and white flour. I use easier-to-digest spelt flour, unsalted natural peanut butter, organic sugar and honey for a less-processed sugar substitute.

1 1/2 cups spelt or whole-wheat
    pastry flour
1 tsp baking soda
1/4 tsp sea salt
1/2 cup unsalted natural peanut butter
1/4 cup unsalted butter
1/3 cup organic sugar
1/3 cup honey
1 large egg
1 tsp pure vanilla extract

MAKES 2.5 DOZEN
HANDS-ON TIME: 15 MINUTES
TOTAL TIME: 25 MINUTES +
10 MINUTES COOLING TIME

Preheat oven to 375°F. Line 2 large baking sheets with parchment paper.

In a large bowl, sift flour, baking soda and salt.

In a stand mixer fitted with a paddle attachment, or in a large bowl using a spatula, cream peanut butter, butter, sugar, honey, egg and vanilla, stopping occasionally to scrape down sides of bowl. Gradually add flour mixture until just combined.

Scoop out dough in 1-tbsp portions, rolling each into a ball. Arrange on prepared baking sheets, leaving 2 inches between each cookie. Dip fork in flour and gently press a crisscross pattern into the tops of cookies, flattening slightly. Bake, switching and rotating the baking sheets halfway through cooking time, until cookies are just golden, 8 to 10 minutes. Allow to cool on baking sheets for 10 minutes, then transfer to wire racks to cool completely.

PER SERVING (1 COOKIE)
BEFORE: 220 CALORIES, 12 G TOTAL FAT
DISH DO-OVER: 86 CALORIES, 4 G TOTAL FAT
NUTRITIONAL INFORMATION: 1.3 G SATURATED FAT,
10.8 G CARBOHYDRATES, 1.2 G FIBRE, 5.5 G SUGAR,
2 G PROTEIN, 58 MG SODIUM, 10 MG CHOLESTEROL

Chocolate Chip Cookies

If I had to pick a favourite recipe from this book, it would be this one. My love of cooking began with my grandma baking chocolate chip cookies. I was far too little to be helpful, I'm sure, but we had so much fun. I can just picture her helping me stand on my little wooden chair so I could reach the countertop and scoop out uneven piles of cookie dough. I'd use that same chair to sit in front of the oven and watch the cookies rise . . . eager to give my grandpa one of my masterpieces straight out of the oven.

2 1/4 cups spelt or whole-wheat flour
1 tsp baking soda
1/4 tsp sea salt
1/2 cup softened unsalted butter
2/3 cup organic sugar
1/2 cup honey
2 large eggs
2 tsp pure vanilla extract
1 cup dark chocolate chips
   (70% cocoa or greater)

MAKES 3.5 DOZEN
HANDS-ON TIME: 15 MINUTES
TOTAL TIME: 25 MINUTES

Preheat oven to 375°F. Line 2 or 3 large baking sheets with parchment paper.

In a medium bowl, sift flour, baking soda and salt.

In a stand mixer fitted with a paddle attachment, or in a large bowl using a spatula, cream butter, sugar, honey, eggs and vanilla, stopping occasionally to scrape down sides of bowl. Gradually add flour mixture until just combined. With a spatula, fold in chocolate chips.

Scoop out dough in 1-tbsp portions, rolling each into a ball. Arrange on prepared baking sheets, leaving 2 inches between each cookie. Bake, switching and rotating the baking sheets halfway through cooking time, until cookies are just golden, 8 to 10 minutes. Allow to cool on baking sheets for 10 minutes, then transfer to wire racks to cool completely.

PER SERVING (1 COOKIE)
BEFORE: 220 CALORIES, 10 G TOTAL FAT
DISH DO-OVER: 98 CALORIES, 4.3 G TOTAL FAT
NUTRITIONAL INFORMATION: 2.4 G SATURATED FAT,
13.1 G CARBOHYDRATES, 1.3 G FIBRE, 7.5 G SUGAR,
1.5 G PROTEIN, 44 MG SODIUM, 15 MG CHOLESTEROL

Double Chocolate Cake

It's relatively easy to sneak some calorie-reducing ingredients — like applesauce, Greek yogurt and egg whites — into a gooey chocolate cake. I dare anyone to pick this cake out of a healthy desserts lineup! Note that the icing must be prepared in advance so the layers don't slide off each other.

ICING

1 1/2 cups non-fat plain Greek yogurt
1/4 cup unsweetened cocoa powder (Dutch-process is best)
4 oz dark chocolate (70% cocoa or greater), chopped, melted and cooled to room temperature
1/2 cup organic icing sugar

CAKE

2 1/2 cups whole-wheat pastry flour
1 cup unsweetened cocoa powder (Dutch-process is best)
1 tsp baking powder
1 tsp baking soda
1/4 tsp sea salt
1 1/4 cups unsweetened applesauce
1 cup non-fat plain Greek yogurt
1/3 cup honey
1/3 cup organic sugar
1/3 cup unsalted butter
2 tsp pure vanilla extract
1 1/2 cups egg whites (about 12 large)

SERVES 12 (MAKES ONE 9-INCH ROUND LAYER CAKE)
HANDS-ON TIME: 40 MINUTES
TOTAL TIME: 1 HOUR + 12 HOURS CHILLING TIME

Note: What is a crumb coat? This is a thin preliminary layer of icing that traps all the loose crumbs, so the final layer of icing glides on smoothly.

Prepare icing: In a stand mixer fitted with a whisk attachment, or in a bowl using a whisk, combine yogurt, cocoa powder, melted chocolate and icing sugar until smooth. Cover and refrigerate for at least 12 hours, to firm up.

Preheat oven to 375°F. Grease and flour two 10-inch cake pans.

Prepare cake: In a medium bowl, whisk together flour, cocoa powder, baking powder, baking soda and salt.

In a food processor, pulse applesauce, yogurt, honey, sugar, butter and vanilla until smooth. Gradually mix into dry ingredients until just combined; do not overmix.

In a separate dry bowl, using an electric beater on high speed, whisk egg whites until soft peaks form. Using a spatula, fold egg whites into batter. (Batter should seem a little lumpy; do not overmix.)

Pour batter into prepared cake pans. Bake for 20 to 25 minutes, until a toothpick inserted in the centre comes out almost clean. Transfer pans to wire racks to cool for 20 minutes, then turn out cakes onto wire racks to cool completely.

Remove icing from the fridge and allow to warm at room temperature until easily spreadable, about 1 hour. Using a serrated knife, slice a small portion off the top of each cake so that the top is flat. Place 1 cake on a stand or flat plate; using an offset or regular spatula, spread a layer of icing over cut side. Place remaining cake cut side down on top of iced cake. Thinly spread about one-third of remaining icing all over cake to form a crumb coat (see Note). Refrigerate for about 1 hour until set, leaving remaining icing at room temperature. Once crumb coat has set, cover cake with remainder of icing. Serve immediately or refrigerate, bringing cake to room temperature before serving.

PER SERVING
BEFORE: 600 CALORIES, 32 G TOTAL FAT
DISH DO-OVER: 339 CALORIES, 10.3 G TOTAL FAT
*NUTRITIONAL INFORMATION: 6 G SATURATED FAT,
53 G CARBOHYDRATES, 7.1 G FIBRE, 25.8 G SUGAR,
13.2 G PROTEIN, 236 MG SODIUM, 17 MG CHOLESTEROL*

Chocolate Chip Cookie Dough Ice Cream

Thanks to my grandma and our chocolate chip cookie baking hobby, I likely ate more raw cookie dough as a child than most kids, and cookie dough ice cream instantly brings out that little kid in me. This egg-free version of my chocolate chip cookie recipe is safe to eat raw. One word of warning: You may have to make extra. When I was testing this recipe, I couldn't resist sneaking into the freezer for a few bites here and there.

COOKIE DOUGH

3/4 cup spelt or whole-wheat flour
Pinch sea salt
1/3 cup softened unsalted butter
1/3 cup organic sugar
3 tbsp cup honey
2 tbsp evaporated milk
1/2 tsp pure vanilla extract
1/2 cup dark chocolate chips
     (70% cocoa or greater)

ICE CREAM

1 tsp unflavoured gelatin powder
1 can (13 oz/354 mL) low-fat
     evaporated milk (minus 2 tbsp
     used above)
1/2 cup honey
1 vanilla bean, split in half lengthwise
3 cups non-fat plain Greek yogurt

SERVES 16 (1/2-CUP SERVINGS)
HANDS-ON TIME: 40 MINUTES
TOTAL TIME: 1 HOUR + 5 HOURS,
45 MINUTES FREEZING TIME

Prepare cookie dough: In a medium bowl, sift flour and salt. In a stand mixer fitted with a paddle attachment, or in a large bowl using a spatula, cream butter, sugar, honey, milk and vanilla extract, stopping occasionally to scrape down sides of bowl. Gradually add flour mixture until just combined. With a spatula, fold in chocolate chips.

On a parchment-lined baking sheet, roll out dough 1/2 inch thick. Cover and refrigerate until firm, about 30 minutes. Cut into 1/4-inch cubes, transfer to a freezer-safe container and freeze for at least 1 hour.

Prepare ice cream: In a small bowl, sprinkle gelatin over 1 tbsp water and let stand until softened, about 5 minutes. In a medium saucepan over medium heat, warm milk, honey and vanilla bean, stirring frequently, until just steaming, about 5 minutes. Whisk in gelatin and let stand for 10 minutes. Remove vanilla bean, scraping any seeds remaining in pod into liquid. Cool to room temperature.

Place yogurt in a large bowl and whisk in vanilla milk until smooth, or use an electric mixer. Transfer mixture to a shallow non-reactive, freezer-safe container. (At this point, if using a commercial ice cream machine, freeze mixture according to manufacturer's instructions. When ice cream has churned, fold in cookie dough pieces.)

Freeze yogurt mixture for about 45 minutes, until it begins to harden slightly around the edges. Scrape down the edges with a spatula, breaking up large chunks, and mix well with a whisk or in a food processor, blending in ice crystals until mixture is creamy again. Return mixture to freezer. Every 30 minutes for 2 to 3 hours, remove from freezer and repeat. Each time, the mixture will get a little harder to whisk, and you may have to switch to a spatula.

After 2 to 3 hours, fold cookie dough chunks into yogurt and return to freezer to harden, about 1 to 2 hours. Ice cream is ready when firm enough to scoop. Best if enjoyed within 1 week. Keep frozen in a resealable freezer-safe container.

Note: If yogurt is too hard to scoop, allow it to soften slightly for a few minutes at room temperature. If mixture becomes icy and firm rather than smooth, place in the fridge for 30 minutes, transfer to a large bowl and mix well with a spatula to soften.

PER SERVING
BEFORE: 290 CALORIES, 15 G TOTAL FAT
DISH DO-OVER: 230 CALORIES, 8.9 G TOTAL FAT
NUTRITIONAL INFORMATION: 5.3 G SATURATED FAT, 29.7 G CARBOHYDRATES, 1.9 G FIBRE,
22 G SUGAR, 8.1 G PROTEIN, 45 MG SODIUM, 15 MG CHOLESTEROL

Mom's Apple Pie

The best types of apples for baking pie are those that are slightly tart and crunchy, such as Granny Smith, Braeburn, Pink Lady, Fuji, Cortland or McIntosh. There are so many varieties available; go ahead and experiment to find your favourite. I like to mix a few varieties together for a balanced flavour. You want an apple that will hold its shape during baking and not turn to mush. Also, since sugar is added to the filling, you don't want an overly sweet apple to start with or the pie will be cloyingly sweet.

CRUST

1 cup whole-wheat pastry flour
1 tsp organic sugar
1/2 tsp sea salt
1/2 tsp baking powder
3 tbsp cold unsalted butter, cubed
3 tbsp non-fat plain Greek yogurt
1 tbsp apple cider vinegar
3 tbsp ice water
1/4 cup egg whites (about 2 large),
    lightly beaten

FILLING

8 cups thinly sliced peeled apples
    (about 7 medium/3 lb)
1/3 cup organic sugar
2 tbsp fresh lemon juice
1/2 tsp ground cinnamon

TOPPING

1/4 cup whole-wheat pastry flour
1/4 cup rolled oats
3 tbsp organic sugar
1/4 tsp ground cinnamon
1/8 tsp freshly grated nutmeg
Pinch sea salt
2 tbsp cold unsalted butter,
    cubed
1 tbsp cold water

SERVES 10 (MAKES ONE 9-INCH PIE)
HANDS-ON TIME: 45 MINUTES
TOTAL TIME: 90 MINUTES +
60 MINUTES CHILLING AND
COOLING TIME

Prepare crust: In a medium bowl, sift or whisk together flour, sugar, salt and baking powder. Using a pastry blender or fork, cut cubed butter into flour until mixture resembles coarse crumbs. Drizzle with yogurt, vinegar and ice water and toss mixture with a fork until a ragged dough forms; do not over-mix. Transfer to a clean work surface lightly dusted with flour and press together just enough to form a disc. Wrap tightly in plastic wrap and refrigerate for at least 30 minutes and up to 1 day.

Roll out pastry to a generous 1/8-inch thickness; fit into a 9-inch pie plate. Trim to leave 3/4-inch overhang; fold extra dough under the edge and pinch to crimp (or use the tines of a lightly floured fork). Brush with egg whites.

Prepare filling: Heat a large non-stick skillet over medium heat. Add apples, sugar, lemon juice and cinnamon. Cook, stirring frequently, until apples are softened and juicy but still retain their shape, about 8 minutes. Remove from heat and cool to room temperature.

Prepare topping: In a medium bowl, stir together flour, oats, sugar, cinnamon, nutmeg and salt to taste. Add cubed butter and drizzle with cold water. Blend using your fingertips until mixture resembles coarse crumbs.

Preheat oven to 425°F.

Pour filling into prepared pie shell and sprinkle with topping. Bake for 15 minutes, then reduce oven temperature to 350°F and bake for another 30 minutes, until crust and topping are golden brown and filling is bubbling. Cool to room temperature for 30 minutes before serving.

PER SERVING
BEFORE: 296 CALORIES, 13 G TOTAL FAT
DISH DO-OVER: 212 CALORIES, 6.3 G TOTAL FAT
*NUTRITIONAL INFORMATION: 3.7 G SATURATED FAT,
37.1 G CARBOHYDRATES, 3.7 G FIBRE, 20 G SUGAR,
3.4 G PROTEIN, 106 MG SODIUM, 16 MG CHOLESTEROL*

Tip: Pick Your Apples

With the exception of Red Delicious, which are far too sweet and mushy for baking, pretty much any apple variety will work in a pie. Keep in mind what you're looking for in your pie, though: If you like tart pies with firm chunks of apples, go for Granny Smith. If you like a sweet, soft pie, McIntosh will do the trick. Personally, I like a little bit of both, so I mix a few varieties together for my pies. Here are my top picks:

Braeburn: Firm and slightly spicy, with red-green skin

Cortland: Tart and crisp, with bright red skin and extra-white flesh

Fuji: Sweet and juicy, with pink and yellow skin

Gala: Sweet, subtle flavour, with striped pink and yellow skin

Golden Delicious: Sweet and crisp, with a yellow skin

Granny Smith: Tart, crisp and juicy, with a bright green skin

Gravenstein: Sweet-tart and crisp, with a striped red and yellow or green skin

Jonagold or Jonathan: Tart, crisp and juicy, with red and yellow skin

McIntosh: Sweet and juicy, with red skin; best paired with a firmer variety

Northern Spy: Extremely crisp, aromatic and slightly sweet, with red-green skin

Pippin: Sweet-tart and firm, with pale green skin

Tip: Keep freshly sliced apples from browning by tossing them with lemon juice. The acidity of the lemon halts the enzyme reaction that causes apples to brown so quickly.

Carrot Cake Cupcakes

Cupcakes took the food-trend world by storm years ago and have now solidified their status as a favourite sweet treat. To make these carrot cake cupcakes moist without a lot of fat, I use applesauce, buttermilk and lots of carrots for extra sweetness. I also substitute coconut oil for butter, because it works so well with the flavours of the cupcake and has fabulous health benefits. Greek yogurt keeps the calories in the icing low, and the tangy flavour complements the sweet little cupcakes perfectly.

CUPCAKES

1 cup unsweetened applesauce
1 cup organic sugar
3/4 cup coconut oil
1/2 cup 1% buttermilk
1/4 cup egg whites (about 2 large)
1 large egg
1 tsp pure vanilla extract
2 cups whole-wheat pastry or
    spelt flour
2 tsp baking soda
1 tsp ground cinnamon
1/2 tsp ground ginger
1/2 tsp sea salt
4 cups grated peeled carrot
    (about 3 large)
1 cup raisins
1/2 cup coarsely chopped walnuts

ICING

1 cup low-fat cream cheese, softened
1/2 cup non-fat plain Greek yogurt
1/3 cup organic icing sugar
1 tsp pure vanilla extract

SERVES 24 (MAKES 2 DOZEN)
HANDS-ON TIME: 35 MINUTES
TOTAL TIME: 45 MINUTES +
2 HOURS CHILLING TIME

Tip: If you don't have a piping bag, use a large resealable bag. Using a spatula, scoop icing into bag. Twist the bag just above the level of icing — this will help push the icing through when you squeeze the bag. Snip off a small piece of the bottom corner when ready to use.

Preheat oven to 350°F.

Prepare cupcakes: In a stand mixer fitted with a whisk attachment, combine applesauce, sugar, coconut oil, buttermilk, egg whites, egg and vanilla until fully incorporated and smooth, about 1 minute. Alternatively, use a large bowl and a whisk.

In a separate bowl, whisk together or sift flour, baking soda, cinnamon, ginger and salt.

If using a stand mixer, switch to a paddle attachment, or using a spatula, add flour, carrots, raisins and walnuts. Mix on low speed (or fold in) until just incorporated; do not overmix.

Line two 12-cup muffin pans with cupcake liners. Using an ice cream scoop or two spoons, fill liners just over three-quarters full. Bake for 20 to 25 minutes, until a toothpick inserted in centre comes out almost clean. Allow to cool completely on wire racks.

Prepare icing: While cupcakes are baking, in a stand mixer fitted with a whisk attachment, or in a food processor or in large bowl using a whisk, combine cream cheese, yogurt, icing sugar and vanilla until smooth. Transfer to a piping bag fitted with a large round or star tip. Refrigerate for at least 2 hours and ideally overnight. [*Make-ahead:* Prepare 24 hours in advance and refrigerate until needed. Cupcakes will keep for 3 to 4 days if un-iced until just before serving.]

Once cupcakes are completely cool, decorate tops with icing. Enjoy immediately or cover and refrigerate until ready to serve. Iced cupcakes will keep for up to 2 days.

PER SERVING
BEFORE: 325 CALORIES, 16 G TOTAL FAT
DISH DO-OVER: 214 CALORIES, 10.6 G TOTAL FAT
*NUTRITIONAL INFORMATION: 7.2 G SATURATED FAT,
26.9 G CARBOHYDRATES, 2.6 G FIBRE, 15.9 G SUGAR,
3.9 G PROTEIN, 193 MG SODIUM, 14 MG CHOLESTEROL*

Whoopie Pies

Whoopie pies are a fun dessert option that's part cookie, part cake. They're basically little cakes sandwiched together with a creamy filling — traditionally, chocolate cake with a fluffy white filling. History claims that these were first baked by Amish women as treats for their families and garnered the name whoopie pies because when men and children opened their lunchbox and found one, they exclaimed, "Whoopie!"

CAKES

1/3 cup unsalted butter
1/2 cup organic sugar
3/4 cup 1% buttermilk
1/2 cup unsweetened applesauce
3 large egg whites
1 tsp pure vanilla extract
1 1/2 cups whole-wheat pastry or
    spelt flour
1/2 cup cocoa powder
2 tsp baking soda
1/2 tsp sea salt

FILLING

1 cup low-fat cream cheese, softened
1/2 cup non-fat plain Greek yogurt
1 tsp pure vanilla extract
2/3 cup organic icing sugar
1 cup no-sugar-added strawberry jam

MAKES 1 DOZEN
HANDS-ON TIME: 30 MINUTES
TOTAL TIME: 40 MINUTES +
30 MINUTES CHILLING TIME

Preheat oven to 350°F. Line a large baking sheet with parchment paper.

Prepare cakes: In a stand mixer fitted with a paddle attachment, cream butter and sugar until smooth, about 1 minute. Alternatively, use a large bowl and a spatula. Add buttermilk, applesauce, egg whites and vanilla; mix well.

In a separate bowl, whisk together or sift flour, cocoa powder, baking soda and salt. Add flour mixture to applesauce mixture and fold using the paddle attachment (or by hand using a spatula), until just combined; do not overmix.

Scoop into 2-tbsp balls and place on prepared baking sheet, set about 2 inches apart.

Bake for 12 to 14 minutes. Cool on baking sheet for 5 minutes, then transfer to wire racks to cool completely.

Meanwhile, prepare filling: In a stand mixer fitted with a whisk attachment, on medium speed, roughly combine cream cheese, yogurt, vanilla and icing sugar. Increase speed to medium-high and mix until smooth. Alternatively, combine in a food processor or in a large bowl using a whisk. Transfer filling to a resealable container and refrigerate for at least 30 minutes.

To assemble whoopie pies, scoop 2 tbsp filling onto flat side of one cake. Top with 2 tsp jam. Sandwich filling with a second cake, flat side down. Repeat with remaining cakes and filling. [*Make-ahead:* Whoopie pies can be prepared ahead, covered and refrigerated for up to 48 hours.]

PER SERVING (1 SANDWICH)
BEFORE: 450 CALORIES, 24 G TOTAL FAT
DISH DO-OVER: 296 CALORIES, 9.5 G TOTAL FAT
*NUTRITIONAL INFORMATION: 5.8 G SATURATED FAT,
47.6 G CARBOHYDRATES, 3.6 G FIBRE, 32.4 G SUGAR,
6.7 G PROTEIN, 435 MG SODIUM, 26 MG CHOLESTEROL*

Crème Brûlée

The classic version of this fancy pudding is simplicity at its best — 35% cream, eggs, vanilla and sugar — so I find it almost criminal that something so minimalist can set you back 36 grams of fat in a single serving. I swap cream for 2% milk to keep some of the creaminess, use cornstarch to thicken, drastically reduce the eggs . . . and *voilà!* A velvety, creamy treat.

2 cups 2% milk or unsweetened
  plain almond milk
2 tbsp cornstarch
1 vanilla bean, split in half lengthwise,
  or 1 tsp pure vanilla extract
1 cinnamon stick
3 large egg yolks
1/4 cup organic sugar + 2 tbsp for
  topping
1/4 cup fresh blueberries
12 fresh raspberries

SERVES 6
HANDS-ON TIME: 25 MINUTES
TOTAL TIME: 1 HOUR, 5 MINUTES +
3 HOURS CHILLING TIME

Tip: If you don't have a kitchen blow torch, you can caramelize the sugar on top using your oven's broiler. Position rack in top third of oven and turn broiler to high. Broil custards for 2 to 4 minutes, until sugar bubbles and darkens, removing ramekins when ready, one at a time if necessary. Bring crème brûlées to room temperature for 20 minutes before serving. Garnish with fresh berries. [*Make-ahead:* Caramelized Crème Brûlée can be prepared up to 3 hours in advance.]

Preheat oven to 300°F.

In a small bowl, mix 1/4 cup milk with cornstarch.

In a medium saucepan, heat remaining 1 3/4 cups milk, vanilla bean and cinnamon stick over medium heat. Cook, stirring frequently, until steaming, about 8 minutes. While milk is warming, in a small bowl, whisk together egg yolks and 1/4 cup sugar until smooth; set aside. Give cornstarch mixture a stir (the cornstarch will have settled) and stir into warmed milk. Continue to heat until thickened and sauce coats the back of a spoon. Allow to cool slightly; discard vanilla bean and cinnamon stick.

Very slowly, about 2 tbsp at a time, pour warmed milk into egg mixture. Continue adding about half of milk in small additions until eggs are slightly warmed. Pour egg mixture into remaining milk and gently whisk to combine.

Divide among six ramekins or custard cups (about 1/3 cup each). Place in two large, shallow pans and pour in enough boiling water to come halfway up ramekins (to make a bain-marie, see Note on page 200).

Bake for 30 to 35 minutes or until edges are set but centres still wobble and a thin knife inserted in centre comes out creamy. Remove ramekins from water and set on a baking rack to cool. Cover and refrigerate for at least 3 hours, or until chilled and set, up to 48 hours. [*Make-ahead:* Prepare and refrigerate for up to 2 days.]

Transfer ramekins to baking sheet and sprinkle remaining 2 tbsp sugar over custards. Use a kitchen blow torch to caramelize the sugar (or see Tip for oven broiling method).

PER SERVING
BEFORE: 425 CALORIES, 36 G TOTAL FAT
DISH DO-OVER: 117 CALORIES, 4.2 G TOTAL FAT
*NUTRITIONAL INFORMATION: 1.4 G SATURATED FAT,
14.9 G CARBOHYDRATES, 0 G FIBRE, 12.7 G SUGAR,
4 G PROTEIN, 42 MG SODIUM, 103 MG CHOLESTEROL*

Breakfasts

Sticky Buns

These buns instantly transport me back to my childhood. My grandma and I made sticky buns with any dough leftover from whatever we were baking that day. No one will believe that these irresistible, fluffy treats are guilt-free. I use 1% milk, organic sugar and whole-wheat pastry flour to cut the calories and fat. Honey keeps the sticky topping moist without adding a ton of butter. Be sure to use instant yeast.

DOUGH

3 cups whole-wheat pastry or
   spelt flour, plus 1/3 cup for dusting
1 package (1/4 oz/7 g) instant yeast
2 tbsp organic sugar
1/2 tsp sea salt
1 1/2 cups 1% milk, warmed to
   105–115°F
1 large egg, lightly beaten
1/4 cup unsalted butter, melted

FILLING

1/3 cup lightly packed organic
   brown sugar
1 tbsp ground cinnamon
3 tbsp unsalted butter, melted

TOPPING

1/3 cup organic lightly packed
   brown sugar
1/4 cup honey
3 tbsp unsalted butter
1/3 cup coarsely chopped pecans

MAKES 12 BUNS
HANDS-ON TIME: 50 MINUTES
TOTAL TIME: 1 HOUR, 15 MINUTES
+ 90 MINUTES RISING TIME

Prepare dough: In a stand mixer fitted with a whisk attachment, on low speed, or in a large bowl using a whisk, combine flour, yeast, sugar and salt. In a separate bowl, whisk together milk, egg and melted butter. If using a stand mixer, switch to a dough hook attachment and keep speed on low. Slowly pour in wet ingredients and mix until just combined, smooth and slightly sticky. Increase speed to medium and knead for about 3 minutes, until smooth (about 6 minutes if kneading by hand). Transfer dough to a clean floured work surface and form into a ball.

Mist bowl with cooking spray. Return dough to bowl, cover with a clean damp kitchen towel or plastic wrap and let rise at room temperature for 1 hour, until doubled in size. Punch down dough, cover and let rise for another 30 minutes.

Prepare filling: In a small bowl, mix together brown sugar and cinnamon.

Prepare topping: In a small saucepan, combine brown sugar, honey and butter and warm over low heat until melted and bubbling, about 5 minutes. Mist a 9- × 13-inch baking dish with cooking spray. Pour mixture into pan, spreading evenly. Sprinkle with pecans.

Place dough on a clean, floured work surface and roll into a 12- × 18-inch rectangle, with a long side facing you. Brush dough with melted butter for filling and sprinkle with cinnamon sugar, leaving a 1/2-inch border at the top edge. Brush top edge with a little water to help seal after rolling.

Starting at the long edge facing you, roll dough into a cylinder, placing seam side down on work surface. To make 12 even rolls, using a very sharp chef's knife or serrated knife, cut cylinder in half. Cut each half in half again and then each piece into 3 even rolls. Arrange rolls cut side up in baking dish. Bake for about 25 minutes, until rolls are golden brown. (*Continued overleaf*)

Place a parchment-lined baking sheet directly over top of pan and very carefully, pressing sheet to rolls, invert to release rolls from pan. Scrape any topping mixture left in pan onto sticky buns. Let cool slightly at room temperature for 10 to 15 minutes before serving.

Note: Hot sugar can burn you if not handled properly. It is important to invert the pan carefully, and to be sure the kiddies aren't underfoot. Also resist the urge to grab a taste right out of the oven: the sugar topping can be extremely hot.

Tip: Sticky buns are best served the day they are baked. Allow leftover buns to cool completely, then cover and store at room temperature for up to 2 days. Serve at room temperature or reheat, warming individual servings in a microwave on medium for about 30 seconds. Microwaves vary, so adjust time accordingly.

PER SERVING (1 BUN)
BEFORE: 813 CALORIES, 32 G TOTAL FAT
DISH DO-OVER: 314 CALORIES, 13 G TOTAL FAT
NUTRITIONAL INFORMATION: 6.6 G SATURATED FAT, 45.5 G CARBOHYDRATES, 4.8 G FIBRE, 21.4 G SUGAR, 5.2 G PROTEIN, 120 MG SODIUM, 42 MG CHOLESTEROL

Chocolate Hazelnut Banana French Toast

You don't need a lot of maple syrup here because of the sweet banana and chocolate hazelnut spread.

8 large egg whites

2 large eggs

1/4 cup 1% milk

1 tsp pure vanilla extract

1/8 tsp ground cinnamon

1 8-inch wedge unsliced whole-wheat challah or other whole-grain bread

1/2 cup Chocolate Hazelnut Spread (page 227)

2 ripe bananas, thinly sliced

1/4 cup pure maple syrup

2 tbsp organic icing sugar

SERVES 4
HANDS-ON TIME: 50 MINUTES
TOTAL TIME: 50 MINUTES

Tip: Don't crowd the pan or flipping the toast will be tricky. Work with 2 pieces at a time if necessary and keep finished toast warm on a baking sheet in a 200°F oven.

Whisk together egg whites, eggs, milk, vanilla and cinnamon. Pour into a large shallow dish (a 9- × 13-inch dish works well; if you use a smaller dish, the egg mixture may seep into the filling during the coating process).

Cut bread into 4 large slices. Carefully cut a pocket into each slice by cutting toward the centre from one of the edges, leaving 3 sides attached. Stuff 2 tbsp chocolate hazelnut spread and one-quarter of the banana slices into each pocket.

Heat a large non-stick skillet over medium heat; mist with cooking spray. Place each sandwich in egg mixture, allowing bread to soak up egg for 30 seconds, then turning to coat other side. Using a spatula, transfer sandwiches to pan. Cook for about 4 minutes per side, flipping once, until bread is golden brown and filling is warm. Arrange on serving plates, then drizzle with maple syrup and dust with icing sugar.

PER SERVING
BEFORE: 900 CALORIES, 39 G TOTAL FAT
DISH DO-OVER: 581 CALORIES, 17.4 G TOTAL FAT
NUTRITIONAL INFORMATION: 4.4 G SATURATED FAT, 82.1 G CARBOHYDRATES, 10 G FIBRE, 36.7 G SUGAR, 26 G PROTEIN, 530 MG SODIUM, 94 MG CHOLESTEROL

Chocolate Hazelnut Spread

The first time I had the packaged spread was as a teenager while I was babysitting. The kids kept asking for "yummy chocolate stuff," and I had no idea what they wanted because I'd never tasted it! My mom wouldn't buy it because the main ingredient is refined white sugar. Here, I've replaced the refined sugar with just a touch of honey, so you taste the hazelnuts and chocolate first, not just sugar. Since the Chocolate Hazelnut Banana French Toast recipe (page 225) calls for only 1/2 cup, you'll have lots leftover for snacking.

1 cup hazelnuts
4 oz chopped dark chocolate
    (70% cocoa or greater)
1/3 cup 1% milk
1/3 cup non-fat plain Greek yogurt
3 tbsp honey or pure maple syrup
2 tbsp unsweetened cocoa powder
    (Dutch-process is best)
Pinch sea salt

MAKES 1 1/2 CUPS
HANDS-ON TIME: 25 MINUTES
TOTAL TIME: 25 MINUTES

Preheat oven to 300°F. Arrange hazelnuts on a baking sheet and roast for about 10 minutes, until skins are dark brown and split. Wrap in a clean kitchen towel and let rest for 2 minutes. Rub nuts in towel to remove skins (don't worry if some are still attached). Transfer nuts to a food processor, discarding skins.

Melt chocolate in a heatproof bowl placed over a pot of barely simmering water. Make sure water does not touch bottom of bowl. Transfer to food processor with nuts. Add milk, yogurt, honey, cocoa powder and salt; purée until blended and smooth, scraping down sides of bowl with a spatula as needed. Transfer to a resealable container, cover and refrigerate for up to 1 week.

PER SERVING (2 TBSP)
BEFORE: 200 CALORIES, 12 G TOTAL FAT
DISH DO-OVER: 152 CALORIES, 11.1 G TOTAL FAT
NUTRITIONAL INFORMATION: 2.9 G SATURATED FAT, 11.7 G CARBOHYDRATES, 2.6 G FIBRE, 7.5 G SUGAR, 3.3 G PROTEIN, 8 MG SODIUM, 1 MG CHOLESTEROL

Chocolate Chip Pancakes

A big stack of fluffy pancakes is the perfect way to start off any leisurely Sunday. I've swapped out all-purpose flour for spelt and use egg whites and 1% buttermilk to lighten up the batter. The big difference comes from not cooking and slathering them in tons of butter but using a slight mist of cooking spray and a little Greek yogurt on top for creaminess.

2 cups spelt or whole-wheat flour
1 tsp baking powder
1/2 tsp baking soda
1/8 tsp ground cinnamon
Pinch sea salt
1/3 cup egg whites (about 3 large)
1 large egg
1/2 cup 1% buttermilk
2 tbsp honey
1/2 cup dark chocolate chips
    (70% cocoa or greater)
1/2 cup non-fat plain Greek yogurt
2/3 cup pure maple syrup
1 cup fresh raspberries (optional)

SERVES 4 (MAKES ABOUT
16 PANCAKES)
HANDS-ON TIME: 30 MINUTES
TOTAL TIME: 30 MINUTES

Preheat griddle or large non-stick skillet to medium-high heat and oven to 200°F.

In a large bowl, whisk together flour, baking powder, baking soda, cinnamon and salt.

In a separate bowl, whisk together egg whites, egg, buttermilk and honey until smooth. Add wet ingredients to dry ingredients and mix with a spatula or wooden spoon until just lumpy. Stir in chocolate chips.

Mist griddle with cooking spray and scoop ladlefuls of batter onto griddle about 3 inches apart. Cook for about 2 minutes, until undersides are golden and bubbles on top have burst. Flip and cook for another 1 minute, until undersides are golden. Transfer to a baking sheet and keep warm in oven, uncovered, until ready to serve. Don't stack, just overlap slightly if necessary.

To serve, stack 4 or 5 pancakes on each plate and top with a dollop of yogurt. Drizzle with maple syrup and garnish with raspberries (if using).

PER SERVING
BEFORE: 766 CALORIES, 22 G TOTAL FAT
DISH DO-OVER: 594 CALORIES, 11.6 G TOTAL FAT
*NUTRITIONAL INFORMATION: 5.2 G SATURATED FAT,
101.8 G CARBOHYDRATES, 9.7 G FIBRE, 48.9 G SUGAR,
17.3 G PROTEIN, 341 MG SODIUM, 50 MG CHOLESTEROL*

The Best Banana Bread

If you're anything like me, you have half a freezer full of black-skinned bananas, and the pile never seems to diminish. This recipe will help cull the herd. I use four very ripe bananas to cut the butter, eggs and sugar, keeping the bread moist and decadent tasting.

2 cups whole-wheat or spelt flour
1 cups walnuts, toasted and cooled
1/2 cup organic sugar
1 tsp baking soda
1/2 tsp sea salt
4 very ripe bananas
2 large eggs, at room temperature,
   lightly beaten
1/2 cup non-fat plain Greek yogurt
1/4 cup unsalted butter, melted
   and cooled
1 tsp pure vanilla extract

SERVES 12 (MAKES 1 LOAF)
HANDS-ON TIME: 20 MINUTES
TOTAL TIME: 1 HOUR, 15 MINUTES
+ COOLING TIME

Preheat oven to 375°F.

In a large bowl, whisk together flour, walnuts, sugar, baking soda and salt.

In a second bowl and using a fork, mash bananas. Add eggs, yogurt, butter and vanilla. Using a spatula, gently fold banana mixture into dry ingredients until batter is thick and chunky; do not overmix.

Lightly mist a non-stick loaf pan with cooking spray. Scoop batter into pan, smoothing top with spatula. Bake for 55 to 60 minutes, until a wooden skewer or thin knife inserted in centre comes out clean. Remove from oven and let rest in pan for 5 minutes. Remove from pan and transfer to a wire rack to cool completely before serving.

Wrapped in parchment paper and then in foil, bread can be stored for up to 2 days at room temperature or refrigerated for up to 1 week.

PER SERVING
BEFORE: 390 CALORIES, 15 G TOTAL FAT
DISH DO-OVER: 251 CALORIES, 11.5 G TOTAL FAT
*NUTRITIONAL INFORMATION: 3.4 G SATURATED FAT,
33.8 G CARBOHYDRATES, 3.8 G FIBRE, 13.8 G SUGAR,
6.7 G PROTEIN, 186 MG SODIUM, 41 MG CHOLESTEROL*

Scones

Scones are such a classic brunch staple that I had to provide a version that wouldn't weigh you down. I use spelt flour, oats and buttermilk to keep them light and soft.

1 3/4 cups spelt or whole-wheat flour
1 cup rolled oats
3 tbsp organic sugar
1 tbsp lemon zest
1 1/2 tsp baking powder
1/2 tsp baking soda
1/2 tsp sea salt
5 tbsp chilled unsalted butter,
    cut into small pieces
3/4 cup 1% buttermilk, plus extra
    for brushing
1 large egg white
1/4 tsp pure vanilla extract
1/3 cup dried cranberries
2 tsp turbinado sugar

MAKES 12 SCONES
HANDS-ON TIME: 25 MINUTES
TOTAL TIME: 40 MINUTES

Preheat oven to 425°F. Line a large baking sheet with parchment paper.

In a large bowl, whisk together flour, oats, sugar, lemon zest, baking powder, baking soda and salt. Cut in butter with a pastry blender or two knives until mixture resembles coarse crumbs.

In a small bowl, combine 3/4 cup buttermilk, egg white and vanilla. Add buttermilk mixture to flour mixture, stirring just until moist (dough will be soft). Turn dough out onto a floured work surface. Sprinkle dough with cranberries. With floured hands, knead four times or just until the cranberries are incorporated. Pat dough into an 8-inch round on prepared baking sheet. Using a knife to make shallow cuts (do not cut through the dough), divide the dough into 12 equal wedges. Brush about 2 tsp buttermilk over top, then sprinkle with turbinado sugar.

Bake for 16 to 18 minutes or until golden. Serve warm, or cool on wire racks. Will keep at room temperature, covered, for 2 days or refrigerated for up to 1 week.

PER SERVING
BEFORE: 390 CALORIES, 18 G TOTAL FAT
DISH DO-OVER: 181 CALORIES, 6.5 G TOTAL FAT
NUTRITIONAL INFORMATION: 3.4 G SATURATED FAT, 25.8 G CARBOHYDRATES, 3.3 G FIBRE, 6.9 G SUGAR, 4.6 G PROTEIN, 179 MG SODIUM, 29 MG CHOLESTEROL

Eggs Benedict

Think eggs Benny are off the list? Think again! I've replaced the copious amounts of butter and most of the egg yolks in the traditional sauce with buttermilk and one egg yolk.

4 slices peameal bacon

3/4 cup 1% buttermilk

1 tbsp cornstarch

5 large eggs

2 tbsp fresh lemon juice

2 tbsp unsalted butter

Pinch cayenne pepper

Sea salt and freshly ground
   black pepper

1 tbsp white vinegar

2 cups lightly packed baby arugula

2 whole-wheat or multigrain
   English muffins, split and toasted

1 tbsp chopped fresh chives

SERVES 4
HANDS-ON TIME: 30 MINUTES
TOTAL TIME: 30 MINUTES

PER SERVING
BEFORE: 1020 CALORIES,
57 G TOTAL FAT
DISH DO-OVER: 251 CALORIES,
13.2 G TOTAL FAT
*NUTRITIONAL INFORMATION:
5.9 G SATURATED FAT, 19.8 G
CARBOHYDRATES, 2.7 G FIBRE,
6 G SUGAR, 14.4 G PROTEIN,
539 MG SODIUM,
208 MG CHOLESTEROL*

Heat a medium non-stick pan over medium heat; mist with cooking spray. Cook bacon, turning once, until lightly browned. Remove from heat and cover to keep warm.

While bacon is cooking, bring a medium saucepan about two-thirds full of water to a boil, then reduce heat to medium until just barely simmering.

In a medium heatproof bowl, whisk 3 tbsp buttermilk with cornstarch until smooth. Add remaining buttermilk and set bowl over pan of heated water. Do not allow water to touch bottom of bowl. Stir frequently for about 4 minutes, until buttermilk is just steaming.

Separate 1 egg, reserving white for another use, and place yolk in a small bowl. Add lemon juice and whisk to combine. Whisk in 1/4 cup steaming buttermilk, drizzling it in a slow, steady stream. Transfer egg yolk mixture to bowl of steaming buttermilk, whisking constantly until sauce is thick enough to coat the back of a spoon, about 1 minute. Remove bowl from saucepan, leaving saucepan on heat. To buttermilk mixture, whisk in butter, cayenne, salt and pepper until combined. Set aside and cover to keep warm.

Add enough water to saucepan to bring it back to two-thirds full. Increase heat until water is just steaming and small bubbles are forming on bottom of pan. Reduce heat to medium-low and stir in vinegar. Crack 1 egg into a small bowl. Hold bowl near the surface of the water and gently pour egg into the water. Repeat with remaining eggs, one at a time, noting order of eggs. Set a timer for 4 minutes and allow eggs to cook undisturbed. Using a slotted spoon, remove each egg in the order you dropped it into pan and gently place on a kitchen towel–lined plate.

While eggs are poaching, toss arugula with remaining 1 tbsp lemon juice and season with salt and pepper.

Arrange each muffin half, cut side up, on a serving plate. Top with 1 slice bacon and a few leaves of arugula. Using a slotted spoon, gently place each egg on arugula. Give sauce a quick stir and pour over eggs. Garnish with chives.

Huevos Rancheros

Huevos Rancheros are a perfect excuse to eat tacos for breakfast, but the regular version can weigh you down with sour cream, fried tortillas, refried beans and cheese. Here, the black beans are lightly sautéed and mashed, instead of being fried in lard, the tortillas are baked not fried, and I've swapped in a combo of egg whites and whole eggs for the scrambled eggs to easily cut a lot of fat.

4 6-inch corn tortillas

PICO DE GALLO
2 Roma tomatoes, seeded and diced
1/4 white onion, diced
1/4 jalapeño pepper, seeded and diced
Juice of 1 lime
3 tbsp chopped fresh cilantro
Sea salt and freshly ground
    black pepper

BLACK BEANS
1/2 medium red onion, diced
3/4 jalapeño pepper, seeded and diced
1 tsp chili powder
1/2 tsp ground cumin
1 cup black beans, drained and rinsed
1/4 cup jarred all-natural tomato sauce
1/4 cup water

SCRAMBLED EGGS
1/2 medium red onion, diced
8 large egg whites
2 large eggs
3 tbsp 1% milk

TOPPING
1/2 cup shredded low-fat aged cheddar
    cheese
1/2 cup non-fat plain Greek yogurt

SERVES 4
HANDS-ON TIME: 35 MINUTES
TOTAL TIME: 35 MINUTES

Tip: If you prefer soft tortillas, simply wrap them in paper towel and microwave on high for just under 1 minute, flipping parcel once during cooking.

Prepare pico de gallo: In a medium bowl, mix together tomatoes, white onion, jalapeño, lime juice and cilantro. Season with salt and pepper.

Prepare black beans: Heat a large non-stick skillet over medium heat; mist with cooking spray. Add red onion and jalapeño and cook, stirring frequently, until softened, about 3 minutes. Add chili powder and cumin and cook, stirring constantly, until fragrant, about 1 minute.

Preheat oven to 400°F. Mist tortillas with cooking spray and arrange in a single layer on a baking sheet. Bake until just crispy, about 5 minutes. Keep warm.

Meanwhile, add beans, tomato sauce and water to pan with onion, stirring to incorporate. Cook, stirring frequently, until liquid is bubbling, about 2 minutes. Reduce heat to medium-low and coarsely mash beans using a wooden spoon or potato masher. Remove from heat and season with salt and pepper. Cover to keep warm.

Prepare scrambled eggs: Wipe skillet clean (or use a second skillet) and warm over medium heat; mist with cooking spray. Add red onion to pan and cook, stirring frequently, until softened, about 3 minutes. Meanwhile, in a medium bowl, whisk together egg whites, eggs and milk. Add to skillet and cook for about 2 minutes, until eggs are just set, scraping a spatula over bottom of pan so that large, soft curds form.

To serve, place 1 tortilla on each plate. Top with bean mixture, eggs, pico de gallo, cheddar and yogurt.

PER SERVING
BEFORE: 1110 CALORIES, 65 G TOTAL FAT
DISH DO-OVER: 248 CALORIES, 8.1 G TOTAL FAT
*NUTRITIONAL INFORMATION: 3.9 G SATURATED FAT,
23.5 G CARBOHYDRATES, 5.8 G FIBRE, 8.2 G SUGAR,
21 G PROTEIN, 409 MG SODIUM, 109 MG CHOLESTEROL*

Sausage & Egg Muffins

Skip the drive-through! This simple breakfast has become an on-the-fly staple in my house. I make the sausage patties and eggs ahead of time and assemble in the morning.

We had a special group of "recipe testers" for this book when photographer and food-styling couple, Mike and Mia, and their three girls were around. Their daughter Lia had her eyes on these sausage patties right from the get-go. After her first bite she exclaimed, "I have two words, Mommy: JACK . . . POT!" I think that says it all.

1 medium zucchini
2 extra-lean turkey or chicken sausages (3 oz each), casings removed
1 cup egg whites (about 8 large)
2 large eggs
Sea salt and freshly ground black pepper
4 whole-wheat or multigrain English muffins, split and toasted
1/2 cup shredded low-fat aged cheddar cheese
4 tbsp Homemade Ketchup (page 19) or organic ketchup

SERVES 4
HANDS-ON TIME: 30 MINUTES
TOTAL TIME: 30 MINUTES
(KETCHUP NOT INCLUDED)

Grate zucchini and squeeze very dry in a clean kitchen towel or paper towel.

In a bowl and using your hands, combine zucchini and sausages. Divide mixture into 4 balls and shape into 1/2-inch-thick patties.

In a medium bowl, whisk together egg whites and eggs.

Heat a large non-stick skillet over medium-high heat; mist with cooking spray. Cook patties, turning once, for about 6 minutes, until browned and cooked through. Remove from heat and cover to keep warm.

Wipe skillet clean, return to medium heat and mist with cooking spray. Add eggs to skillet and cook for about 2 minutes, until eggs are just set, scraping a spatula over bottom of pan so that large, soft curds form. Season with salt and pepper.

To assemble sandwiches, place 1 patty on the bottom half of each English muffin. Top with eggs, cheese and ketchup, and sandwich with muffin tops.

PER SERVING
BEFORE: 440 CALORIES, 26 G TOTAL FAT
DISH DO-OVER: 324 CALORIES, 8.8 G TOTAL FAT
NUTRITIONAL INFORMATION: 2.9 G SATURATED FAT, 36.3 G CARBOHYDRATES, 5.5 G FIBRE, 12.6 G SUGAR, 26.5 G PROTEIN, 943 MG SODIUM, 122 MG CHOLESTEROL

Beverages

Milkshakes

As a kid, I always wanted a milkshake when we went out for dinner, but my savvy mom knew how much sugar and fat were in them, so it was a rare treat. Most low-fat milkshakes use frozen yogurt, which varies widely in fat, sugar and calories. I opt for non-fat Greek yogurt instead and freeze it in ice cube trays ahead of time. When you're craving the nostalgia of a thick creamy shake, this recipe's got you covered.

VANILLA

2 cups non-fat plain Greek yogurt

1 1/2 cups skim milk or unsweetened plain almond milk

1/3 cup honey or organic sugar

2 tsp pure vanilla extract

1/2 cup Do-Over Whipped Cream (page 24)

SERVES 2
HANDS-ON TIME: 25 MINUTES
TOTAL TIME: 40 MINUTES +
4 HOURS CHILLING TIME

VANILLA MILKSHAKE
**BEFORE: 650 CALORIES,
27 G TOTAL FAT
DISH DO-OVER: 407 CALORIES,
0.2 G TOTAL FAT**
*NUTRITIONAL INFORMATION:
0.2 G SATURATED FAT,
70.8 G CARBOHYDRATES,
0.1 G FIBRE, 65.3 G SUGAR,
31.5 G PROTEIN, 177 MG SODIUM,
18 MG CHOLESTEROL*

Freeze yogurt in ice cube trays until firm, about 4 hours or overnight. [*Make-ahead:* Prepare up to 2 weeks in advance; store in a resealable freezer bag or container.]

In a blender, purée ingredients until smooth and thick. Pour into tall glasses and top with whipped cream.

OTHER FLAVOUR OPTIONS:

Chocolate
Reduce vanilla to 1 tsp. Add 3 tbsp unsweetened cocoa powder. (Dutch-process is best.)

Strawberry
Reduce yogurt to 1 cup and vanilla to 1 tsp. Add 2 cups sliced fresh strawberries (about 10 medium).

Cookies 'n' Cream
Purée vanilla flavour ingredients until smooth, add 1/2 cup coarsely crumbled gluten-free chocolate vanilla crème sandwich cookies (about 4) and pulse to combine.

CHOCOLATE MILKSHAKE
**BEFORE: 730 CALORIES, 27 G TOTAL FAT
DISH DO-OVER: 418 CALORIES, 1.2 G TOTAL FAT**
*NUTRITIONAL INFORMATION: 0.9 G SATURATED FAT,
75 G CARBOHYDRATES, 2.5 G FIBRE, 65.2 G SUGAR,
32.9 G PROTEIN, 179 MG SODIUM, 18 MG CHOLESTEROL*

STRAWBERRY MILKSHAKE
**BEFORE: 750 CALORIES, 27 G TOTAL FAT
DISH DO-OVER: 385 CALORIES, 0.7 G TOTAL FAT**
*NUTRITIONAL INFORMATION: 0.3 G SATURATED FAT,
77.7 G CARBOHYDRATES, 3.8 G FIBRE, 70.4 G SUGAR,
20.7 G PROTEIN, 137 MG SODIUM, 11 MG CHOLESTEROL*

COOKIES 'N' CREAM MILKSHAKE
**BEFORE: 690 CALORIES, 33 G TOTAL FAT
DISH DO-OVER: 510 CALORIES, 4.5 G TOTAL FAT**
*NUTRITIONAL INFORMATION: 2.4 G SATURATED FAT,
88.1 G CARBOHYDRATES, 1 G FIBRE, 75 G SUGAR,
32.3 G PROTEIN, 255 MG SODIUM, 18 MG CHOLESTEROL*

Eggnog

Cut the fat and increase the merriment with this holiday favourite. Here, I replace cream, refined white sugar and egg yolks with skim milk, mostly egg whites and honey, and use cornstarch to thicken the mixture without adding fat.

6 cups skim milk

1 tbsp cornstarch

4 large eggs

1/2 cup egg whites (about 4 large)

3/4 cup honey

1/4 tsp freshly grated nutmeg,
    plus more for garnish

1 vanilla bean, halved lengthwise

8 oz dark rum (optional)

SERVES 8
HANDS-ON TIME: 15 MINUTES
TOTAL TIME: 15 MINUTES
+ 2 HOURS CHILLING TIME

In a medium saucepan, whisk together 1/4 cup milk and cornstarch. Whisk in eggs, egg whites, honey and nutmeg until smooth. Whisk in remaining milk, reserving 1 cup, and add vanilla bean. Turn heat to medium and bring mixture to a simmer, being careful that it doesn't boil. Simmer, stirring constantly with a wooden spoon, until thick enough to coat the back of spoon, about 8 minutes.

Remove from heat and stir in reserved milk to stop the cooking. Remove vanilla bean, transfer to a resealable container and refrigerate for at least 2 hours. (It will keep for up to 2 days.)

Served chilled with rum (if using) and sprinkled with nutmeg.

PER SERVING
BEFORE: 321 CALORIES, 22 G TOTAL FAT
DISH DO-OVER: 207 CALORIES, 2.7 G TOTAL FAT
*NUTRITIONAL INFORMATION: 1 G SATURATED FAT,
36.6 G CARBOHYDRATES, 0.1 G FIBRE, 35.8 G SUGAR,
10.8 G PROTEIN, 134 MG SODIUM, 95 MG CHOLESTEROL*

Mango Lassi

My favourite beverage with spicy Indian food is a refreshing mango lassi, to balance out the intense layers of flavour from the fragrant spices. Instead of the traditional version with full-fat yogurt, refined white sugar and whole milk, my version stays just as creamy and sweet with non-fat Greek yogurt, skim milk and honey.

2 ripe large mangoes, peeled, pitted and
  diced, or 2 cups frozen mango chunks
1 1/2 cups ice cubes
1 cup non-fat plain Greek yogurt
1/2 cup skim milk
2 tbsp honey
1 tsp rose water (optional)
1/8 tsp ground cardamom (optional)
Pinch sea salt

SERVES 2
HANDS-ON TIME: 10 MINUTES
TOTAL TIME: 10 MINUTES

In a blender, purée all ingredients until very smooth. Pour into glasses and serve immediately.

PER SERVING
BEFORE: 247 CALORIES, 6.5 G TOTAL FAT
DISH DO-OVER: 290 CALORIES, 0.6 G TOTAL FAT
NUTRITIONAL INFORMATION: 0.2 G SATURATED FAT, 61.3 G CARBOHYDRATES, 3.8 G FIBRE, 54 G SUGAR, 15.1 G PROTEIN, 74 MG SODIUM, 8 MG CHOLESTEROL

Blended Iced Mocha

Save yourself a few bucks and make this better-for-you version at home. The key here is xanthan gum, which can be purchased online or at most grocery, health or bulk food stores. It makes the mixture thick and frothy, just like at your local coffee shop. A little goes a long way, so a small bottle will last for months.

2 cups ice cubes
1 cup double-strength brewed coffee
1 tbsp unsweetened cocoa powder
  (Dutch-process is best)
1 cup skim milk or unsweetened
  plain almond milk
3 tbsp honey or organic sugar, plus
  more to taste
1/8 tsp xanthan gum
1/2 cup Do-Over Whipped Cream
  (page 24)

SERVES 2
HANDS-ON TIME: 25 MINUTES
TOTAL TIME: 40 MINUTES

In a blender, purée ingredients until smooth. Pour into glasses and garnish with whipped cream.

PER SERVING
BEFORE: 400 CALORIES, 15 G TOTAL FAT
DISH DO-OVER: 164 CALORIES, 0.5 G TOTAL FAT
NUTRITIONAL INFORMATION: 0.4 G SATURATED FAT, 37.3 G CARBOHYDRATES, 1 G FIBRE, 35.8 G SUGAR, 6.3 G PROTEIN, 79 MG SODIUM, 3 MG CHOLESTEROL

Margarita

Margaritas seem like a pretty innocent choice, calorie-wise. But many are made with copious amounts of sugar and juice from concentrate, and have enough salt on the rim to keep you bloated for a week. My do-over version takes care of all this by swapping white sugar with honey, using freshly squeezed juices and rimming only one-quarter of the glass with salt. I like my margaritas on the rocks, but you can easily make a slushy frozen version by combining all the ingredients in a blender. Be sure to use 100% agave tequila without any added sugar (see page 14).

4 ice cubes

3 oz 100% agave tequila (blanco or reposado)

1/3 cup fresh lime juice

1/4 cup fresh orange juice

2 tbsp honey

1/2 lime, cut into 3 wedges

SERVES 2
HANDS-ON TIME: 5 MINUTES
TOTAL TIME: 5 MINUTES

If salting glass rims, pour salt into a small shallow dish. Run lime wedge around one-quarter of the rim of each glass. One at a time, dip wet rim into salt at a 45-degree angle; rotate glass to coat rim about 1/4-inch deep.

Place ice cubes in a cocktail shaker and add tequila, lime juice, orange juice and honey. Seal and shake well. Fill each glass with ice, strain margarita into glasses and garnish each with a lime wedge.

PER SERVING
BEFORE: 280 CALORIES, 0 G TOTAL FAT
DISH DO-OVER: 182 CALORIES, 0.1 G TOTAL FAT,
*NUTRITIONAL INFORMATION: 0 G SATURATED FAT,
24.1 G CARBOHYDRATES, 0.1 G FIBRE, 20.7 G SUGAR,
0.4 G PROTEIN, 2 MG SODIUM, 0 MG CHOLESTEROL*

Piña Colada

This creamy tropical treat can be one of the biggest saboteurs on a cocktail menu thanks to the offending ingredients: cream, coconut milk and refined white sugar. I've swapped those out for coconut water, light coconut milk and lots of sweet ripe pineapple. The result? A creamy, refreshing, bikini-worthy bevvie.

1/2 cup unsweetened shredded coconut

2 cups ice cubes

2 cups diced ripe fresh pineapple

1/2 cup coconut water

1/4 cup light coconut milk

4 oz white rum

4 oz dark rum

1 lime, juiced

4 wedges of fresh pineapple or lime for garnish

1 tbsp toasted coconut for garnish (optional)

SERVES 4
HANDS-ON TIME: 15 MINUTES
TOTAL TIME: 18 MINUTES

Heat oven to 350°F. Spread coconut on a parchment-lined baking sheet and toast in oven for about 3 minutes, until golden. Transfer to a shallow dish.

In a blender, purée ice, pineapple, coconut water, coconut milk, and white and dark rum until smooth.

Pour lime juice into a small shallow dish. Dip rim of a glass into juice at a 45-degree angle; rotate the glass to coat rim in juice about 1/4-inch deep. Repeat in dish of toasted coconut, coating rim. Repeat with remaining glasses. Pour piña colada into glasses and garnish each with a slice of lime or pineapple. Add a sprinkling of toasted coconut, if desired.

Note: For a virgin piña colada, eliminate rums and add an extra 1/2 cup coconut water.

PER SERVING
BEFORE: 550 CALORIES, 18 G TOTAL FAT
DISH DO-OVER: 254 CALORIES, 6.5 G TOTAL FAT
|NUTRITIONAL INFORMATION: 5.7 G SATURATED FAT,
19.1 G CARBOHYDRATES, 3.3 G FIBRE, 13.1 G SUGAR,
1.4 G PROTEIN, 39 MG SODIUM, 0 MG CHOLESTEROL

Strawberry Daiquiri

Fruity rum drinks are just the ticket in the summer, but two boozy daiquiris can add up to over 500 calories! Most mixes are loaded with refined sugar. Ditch the mix for my refreshing version of the original using only a little honey in place of refined white sugar.

2 cups ice cubes

20 ripe medium strawberries,
    stemmed and halved (about 4 cups)

3 tbsp honey

1/2 cup unsweetened pomegranate
    juice

1/4 cup fresh lime juice

4 oz light rum

4 strawberries, sliced halfway through
    centre from bottom, for garnish

4 thin lime wheels (or wedges),
    for garnish

SERVES 4
HANDS-ON TIME: 10 MINUTES
TOTAL TIME: 10 MINUTES

In a blender, purée ice, strawberries, honey, pomegranate juice, lime juice and rum (if using) until smooth and slushy. Pour into glasses and garnish each with a strawberry and lime wheel.

Serving Suggestion: For a virgin daiquiri, eliminate rum and add another 1/4 cup unsweetened pomegranate juice.

PER SERVING
BEFORE: 250 CALORIES, TOTAL 0 G TOTAL FAT
DISH DO-OVER: 156 CALORIES, 0.2 G TOTAL FAT
*NUTRITIONAL INFORMATION: 0 G SATURATED FAT,
24.7 G CARBOHYDRATES, 1.6 G FIBRE, 21.2 G SUGAR,
0.7 G PROTEIN, 6 MG SODIUM, 0 MG CHOLESTEROL*

Rum Punch

Rum punch is an addictive concoction served all over the Caribbean, especially in the West Indies, where many recipes are passed down from generation to generation. Punch comes from the Indian word *panch*, meaning "five" and referring to the ingredients: sour, sweet, strong, weak and spiced. There's an old rhyme that describes the mix: "One of sour, two of sweet, three of strong, four of weak, a dash of bitters and a sprinkle of spice, serve well chilled with plenty of ice." I've mostly stuck to the traditional ratios but lightened up the rum and subbed freshly squeezed juice for simple syrup made from refined sugar. Also, I've used coconut water for the "weak" ingredient. This lightens the calories and makes the punch much less syrupy than most other versions, but be forewarned: this is a deceptively strong drink.

3/4 cup light rum
1 1/2 cups coconut water
1 cup fresh orange juice
1/2 cup fresh lime juice
1/2 cup pineapple juice
2 dashes bitters
Freshly grated nutmeg
4 lime twists for garnish

SERVES 4
HANDS-ON TIME: 5 MINUTES
TOTAL TIME: 5 MINUTES + 1 HOUR CHILLING TIME

Mix together rum, coconut water, orange juice, lime juice, pineapple juice and bitters in a large pitcher. Cover and refrigerate for about 1 hour, or overnight. Pour into tall glasses filled with ice and garnish with freshly grated nutmeg and a twist of lime.

PER SERVING
BEFORE: 233 CALORIES, 0.2 G TOTAL FAT
DISH DO-OVER: 169 CALORIES, 0.4 G TOTAL FAT
NUTRITIONAL INFORMATION: 0.2 G SATURATED FAT, 17.5 G CARBOHYDRATES, 1.2 G FIBRE, 12.5 G SUGAR, 1.3 G PROTEIN, 96 MG SODIUM, 0 MG CHOLESTEROL

Acknowledgments

The expression "it takes a village to raise a child" rings very true with a cookbook, which, as any author can attest to, becomes your baby during its creation. I could not have done it without my talented and passionate team, family and friends. Writing a cookbook has been a dream and goal of mine for such a long time. I cannot thank you all enough:

Mom and Dad — How can anyone sum up in a few sentences their appreciation for their parents and all they do? Well, I can't, but very simply, thank you for your love and unwavering support, even when becoming a cook seemed like a crazy idea. I love you.

My grandparents — I miss you all dearly. Revisiting our stories as I wrote this book brought tears to my eyes every time. I'll cherish the memories forever, and I love you more than you'll ever know.

My sisters, Carol and Susan — No idea where this gene for silliness and chatter comes from, but because of the three of us, family gatherings are far from quiet affairs! Thank you for all the laughs, for being the best sisters ever and for always being there to cheer me on. I love you both so much.

Mark — thank you for putting up with perpetual kitchen chaos and all my crazy ideas! One day I'll get you your very own stove to fold laundry on. xo

Brad Wilson, editorial director — When we first met, I bet you thought I was a chatterbox lunatic. I'd prattle on, and you would listen and interject when I took a moment to breathe. Your patience is staggering. Even at the 11th hour, your extreme calm never wavered. It's quite amazing! Thank you, Brad, for believing in me and bringing *Dish Do-Over* to life. I learned so much throughout this process. I'm deeply grateful for this opportunity and for all the laughs along the way. I'm looking forward to seeing if Sam, your book-eating dog, likes the taste of this one!

Noelle Zitzer, senior managing editor — Much like Brad, Noelle must have nerves of steel to put up with all of us crazy chefs and authors. How she balances the sheer volume of books on her plate is mind-boggling. Thank you, Noelle, for your hard work, dedication and gentle approach in pulling all the pieces together.

Judy Phillips, freelance editor — Copy editing is a job I could never be a pro at, so I'm very happy you are! Thank you for your relentless pursuit of consistency and great attention to detail. I hope your nightmares about panko have subsided!

Tracy Bordian, editor "at large" — Proofreading is another job I could never tackle, so I am very grateful to have had you on the team. After a few rounds of edits, layout changes and so on, I found it quite amazing to see the amount of detail involved in proofreading a book. Thank you, Tracy, for your incredible work.

Lisa Bettencourt, designer — Lisa, you brought the entire vision of *Dish Do-Over* together and made it simple, elegant and beautiful. I had an idea of how I wanted the book to look, but this is beyond what I envisioned. Thank you so much!

Maylene Loveland, senior publicist — Writing a cookbook means nothing if no one knows about it. I'm very fortunate to have Maylene at the helm of the publicity side of things. Thank you for getting *Dish Do-Over* in everyone's hands.

Ruth Pincoe, indexer — You were one of my favourite guests when I ran a cooking school downtown a few years ago. We often talked about cookbooks; it was exciting when we featured an author you had worked with. So I was thrilled when Noelle told me that you would be providing the *Dish Do-Over* index — such an important part of any cookbook. Thank you, Ruth!

Mike McColl, photographer at Photos with Sauce (photoswithsauce.ca) — I was thrilled when you and your food stylist wife, Mia, agreed to work with me on *Dish Do-Over*. As a chef turned photographer, you shoot real food, with no digital retouching trickery, and have a great artistic eye. Thank you, Mike, for the daily music selection, for all the little extras (like painting picnic tables) and most of all for capturing the recipes so perfectly.

Mia Bachmaier, principal food stylist at Photos with Sauce — An extremely talented chef, you put your heart into whatever project you take on. Food styling seems to come naturally to you, and I couldn't have been more confident in having you in charge of the kitchen. You and Mike are wonderful and so easy to work with — I'm looking forward to our next project together! Thank you, Mia, for all the crazy shopping trips and fancy coffees, and for making the recipes look so delicious.

Lia, Ella and Luci McColl — You three would roar in like a herd of teeny elephants, looking for an after-school snack and inspecting the goodies in the kitchen. Thank you, ladies, for being the best crew of taste-testers ever! Special thanks to Lia for picking out the perfect blue colour for the picnic table, and big thanks to all of you girls for letting us use your beautiful hand-painted bowls on page 140! The Macaroni & Cheese photo is one of my favourites because of them.

Gillian Watts — You came through for me in spades when I needed you, always sending back beautifully written and edited copy, often with thoughtful notes and additions. Gillian, thank you for deciphering my chicken scratch and for understanding exactly what was needed!

Sabrina Falone — When I was the food producer at *Steven and Chris* and you were our food stylist, you ran the kitchen like a well-oiled machine! Thanks, Sabrina, for jumping in right away to help with *Dish Do-Over*, with your super-efficient research skills. Thanks, too, for always being there with a smile.

Lisa Rollo — When I needed some research help, I put together a little team of ladies, which included you, on Mia's referral. Lisa, thank you for your diligent work and attention to detail.

Sarah Schlow — I'm so glad that my friend Catherine Mangosing introduced us. Writing a tagline for a book is a critical job — one that calls for a pro. It is extremely important to capture, in one short sentence, both the tone of the book and people's attention. Thank you, Sarah, for coming up with such creative one-liners; you conveyed the essence of *Dish Do-Over* perfectly!

Lauren Cameron — You came to me on a referral from my days at the *Canadian Living* Test Kitchen. Thank you, Lauren, for doing anything that was asked, from washing dishes to researching nutritional information. I'm grateful for your hard work and positive attitude.

M.K. and P.S. — A most heartfelt thank you for your warm hospitality and for allowing us to invade your beautiful home. See you in the sun!

Valeria Nova, makeup artist at Two Chicks and Some Lipstick (twochicksandsomelipstick.com) — For anyone who wants perfect hair and makeup, you're the go-to gal! You and your business partner, Lori Fabrizio, amaze me with your artistic talent and knack for giving women a naturally glamorous look, one that is never overdone and always perfect. Thank you, Val, for all our make-up chair chit-chats and for always taking such excellent care of me.

Lindsay Agnew, Lindsay Agnew Style (lindsayagnew.com), set decorator (kitchen photos) — Linds, I don't understand how you pull together a room so effortlessly, giving it 10 different looks, but you have an amazing gift! Thank you for showing up to our set with your car jammed full of gorgeous props, and for somehow knowing exactly how my book's kitchen should look.

Tara Williams, wardrobe stylist — I love your style, your passion for thrift-shop browsing and your impeccable eye for detail. Thank you for the marathon shopping missions and for putting my look together. Please forgive me for using that "bad collar" shot . . .

Grace Meat Products in Toronto — Thank you, Joel Gold and the Grace Meats team, for providing all the beautiful meat in the book!

Krys Roman, Rosewood Estates Winery — Thanks to you and your family for your delicious, unpasteurized, hand-crafted wildflower honey.

Marc and Sharyn Joliat, at Info Access (1988) Inc. — One of the toughest parts of this book for me was gathering the nutritional information. Marc and Sharyn, thank you for your incredible attention to detail and your dedication in completing this project, even while on vacation!

Steven Sabados and Chris Hyndman, of CBC's *Steven and Chris* — You are two of the most fabulous men I know — larger than life, extremely talented and both with hearts of gold. To work with passionate people like you is a gift; I am very lucky. You changed my life by welcoming me to your team, trusting me to help support your brand and passion. Thank you for all the laughs and for always being yourselves.

Rick Matthews, executive producer of CBC's *Steven and Chris* — You somehow knew that I could be a food television producer, even though the idea had never crossed my mind. That life-changing decision helped forge the career path I'm on today and brought many wonderful people into my life, both personally and professionally. Thank you, Rick, for years of support and for helping make the dream of a *Dish Do-Over* cookbook a reality.

Amrita Singh (prettyfrugalliving.com) — Thank you for always being there to listen to my endless chatter, for helping me sort through the grey areas to make smart decisions, for being my TV mentor, for introducing me to Brad, for pulling the *Steven and Chris* "Dish Do-Over" brand together, and especially for being the social convenor of our little crew!

Karen Bower — Thank you for your support in uniting HarperCollins Canada and the CBC in this adventure and for putting *Dish Do-Over* in the CBC store! I believe we broke new ground in this partnership, and you made the process simple and seamless.

The *Steven and Chris* team — Time and time again, the celebrity chefs we had as guests on the show would comment on how the team at *Steven and Chris* was one of the happiest and most professional crews they had ever come across. Leaving my full-time position on the show to write this book was bittersweet, with lots of happy tears. Thank you for Fast Food Fridays, the loud lift and all the laughs. Still working on my inside voice . . .

The *Steven and Chris* viewers — Thank you for not only watching, but also sending your letters and "Dish Do-Over" requests, and for making my recipes at home! Without your support, this book would not be in your hands right now.

Index